UNRAVELLING SOCIAL POLICY

Unravelling Social Policy

Theory, Analysis, and Political Action towards Social Equality

Revised and Enlarged Edition

DAVID G. GIL

SCHENKMAN PUBLISHING COMPANY
Cambridge, Massachusetts

TO EVA,
GIDEON AND DANIEL

CONTENTS

List of Charts and Tables   viii

Foreword by Charles I. Schottland   ix

Preface to Second Edition   xi

Acknowledgements   xiii

Introduction   xv

**PART I   THEORY AND METHOD OF SOCIAL POLICY
           ANALYSIS AND SYNTHESIS**   1

CHAPTER ONE
Current Views of Social Policy   3

CHAPTER TWO
A Conceptual Model of Social Policies   11

CHAPTER THREE
A Framework for Analysis and Synthesis of Social Policies   31

**PART II   AN ILLUSTRATION OF SOCIAL POLICY
            ANALYSIS AND SYNTHESIS**   57

CHAPTER FOUR
Mothers' Wages, Children's Allowances, Parents' Wages—
Analysis and Synthesis of a Social Policy Cluster   59

PART III   SOCIAL POLICIES AND SOCIAL PROVISION   137

CHAPTER FIVE
Resolving Issues of Social Provision in Our Society   139

**EPILOGUE   POLITICAL ACTION TOWARD SOCIAL
             EQUALITY**   175

Implications for Social and Political Action   177

Notes   195

Index   205

LIST OF CHARTS AND TABLES

CHART 2.1   A Conceptual Model of Social Policies   25

CHART 2.2   Natural and Societal Forces Limiting, Influencing, and Interacting with the Key Processes and General Domain of Social Policies   29

CHART 3.1   Framework for Social Policy Analysis and Synthesis   33

TABLE 4.1   Total Money Income of Families with Children under 18 — 1969   71

TABLE 4.2   Mothers' Wages and Children's Allowances Compared with 1970 Nonfarm Poverty and Near Poverty Thresholds for Female-Headed Household   75

Foreword

"Social policy" is now a hit theme in academic and political arenas throughout the world.[1] Increasingly, students of government and society, generally, are seeking to understand the forces and processes which establish or change social policies, to predict the consequences of social policies, and to establish goals for the "good society" toward which social policies should lead us.

In spite of the world-wide interest in this issue, there has been little systematic analysis of social policy or even agreement as to its definition. In this volume David Gil attempts such analysis and definition. He develops a model against which a specific social policy might be analyzed and assessed.

Readers of this book may disagree with many of Gil's observations and comments and even with his basic goals centering around his concept of equality and egalitarianism. But his simple formulation of a model and a methodology of analysis of social policies is a significant step forward in the attempts to develop a more scientific approach to the study of social policy.

Social policies, which determine a country's programs and services in such matters as income distribution, employment, education, health services, housing, and levels of living (to mention only a few) are too important in the lives of all people to be left to chance or as a response to individual or group interests without objective analysis. What are the basic goals of our society, or rather, what are the goals which we should strive for in our society? How does any specific policy relate to these goals? These are fundamental questions which do not receive enough attention in today's political arenas.

As a former official in the Federal Government, I have seen major social programs established on the basis of the conviction of a single important official or a single case brought to the attention of a member of Congress, or on the basis of pressure from a small special interest group, without any in-depth analyses or consideration of ultimate consequences. As a result, the "unintended consequences" of such action make lively case histories for academic studies.

A semantic or definitional stumbling block in analyzing social policy has been the fact that many students of social policy relate the very term to a "desirable" or "good" goal or activity. This distorts attempts at objective analyses. Totalitarian governments may have well-established and accepted social policies which would not be considered "desirable" or "good" in a democratic society. The model proposed herein has a neutral quality, making it useful for analyses of any social policy. Likewise, it is useful whether considering "holistic" or overall social policies or whether it is used to analyze "piecemeal engineering" proposals — the latter being the more likely and numerous in today's complicated society.

Dr. Gil's model and methodology is a beginning attempt at some rationality and systematic appraisal of social policies. It will undoubtedly be improved upon in the years to come. Its contribution lies in its innovative proposals upon which a more sophisticated scientific analysis of social policy can be built. It is, therefore, an important and significant step forward in our efforts to develop more effective ways of assessing and predicting the results of proposals in the social policy arena.

Charles I. Schottland, Professor of Law and Social Welfare and former President, Brandeis University; former United States Commissioner of Social Security; President, International Council on Social Welfare.

Preface to Second Edition

Publication of a second edition of *Unravelling Social Policy* provides an opportunity for reflection. It is also a source of mixed feelings: satisfaction upon realizing that readers' interest did exceed the estimates of the publisher, and regrets at shortcomings of the book, which I would write differently now, given insights gained since completing the manuscript in 1971.

An author is not necessarily done with a book when he sends it to the printer. This is certainly true for this work which reflects one stage in a search for strategies of reason aimed at survival and self-actualization of people everywhere. The inevitably unfinished character of this search has caused occasional misunderstandings of the thrust of this book. Hence some explanations seem indicated.

As suggested by the title, my central purpose in writing this book was to unravel the nature and dynamics of social policies in any human society and to develop a conceptual model of these policies from a holistic-evolutionary perspective. This involved discerning the common domains of all social policies, their key variables, and the forces which affect and constrain the evolution of social policies. Related to this central, theoretical focus is a methodological one, to derive from the conceptual model a framework for systematic analysis of past and present social policies, and for synthesis of alternative systems of social policies.

The use of the framework is demonstrated in Part II of the book in an analysis of one particular cluster of social policies, mothers' wages, parents wages, and children's allowances. Some reviewers concluded, erroneously, that this illustrative analysis amounted to a veiled advocacy of these policies. I wish to emphasize here that this had not been my intention.

The final focus of the book was not part of the original plan. It emerged when I realized, while working on the conceptual model and the analytic framework, that policy analysis per se accomplishes nothing, and that meaningful changes of systems of social policies were predicated upon philosophical and political practice rather than upon professional analysis and administrative practice. Hence, I explored in the Epilogue implications of the conceptual model of social policies for a theory of political practice toward the development of egalitarian, libertarian, humanistic, democratic social orders.

My studies after writing *Unravelling Social Policy* have deepened my insights into the nature and dynamics of social policies and political practice, and into the central importance of social values and their reciprocal relationship with social policies and societal institutions. I decided however, not to integrate these further studies throughout the present volume which is reflective of one stage in my explorations. Interested readers are referred to a new book of essays, *The Challenge of Social Equality*,° written over recent years. One of these essays, "Resolving Issues of Social Provision," has been included in this second edition as Part III, Chapter 5, to illustrate approaches derived from the conceptual model of social policies.

David G. Gil

Lexington, Mass., December 26, 1975

°Cambridge, Mass., Schenkman Publishing Co., 1976.

Acknowledgements

Research for this book was conducted within the Social Policy Study Program at the Florence Heller Graduate School for Advanced Studies in Social Welfare, Brandeis University. The Social Policy Study Program is supported by the Office of Child Development of the U. S. Department of Health, Education, and Welfare under Research Grant No. PR-288-1. The generous assistance of the Office of Child Development is gratefully acknowledged herewith.

I wish to thank Dr. Charles P. Gershenson, Director of Research of the Office of Child Development, for his encouragement throughout the stages of this study; Ms. Ann Orlov, Editor for the Behavioral Sciences at Harvard University Press, for suggesting the writing of this book; Charles I. Schottland, President of Brandeis University, and my colleagues at the Heller School, especially Professors Roland Warren, Pamela Roby, Carol Brown, Michael Brower, Barry Friedman, and Leonard Hausman, whose critical comments and counsel helped clarify my thinking; Professor Richard M. Titmuss of the London School of Economics, Professor Peter Townsend of the University of Essex, and Dean Alvin L. Schorr of New York University, whose pioneering studies of social policies inspired my own explorations in this field. I also owe special thanks to my research associates, Robert Colbourne and Uri Davis, and to these students in my Seminar at the Heller School; Sheldon Gelman, Brin Hawkins, Janet Kernodle, Bruce Lagay, Jesse McClure, Ann McInvale, Malcolm Morrison and Arthur Naparstek. Their challenging questions and comments contributed immensely to the development of my own thinking on matters of social policy. Thanks are also due to Mrs. Virginia Normann for her patience, understanding and skill in preparing the manuscript, and to my wife, Eva, for her patience and understanding in listening to, commenting on, and improving my work.

D.G.G.

Lexington, Mass.
September 15, 1971

Introduction

Social policy issues are constant items on the public agenda of the United States, on local, state, and national levels. In spite of this widespread public concern with matters of social policy, however, our society lacks a comprehensive and·internally consistent system of social policies, one that would be conducive to the realization of the inherent human potential of all its members. The United States is not at all unique in this respect. Social policy questions are, and have been, objects of public concern in every known human society throughout man's evolution, but comprehensive, and truly satisfactory solutions to these questions have usually eluded his grasp.

One frequently identified obstacle to the development of a comprehensive and consistent social policy system in this and other countries is the fragmented, parochial, and incremental approach pursued by various self-serving groups in the "social marketplace" in efforts to change conditions which they consider undesirable in terms of their perceived interests. Some social.scientists suggest that this tendency to fragmentation, parochialism, and incrementalism in the development of social policies is an intrinsic aspect of democracy in a complex and pluralistic society, and that it therefore could not be eliminated entirely, although its scope could be reduced. Other scholars, including this author, reject such a narrow conception of democracy and of human potential.

A second, perhaps more fundamental, obstacle to the development of a coherent social policy system is hardly ever mentioned. This obstacle is the curious lack of clarity and agreement as to what social policy actually is, and what its domain and functions are within society.

Correlatively, there is also insufficient comprehension of the nature of the key processes through which social policy systems operate, of interactions among these key processes, and of their consequences for the quality and circumstances of life in society, and for human relations and experience.

This book attempts to tackle both these obstacles on theoretical, methodological, philosophical, and political levels. As for the latter obstacle, which is essentially on the level of theory and method, this study develops, and illustrates the use of, a conceptual model of social policies and a framework for systematic analysis and synthesis of such policies. Concerning the former obstacle, which is philosophical and political in nature, the study explores implications of the proposed conceptual model of social policies for an alternative approach to political action aimed at structural social change toward an egalitarian, humanistic social order.

The conceptual model of social policies and the analytic framework constitute a theoretical base and a method, respectively, for facilitating insights into the dynamics and consequences of past, extant, and newly generated social policies, and of the political processes within which these policies evolve. The model and framework should, therefore, enable governmental and other formal and informal societal units to engage in analysis and development of social policies in a more effective manner than is possible at present, and to design more comprehensive and internally less inconsistent systems of social policies.

Social policy analysis is, of course, carried on constantly by many individuals and groups, within and outside governmental agencies. However, those who engage currently in such analyses lack a systematic and comprehensive approach which is widely accepted for the purpose. Existing approaches to social policy analysis differ along several dimensions. First, they differ in the definition of the concept "social policy." Many analysts proceed in their work without clarifying the meaning of this concept, while others define it in vague terms. Next, analytic approaches differ in the nature and scope of the questions and foci examined in the analysis of specific social policies and their consequences, and also in the skills, scholarly competence, and resources of the analysts themselves. Finally, analysts differ in overt and covert value premises. Different combinations along these dimensions yield a large number of analytic approaches and it is therefore not surprising that social policy analyses, and predictions derived from such analyses, tend to vary widely. In view of this current state of the "art" of social policy analysis, it seems highly desirable to develop a more systematic approach which should lead to similar factual conclusions when employed by different analysts in the analysis of the same policy, irrespective of their individual value orientations.

It should be emphasized, however, right at the outset, that the approach to social policy analysis and development presented in this book is not meant to produce "automated solutions" to policy issues faced by decision-makers in and outside the government, or to relieve them of the responsibility to weigh against value premises or political considerations factual conclusions reached by means of the proposed approach. Social policy analysis is not expected to provide definitive answers to moral and value dilemmas. An effective analytic approach should, however, enable analysts to identify aspects of social policy issues which require moral and value choices, and to distinguish these from other aspects which can be decided on the basis of factual information.

Designing new and more adequate social policies and gaining insights into their dynamics and consequences with the aid of the conceptual model and the analytic framework constitute, however, only first, albeit essential, steps toward comprehensive, internally consistent, and humanly satisfying systems of social policies. Understanding must be followed by consistent political action if significant social changes suggested by systematic policy analysis are ever to become social realities. Policy analysis and synthesis lead thus, willy-nilly, to questions concerning strategies of political action for social change. To explore these crucial questions the focus of the book shifts in the concluding section from theoretical and methodological considerations of the conceptual model and the analytic framework to a philosophical inquiry into implications of that model for political action toward structural social change. This inquiry is a logical necessity if one is interested, as this author happens to be, not merely in gaining knowledge about the dynamics and consequences of various social policies, but in applying this knowledge to the active promotion of changes in the extant social policy system. Clearly, also, a valid conceptual model of social policies constitutes an excellent source for such an inquiry into strategies for political action, since the model's function is to unravel the "mystery" of social policies by identifying their key processes, and the forces and conditions which can bring about variations in the established patterns of these processes.

More specifically, the book's outline is as follows. Part One presents a theory and method for analysis and synthesis of social policies. The first chapter surveys prevailing thinking about social policy among leading writers on this subject. The second chapter articulates the proposed conceptual model of social policies. In the third chapter a framework for systematic policy analysis and synthesis is derived from the conceptual model and the use of this framework is explicated. Part Two is concerned with the application of the proposed theory and method. The fourth chapter illustrates the use of the framework in the analysis of one specific policy proposal, "Universal Mothers' Wages and Children's Allowances," and in the development of two alternative social policies, "Selective Mothers' Wages and Children's Allowances," and "Parents' Wages." In the Epilogue, conclusions are drawn from the theoretical insights implicit in the conceptual model of social policies for political action toward an egalitarian, humanistic social order.

No social scientist is, nor should he ever attempt to be, without value commitments of his own. Try as he may to keep his personal values separate from his scholarly work, he is not likely to succeed completely in these efforts. It seems, therefore, important that social scientists clearly state their individual value orientations in areas relevant to the scholarly pursuit at hand.

This author is firmly committed to social policies which promote the fundamental values enunciated in 1776 in the Declaration of Independence of the United States of America, namely, ". . . that all men are created equal, that they are endowed by their Creator with certain unalienable rights, that among these are life, liberty and the pursuit of happiness. . . ." These values, it would seem, can be realized for all members of a society only when its social policies equalize their rights and opportunities. Equality of rights and opportunities in this context is not to be understood in a narrow, mechanical-quantitative sense, but in accordance with the profound and eloquent exposition by the British philosopher and social scientist R. H. Tawney in his treatise, *Equality,*[1] and George Bernard Shaw's recently discovered lost essays, *The Road to Equality.*[2] Briefly, social equality is one feasible organizing principle for shaping the quality of life and the circumstances of living of individuals and groups in society, as well as for structuring all human relations. The principle of social equality derives from a central value premise according to which every individual and every social group are of equal intrinsic worth and, hence, are entitled to equal civil, political, social, and economic liberties, rights, and treatment, as well as subject to equal constraints. Implicit in this central value premise is the notion that each individual should have the right to freely actualize his inherent human potential, and to lead as fulfilling a life as possible within the reality of, and in harmony with, the natural environment, free of exploitation, alienation, and oppression, and subject only to the general limitation that any individual's and group's rights to freedom and self-actualization must never interfere with the identical rights of all other individuals and groups.

Social equality as conceived here seems predicated upon a social order involving: rationally planned, and appropriately balanced, collective development, utilization, and preservation of all natural resources; equality for all individuals and groups in access to statuses and corresponding roles within the totality of tasks to be performed by society; and equality for all in the distribution of rights to available material and symbolic, life-sustaining and life-enhancing goods and services. It should be reemphasized, though, that since social equality aims at actualization of individual differences in innate potentialities, rather than at monotonous uniformity, it is not meant to be realized by dividing all available resources into identical parts for distribution to every member of society, but through distributive and allocative systems based on thoughtful and flexible consideration of individual differences and needs. Obviously then, a social order based on egalitarian value premises will differ radically from one based on the alternative principle of "social inequality," according to which individuals and groups differ in their intrinsic worth and, hence, are entitled to as much of available goods and services for their own use as they can gain control over through competition with, and exploitation of, other individuals and groups, and of the natural environment.

The value commitments of the author are likely to be sensed throughout this book, especially in the selection and discussion of substantive illustrations such as the Mothers' Wages policy, and in the exploration of implications of the conceptual model of social policies for political action. However, the proposed conceptual model and the framework for social policy analysis are, in the author's best judgment, neutral analytic concepts and instruments which can be utilized by scholars and analysts irrespective of their personal value premises. This is as it should be: analytic tools should conform to criteria of scientific objectivity, but the analysts should maintain their human and social characteristics and responsibilities.

THEORY AND METHOD
OF SOCIAL POLICY ANALYSIS AND SYNTHESIS

CHAPTER ONE

Current Views of Social Policy

Students who examine the literature on social policy in the United States and from across the Atlantic in order to discern the meaning of this widely used concept, soon realize that it lacks a commonly accepted, universally valid definition, and that social scientists and policy analysts differ in their views concerning the domain and functions of social policy, and concerning the key processes through which social policies operate.

Many writers on social policy seem to assume that the concept is self-explanatory, that it conveys the same meaning to every reader, and that it therefore requires no definition. Thus, some of the most perceptive analysts of social policy in the United States have used the term social policy in the titles, and throughout the text, of important books without ever specifying its meaning. Recent illustrations of the tendency to avoid the issue of definition are Alvin Schorr's *Explorations in Social Policy*,[1] S. M. Miller and Frank Riessman's *Social Class and Social Policy*,[2] and Miller and Pamela Roby's *The Future of Inequality*.[3] These significant books reflect their authors' comprehensive view of social policy which goes far beyond conventional social welfare policies and programs. They seem to consider reduction of

3

social inequalities through redistribution of claims, and access, to resources, rights, and social opportunities as core functions of social
policy. Yet, for some unstated reason, these authors choose not to
develop a generally valid definition of the central focus of their in-
quiries. Similarly, the editors and authors of a new and important
journal, *Social Policy*, though using the concept as title of their publication, refrain from defining it.[4] Editorial comment and articles in
Social Policy reveal an implied definition akin to that reflected in the
foregoing books.

Many other authors seem equally reluctant to define social policy
in precise terms. Thus T. H. Marshall, a sociologist at the University
of London, opens his book, *Social Policy*, with the statement: "Social
policy is not a technical term with an exact meaning,"[5] and Howard
E. Freeman and Clarence C. Sherwood, both American sociologists,
express an identical view: "Social policy is a lay term, not a technical
one, and like most such terms, it defies simple definition."[6] Martin
Rein, a prolific writer on social policy issues in the United States,
declares in a collection of his papers: ". . . no formal definitions are
attempted here," and he cites the authority of Gunnar Myrdal for
avoiding the definitional task of "terms such as economics, sociology,
or psychology."[7]

However, in spite of their view that the concept of social policy
cannot, or need not, be defined, these latter authors, and many others
on both sides of the Atlantic, have struggled to define it in abstract and
generally valid terms, and have suggested a wide range of explicit
or implicit definitions. Thus, Freeman and Sherwood develop a four-
layer definition of social policy as a philosophical concept, a product,
a process, and a framework for action, respectively:

"At least four different uses or definitions can be distinguished, however:
1. Social policy as a philosophical concept. In an abstract sense, social
   policy is the principle whereby the members of large organizations and
   political entities collectively seek enduring solutions to the problems
   that affect them — almost the opposite, that is, of rugged individualism.
2. Social policy as a product. Viewed as a product, social policy consists
   of the conclusions reached by persons concerned with the betterment
   of community conditions and social life, and with the amelioration of
   deviance and social disorganization. Often the product is a document
   — what the British call a "white paper" — which lays out the intended
   policy for an organization or political unit.
3. Social policy as a process. Here, social policy is the fundamental
   process by which enduring organizations maintain an element of stability and at the same time seek to improve conditions for their members.

Existing social policies are usually never fully developed; they are continually modified in the face of changing conditions and values.
4. Social policy as a framework for action. As a framework for action, social policy is both product and process. It assumes the availability of a well-delineated policy which is to be implemented within the context of potential changes in the values, structure, and conditions of the group affected."[8]

Rein answers his own question "What is Social Policy?" with a series of progressively more comprehensive definitions, starting with:

"Social policy can be regarded as the study of the history, politics, philosophy, sociology, and economics of the social services. The definition of the term 'social services' involves a stubborn ambiguity. The definition should, at least, be broad enough to encompass services such as education, medical care, cash transfers, housing, and social work. . . ."[9]

Rein subsequently expands his foregoing initial formulation and adopts the more comprehensive orientation reflected in the writings of Richard M. Titmuss, a leading British social policy theorist and analyst.[10] Here is Rein's expanded definition:

"Accordingly it is not the social services alone, but the social purposes and consequences of agricultural, economic, manpower, fiscal, physical development, and social welfare policies that form the subject matter of social policy."[11]

One further definition suggested by Rein is

". . . to define social policy as planning for social externalities, redistribution, and the equitable distribution of social benefits, especially social services."[12]

Eveline M. Burns, a leading analyst of social policy in the United States since the early thirties, views social policy as:

". . . the organized efforts of society to meet identifiable personal needs of, or social problems presented by, groups or individuals . . ."[13]

Charles I. Schottland, another leader in social policy development in the United States, and a former Commissioner of Social Security, suggests the following broad and general definition:

"A social policy is a statement of social goal and strategy, or a settled course of action dealing with the relations of people with each other, the mutual relations of people with their government, the relations of governments with each other, including legal enactments, judicial decisions, administrative decisions, and mores."[14]

Schottland's views on social policy are similar to the following formal definition in a pamphlet on social policy goals issued by the National Association of Social Workers:

"Public Social Policy . . . consists of those laws, policies, and practices of government that affect the social relationships of individuals and their relationship to the society of which they are a part." [15]

Kenneth E. Boulding, an American economist with a long-standing interest in social policy, offers the following formulation in a paper in which he attempted to draw a dividing line between economic and social policy:

". . . it is the objective of social policy to build the identity of a person around some community with which he is associated," . . . "social policy is that which is centered in those institutions that create integration and discourage alienation." [16]

In turning to the views on social policy of British social scientists and policy analysts one finds as broad a range as in the United States. T. H. Marshall, whose doubts concerning the feasibility of defining social policy in precise terms have been quoted earlier, is nevertheless quite ready to commit himself to a specific formulation. He states that social policy

"is taken to refer to the policy of governments with regard to action having a direct impact on the welfare of the citizens, by providing them with services or income. The central core consists, therefore, of social insurance, public (or national) assistance, the health and welfare services, and housing policy." [17]

Richard Titmuss, whose influence has already been noted in Rein's work, presents a more comprehensive view of social policy than Marshall, his colleague at the University of London. Titmuss considers "the direct public provision of services in kind (e.g., education and medical care) and the direct payment of benefits (e.g., retirement and family allowances)" as the "iceberg phenomena of social welfare," and "fiscal welfare and occupational welfare" as "the indirect or submerged parts of the iceberg of social policy." [18] Titmuss' incisive analysis of the foregoing "three components of social policy," the familiar, overt one, and the less familiar, covert ones, is reflected in the following excerpts from a lecture on *The Role of Redistribution in Social Policy* which he delivered in 1964 to the staff of the Social Security Administration of the U. S. Department of Health, Education, and Welfare:

"All three categories of social policy have a great deal in common in terms of redistribution. They are all concerned with changing the individual and family pattern of current and future claims on resources set by the market, set by the possession of accumulated past rights, and set by the allocations made by Government to provide for national defense and other non-market sectors. Social welfare changes the pattern of claims by, for instance, directly providing in kind education or mental hospital care either free or at less than the market cost. Fiscal welfare changes the pattern of claims by taking less in tax (and thus increasing net disposable income) when a taxpayer's child is born, when its education is prolonged, when men have ex-wives to maintain, when taxpayers reach a specified age, and so on. An individual's pattern of claims on resources is today greatly varied through fiscal welfare policy by his or her change in circumstances, family responsibilities and opportunities available (and taken) for prolonged education, home ownership and so on. . . ."

"Occupational welfare, provided by virtue of employment status, achievement and record, may take the form of social security provisions in cash or in kind. Such provisions are legally approved by Government and, as in the case of fiscal welfare, they may be seen as alternatives to extensions in social welfare. Their cost falls in large measure on the whole population. It is thus, like social welfare and fiscal welfare, a major redistributive mechanism."

"A substantial part of these occupational welfare benefits can be interpreted — again like fiscal welfare — as social policy recognition of dependencies; the long dependencies of old age, childhood and widowhood, and such short-term dependencies as sickness and the loss of job rights."[19]

Peter Townsend, a sociologist at the University of Essex, seems to be working on the development of universally valid definitions and conceptions of social policy. His approach, a continuation of Titmuss' penetrating analysis, is illustrated by the following excerpt:

"We must define social policy not just as the strategy of development of the social services as defined by government but as the underlying as well as the professed rationale for institutionalized control of present and future social development. Included would be measures adopted and organized by government but also by industry, voluntary associations, professions and other bodies to meet specifically social objectives — the achievement of social equality or justice, the redistribution of wealth, the adjustment of income to meet the needs of dependency, equality for women, equality for people of different race or religion and so on. It would include employer welfare and fiscal benefits as well as the formally defined public social services. This definition is very wide but something like it seems to me to be inescapable if we are to keep before ourselves the new as well as the old inequalities."[20]

A. Macbeath of The Queen's University in Belfast seems to have come closest to developing a comprehensive, abstract, and universally valid conception of social policy. According to him

"Social policies are concerned with the right ordering of the network of relationships between men and women who live together in societies, or with the principles which should govern the activities of individuals and groups so far as they affect the lives and interests of other people."[21]

The final definition to be quoted in this brief and selective survey of current views on social policy is by Father J. A. Ponsioen of the International Institute of Social Studies in The Hague, Netherlands. In an essay entitled *General Theory of Social Welfare Policy*, Ponsioen examined the "semantics" of social welfare policy. After defining "policy" as

"a continuous and deliberate activity aimed at a remote purpose or ideal which becomes realized progressively according to circumstances, possibilities, resistance, stimulating forces and counter-forces,"

he suggests the following, strongly value-oriented definition of social policy

"as a policy which aims at a continual reform of society in order to eliminate weaknesses of individuals or groups in that society. In its progressive realization it assists the weak people, prevents weaknesses, and constructs or ameliorates good situations."[22]

SUMMARY

The foregoing selection of excerpts from recent writings of leading social theorists, policy analysts, and social welfare program administrators in the United States and overseas reveals a growing trend toward comprehensive and abstract formulations of the concept social policy. While agreement on a universally valid conceptual model of social policies, their common domain, functions, and general processes has not, as yet, been achieved, the essential elements and the broad outlines of such a model can already be discerned in the literature.

Several dilemmas can, however, be identified in current thinking about social policies. Many authors tend to equate social policies with the social services or the policies that shape social welfare programs. While such a conception of social policy may be useful for administrative and legislative purposes, it seems unsatisfactory from the perspective of social theory, mainly because it is dysfunctionally narrow, and also, because the terms social services and social welfare have themselves not been clearly defined, and their use in the definition of social policies thus merely substitutes one vague notion for another.

It may be noted in this context that current views of social welfare services range from a narrow conception according to which these services aim to ameliorate needs and problems of individuals and groups which result from transitional shortcomings of a supposedly self-regulating, free-enterprise economy, to a comprehensive conception, according to which these services comprise a broad array of societal provisions including education, manpower training, health-care, housing, income maintenance, personal social services, treatment of delinquents, recreation, etc. Harold L. Wilensky and Charles N. Lebeaux, who examined this issue several years ago, referred to these two conceptions of social welfare as "the residual and the institutional."[23]

Irrespective of whether authors subscribe to a narrow or a comprehensive conception of social welfare they tend to consider economic issues as a separate policy domain, apart from social policies. This seems to be an arbitrary distinction with untoward consequences for the development of social as well as of economic policies. Implied in this conceptual separation of economic from social policies is a view of the economy, and of economic development and growth as ends in their own rights, rather than as means for the attainment of social ends. Implied in it is also the hypothesis, or rather the illusion, that constant growth of the Gross National Product will result, automatically, in the gradual disappearance of poverty and of poverty-related social problems. Furthermore, viewing social policies as apart from economic policies deprives social policy development of its most potent tools, and consigns to social policies the function of dealing merely in a reactive and ameliorative fashion with the fallout problems of economic policies.

Equating social policies with social welfare services and programs leads also to a fragmentary, "categorical" approach to the analysis and development of social policies. In such an approach specific social policies are conceived of as societal responses to specific social needs or problems such as income insufficiency, child neglect and abuse, poor health and education, substandard housing, delinquency, etc., rather than as elements of a comprehensive system of social policies, all of which, through their combined effects, shape the overall quality of life in a society, the living conditions of its members, and their human relations to one another and to society as a whole. As a consequence of this categorical, fragmented conception of social policies, their underlying common domain and dynamics are usually disregarded, as is the fact that the very needs and problems which specific policies are expected to resolve are themselves the unavoidable consequences of extant and earlier social policies. It should be stressed in this context that a comprehensive conception of social policies reveals them to be the dynamic source of all social problems, for these problems are rooted in the fabric of a society which in turn derives from, and is constantly maintained by, its system of social policies. Social policies are, therefore, not merely potential solutions of social problems but are also their powerful underlying causes.

It seems appropriate to end this review of current thinking about social policies with the observation that several leading authors on the subject have already cut the umbilical cord which, for too long, had linked the conception of social policies to the social services. In doing so these authors have extricated themselves from the web of theoretical and practical difficulties inherent in the linkage of these concepts. The quest for a universally valid conceptual model of social policies seems thus to have entered a new and, theoretically, more promising stage. The continuation of this quest is the subject of the next chapter.

CHAPTER TWO

A Conceptual Model of Social Policies

The aim of this chapter is to develop and articulate a conceptual model of social policies in any human society, and to present arguments in support of the universal validity claimed for that model. Models are abstractions or representations of selected aspects of reality. Their general purpose is to facilitate the understanding of the dynamics of the phenomena they represent. According to a social science dictionary a model is

> "a pattern of relationships, either conceptual or mathematical which is found in some way to imitate, duplicate or analogously illustrate a pattern of relationships in one's observations of the world . . . The value of a model is determined by its usefulness for guiding study. Models are tentative and limited yet they are the building blocks of theory, interpretation, empirical discoveries, prediction, and general scientific progress."[1]

A valid model of social policies should enhance understanding of the general elements, functions, and dynamics of all social policies, facilitate analysis of specific social policies and their consequences, and aid in the development of alternative social policies. Implied in the construction of such a conceptual model is the premise that all social policies, in spite of considerable differences in content, objectives, and scope, are, nevertheless, directly or indirectly concerned with an identical domain of societal existence. Thus, policies dealing with such diverse issues as agriculture, commerce, and industry; conservation, zoning, and housing; health, education, and economic security; manpower, selective service, transportation, and taxation, etc., are assumed to serve underlying common functions. The conceptual model is expected to identify this common domain of all social policies, to specify the processes or key mechanisms which generate variations in the content, objectives, and scope of different social policies, and to trace the relationships among these processes.

An important corollary of the foregoing premise is that social policies are not independent of, but interact with, each other, and consequently constitute a comprehensive system. It is this entire system, rather than any specific social policy, which, through its aggregate effects, shapes the common domain of all social policies. It should be noted, however, that while specific social policies are considered to be contributing elements of a comprehensive system, they are not necessarily assumed to be consistent with each other. On the contrary, inconsistency among the different policies of social policy systems is to be expected because of continuous conflicts of interest among the various groups in a society which underlie the evolution of its social policies.

Before proceeding further with the discussion of the conceptual model of social policy, several key terms need to be defined:

Policies are guiding principles or courses of action adopted and pursued by societies and their governments, as well as by various groups or units within societies, such as political parties and other interest groups, business firms and corporations, labor unions and professional associations, formal and informal voluntary organizations, religious and ethnic groups, geographic entities, family and kinship groups, etc. Single individuals, too, may hold, promote, and pursue specific policies. Specific policies govern, or are intended to govern, specified domains of a society or its subunits. Because of linkages and interactions between the various domains of a society, any policy may affect domains other than the one with which it is primarily concerned. Policies tend to, but need not, be codified in formal legal instruments.

A *society* is a group of interdependent human beings, living usually in territories over which they, collectively, exercise some degree of sovereignty. The membership and ecological base of a society need, however, not be fixed. Members of a society share "a common and at least somewhat distinct culture, . . . have a feeling of unity, and regard themselves as a distinguishable entity." A society functions to maintain itself and to assure its continuity and biologic survival, while over time it also undergoes manifold changes in structure, dynamics, membership, boundaries, values, and culture.[2] The adjective *social* derives its meaning from the noun society, and is consequently defined as having to do with life in society, and with intra-societal relationships among individuals, groups, and society as a whole.

THE COMMON DOMAIN OR FOCUS OF SOCIAL POLICIES

In accordance with the foregoing set of definitions, social policies are a special type of policies, namely, policies which deliberately pertain to the quality of life and to the circumstances of living in society, and to intra-societal relationships among individuals, groups, and society as a whole. And any specific social policy, irrespective of its unique content, objectives, and scope, is thus one discrete instance of this type of policies. The common domain of all social policies can consequently be identified as *the overall quality of life in society, the circumstances of living of individuals and groups, and the nature of all intra-societal human relations.*

The domain identified here as the common focus of all social policies constitutes the core of the conceptual model of social policies. Intrinsic to his conceptual model is the proposition that all extant social policies of a given society, operating together as a system, exert a decisive influence over this entire domain, and that any specific social policy, or any specific cluster of social policies, influences a specific segment within this broad domain. This proposition is supported by observations in all known human societies which indicate that the overall quality of life, the circumstances of living, and the nature of intra-societal human relations do not evolve at random, but tend to follow regular patterns which develop over time out of continuous interaction between (1) natural forces, both physical and biological; (2) man-designed principles and courses of action; and (3) chance events. These man-designed principles and courses of action which interact with natural forces and chance events in shaping the quality of life, the circumstances of living, and the human relations among members of a society are, by definition, its social policies.

From this discussion of the common domain or focus of social policies it is evident that economic factors are central aspects of that domain since they are important determinants of the quality of life in a society, of the circumstances of living of its members, and of their relationship to each other and to society as a whole. Policies dealing with economic issues belong, consequently, to the type of policies defined here as social policies, for they are important means toward attaining societal objectives in the social policy domain. By including economic policies within the social policy system the conceptual dilemmas which have been noted in the discussion of current views of social policy can be avoided.

The phrases "quality of life" and "circumstances of living" in the specification of the common domain or focus of all social policies are easily comprehended by way of common sense, but precise scientific definitions and measurement of these concepts are difficult as they involve not only observable and measurable characteristics, but also subjective perceptions and judgments. For purposes of social policy analysis and development, circumstances of living and the quality of life may be represented by specified sets of biological, demographic, psychological, social, economic, political, cultural, and ecologic indicators to the extent to which such indicators are available.[3] Eventually, measurements on these dimensions will have to be supplemented by valid and reliable indicators of subjective perceptions of the circumstances of living and the quality of life, obtained at regular intervals through specially designed interviews with representative samples of a society.

The number of possible sets of "intra-societal relationships" is large. However, all these relationships fall within the following five reciprocal types:

individual — individual;
individual — group;
individual — total society;
group   — group;
group   — total society.

The term "group" is used here to refer to various social aggregates below the level of a total society such as families, business firms, voluntary associations, neighborhoods, labor unions, political parties, etc.

Human relationships involving individuals and/or groups belonging to different societies are not included in the phrase intra-societal relationships, and are thus not part of the domain of social policy as defined here, although they may influence, and, in turn may be influenced by, social policies. These relationships, as well as the relations between entire societies, belong to the domain of foreign policies. Similarly, an individual's relationship to himself, his inner life, is not included in the domain of social policy. This private domain is, however, influenced by social policies and tends to have considerable influence over them. One further set of relationships not included in the domain of social policies, but also interacting with it, is man's individual and collective relationship to the supernatural. These relationships constitute the domain of religion. It should be noted, however, that man's individual and collective relationship to nature belongs definitely to the domain of social policies since these relationships have a direct impact on the quality and circumstances of life.

THE KEY PROCESSES OF SOCIAL POLICIES

The primary objective of a conceptual model of social policies is to identify the common domain or common focus of all social policies. This objective has been achieved in the preceding section with the specification of the core of the conceptual model. A second objective is to discern the universal, man-designed, generic processes which underlie the operation of all social policies, and to which they can, therefore, be reduced. These processes constitute the dynamic elements of the conceptual model, for through them and their derivatives societies influence the quality of life, the circumstances of living, and the nature of human relations. These processes then are the key mechanisms which generate, through their variations and interactions, the specific contents, objectives, and scope of different social policies.

What then are these universal, man-designed, basic processes by which human societies systematically influence and shape the quality and circumstances of life of their members, and the nature of all intrasocietal human relations? The content, objectives, and scope of policies and activities concerned with the quality of life, the circumstances of living, and human relations vary widely, especially in modern, complex, industrial, and post-industrial societies. They deal with such diverse activities as fishing and hunting; planting and harvesting crops; raising cattle; mining minerals; conserving woods, wildlife, and other natural resources; building houses, schools, factories, hospitals, churches, and jails; constructing highways, bridges, and railroads; manufacturing, distributing, and selling consumer goods; practicing medicine and law; teaching, training, and conducting scientific research; performing diverse governmental functions; writing poetry and music, and painting pictures; etc. In spite of this apparently unlimited diversity all these activities can conceptually be subsumed under one or more of the following three interrelated, universal processes or societal mechanisms:

1. *resource development:* the development of material and symbolic, life-sustaining and life-enhancing resources, goods, and services;
2. *division of labor, and task or status allocation:* the assignment of

individuals and groups to specific tasks which must be performed in order to develop, and distribute throughout society, these life-sustaining and life-enhancing resources, goods, and services, and to assure society's survival; or, in sociological terms, the allocation of individuals and groups to specific statuses within the total array of societal tasks and functions, involving corresponding roles, and prerogatives intrinsic to these roles;

3. *rights distribution:* the distribution, to individuals and groups, of specific rights to material and symbolic, life-sustaining and life-enhancing resources, goods, and services, through general entitlements, task or status specific rewards, and general and specific constraints.

These three basic processes, and specific policies derived from them, vary widely in content, objectives, and scope among different societies living in different geographic settings and ecologic conditions. They vary also over time in the same society and in the same geographic setting as a result of natural, social, cultural, and technological changes. Yet in spite of virtually unlimited variability in the specific content, objectives, and scope of these processes, and the policies generated through them, they do exist in some form in every known human society.

The universality of the interrelated processes of resource development, division of labor and task or status allocation, and rights distribution, seems due to the fact that they are rooted in, and constitute man's collective response, since the dawn of societal evolution, to certain intrinsic characteristics of the human condition. These characteristics are:

1. man's strong, bio-psychological drive to survive and propagate;
2. the relative scarcity of life-sustaining resources available readily in man's natural settings;
3. the necessity for some form of human labor without which sufficient life-sustaining resources could not be obtained from the natural environment;
4. the necessity to devise some system for organizing and assuring the performance of labor essential to the development of these life-sustaining resources; and
5. the necessity to devise some system for the distribution of the life-sustaining resources throughout society.

Because of these intrinsic characteristics of the human condition everywhere and any time, the overall quality and circumstances of life depend primarily on a society's interaction with, and conservation of, its natural environment and, more specifically, on the quality and quantity of the resources, goods, and services it generates through the investment of human labor. And the circumstances of living of individuals and groups, and their relationship to each other and to society as a whole depend largely on their specific statuses within the total array of societal tasks, and on their specific rights to concrete and symbolic goods and services produced by society. These considerations suggest that the processes of resource development, status allocation, and rights distribution are the key variables or key mechanisms of all social policies, and, therefore, the dynamic elements of the conceptual model of social policies. The possibilities of variation in the way these three processes operate and interact with each other in different societies and at different times are numerous, and correspondingly numerous are, therefore, the possible variations of specific social policies and of entire systems of social policies.

In accordance with the conceptual model of social policies developed here any specific social policy reflects one unique position on one or more of these key variables and one unique configuration of interaction between them; and changes of social policies and of entire systems of social policies involve corresponding changes on one or more of the underlying key variables and in the relationship between them. Desired modifications in intra-societal relationships and in the quality and circumstances of living can consequently be achieved by a society by means of appropriate modifications of one or more of the key mechanisms of social policies. This proposition is of crucial importance for social policy analysis and synthesis. For implied in it is the frequently disregarded corollary according to which significant changes in intra-societal human relations and in the quality and circumstances of living will occur only when a society introduces significant modifications in the scope and quality of the resources it develops, and/or in the principles by which it allocates statuses and distributes rights to its members. Social policies which involve no modifications of these key mechanisms, or which involve only slight modifications, can therefore not be expected to bring about significant changes in the quality and circumstances of living and in the nature of human relations in a society. By examining social policies in terms of the key variables identified here, policy analysts can determine whether real and significant changes may be expected from the implementation of these policies, or whether changes would be merely superficial and insignificant — "a new variation on an old, status quo theme."

One further implication of the conceptual model of social policies is that "social problems" perceived by various groups in society concerning the quality or circumstances of life, or concerning intra-societal relationships, are to be understood as intended or unintended consequences of the existing configuration of social policies. Social policies are, therefore, not merely solutions to specified social problems, but all past and extant social policies of a society are causally related to the various social problems perceived in that society at any point in time. This conceptualization of the relationship between social policies and social problems does not negate the significance of specific social policies as potential solutions to perceived social problems. Rather, it provides an expanded theoretical basis for the proposition that valid solutions of social problems require appropriate modifications of the key processes of social policies. Such modifications are viewed as potentially powerful instruments of planned, comprehensive, and systematic social change, rather than merely as reactive measures designed to ameliorate specified undesirable phenomena in an ad hoc, fragmented fashion.

Because of the importance of the three key variables for social policy analysis and synthesis some further clarification concerning them seems indicated.

The first process, resource development, involves societal decisions and courses of action concerning the type, quality, and quantity of all material and symbolic goods and services generated by a society, as well as the ordering of priorities in this sphere. Decisions concerning the selective utilization and preservation of the natural environment are involved in this process, as are decisions concerning the acceptable levels of social, ecological, and economic costs of various productive activities. Further important aspects of the resource development process are investment decisions concerning the allocation of scarce resources to production rather than to consumption, and decisions on storage of resources in the form of savings or inventories for future investment or consumption. Since the totality of rights and right-equivalents available for distribution throughout a society depends on the aggregate of material and symbolic resources, goods, and services generated by it, decisions and actions concerning resource development are of crucial importance for the circumstances of living of individuals and groups of a society. Furthermore, since decisions concerning resource development have complex consequences for the natural environment, not all of which are always sufficiently understood, these decisions have a significant impact on the overall quality of life in a society.

Economists have designed a simple measure of the totality of goods and services produced by a society — the Gross National Product. This index is a rough reflection of a society's resource development. In using this index for policy analysis one must remember, however, that it makes no allowance for the hidden costs and disbenefits which are the unintended by-products of many productive activities. Moreover, the value of goods and services which is entered in the G.N.P. index is their market price which may or may not be an appropriate reflection of their "social value." Thus, one private luxury car may be assigned equal weight in the G.N.P. to one public transportation bus, although the social value of the two vehicles seems to differ considerably.

It should be noted that resource development involves also the generation of symbolic resources, goods and services which tend to be of considerable importance in all known human societies. For as soon as man's essential material needs are met at a subsistence level, he seems to be yearning for a great variety of non-essential material and non-material goods and services. Honors, titles, and other symbols of prestige bestowed by kings, governments and various groups in societies are illustrations of one type of such symbolic goods and services. Art, literature, and music, and their diverse products, illustrate other types of symbolic goods and services for which there was demand throughout history in all known human societies. Symbolic goods are often interwoven with non-symbolic ones. Thus, the luxury car mentioned above clearly serves concrete and symbolic functions and its high market price is partly explained by its serving as a "status symbol."

The second key process of social policies is concerned with a society's organization of the totality of its work load, functions, and "manpower." This process involves societal decisions concerning the division of labor and functions, and the recruitment and preparation of personnel for specific tasks, functions, and positions resulting from this division, or, in technical terms, decisions concerning the assignment of individuals to statuses, and the allocation of statuses to individuals.

The term "status" is used here to refer to specified positions, functions, or tasks within the total work load of a society, such as king, judge, soldier, slave, farmer; veteran, pensioner; child, female, father, wife, orphan, thief.[4] The term does not include the element of "prestige" which tends to be closely associated with status in most societies, but which should be conceptually distinguished from it, since it is not intrinsically related to statuses. Prestige is a "right" distributed by society as an inducement to, or reward for, incumbents of statuses. Any individual occupies usually more than one specific status, and it is possible to describe a person in terms of the cluster of statuses which he occupies at a given point in time and throughout his life span.

Every society has its own unique ways for filling the various positions within the total array of tasks which need to be performed, and for allocating to each individual a specific combination of statuses. These allocative processes are never left entirely to chance but tend to follow regular patterns. Some statuses are allocated on the basis of biological characteristics such as sex, life-cycle stages, blood relationship, skin color, size and other physical properties. The allocation of statuses in complex modern societies involves, however, in addition to biological factors, intricate social mechanisms and criteria including inheritance, nepotism, patronage, merit systems; serfdom, slavery, discrimination; schooling and professional training; etc. Major policy issues concerning status systems are the extent to which access to various statuses is open on an equal basis to all members of a society (it rarely ever is), and the nature of the criteria which determine the selection and allocation of individuals and groups to statuses. Quite obviously, the circumstances of living of individuals and groups in a society, and the manner in which they interact, are dependent in many ways on the specific statuses they occupy.

The term "role" refers to the dynamic aspect of status, that is, the set of tasks and functions which the incumbent of a given status is expected to perform. It is important to note in this context that role expectations are rarely fixed to the last detail. Rather, the role defines a normative range of possible behaviors, and different incumbents of a given status will tend to interpret the role in their individual ways within that range. This variability of role performance seems to be one important avenue of gradual social change. Role allocation is usually a function of status-allocation. However, occasionally the role content of given statuses may be changed during the incumbency of given individuals. In such situations, role allocation involves a certain degree of independence from the allocation of statuses.

"Prerogatives" are a specific type of rights that are attached to a status as a sine-qua-non of role performance, such as the right of a traffic policeman to stop traffic. Prerogatives are conceptually inseparable from status and role and are thus considered to be allocated automatically, along with the allocation of statuses, rather than through the rights-distribution processes. Prerogatives must be distinguished conceptually from rights, which are not essential for the performance of roles and which are distributed as specific "rewards" for status incumbency, or as general "entitlements." Prerogatives are therefore allocated through the status-allocation mechanism, while all other rights, including prestige, are distributed through the third key mechanism of social policies, the one dealing with the distribution of rights.

The third key process of social policies concerns the right of access to the total array of life-sustaining and life-enhancing resources generated by, and available to, a society. A variety of methods are employed for this purpose—rewards, entitlements, and constraints. Together they result in the distribution to every member of society, and to social groups, of varying levels of rights to claim and control resources in the form of material and symbolic goods and services. "Rewards" are rights provided in exchange for the incumbency of a status and the performance of corresponding roles. Salaries, wages, titles, and other forms of prestige, expense accounts, and job-linked pensions are illustrations of this type of rights distribution. "Entitlements" may be universal or categorical. They are rights assigned by virtue of membership in a total society or in a specified social group. Thus, all members of society may be entitled to free speech and to certain public services, such as public health, education, recreation, sanitation, etc., and all children may be entitled to school meals, and war veterans to honors and pensions. The boundary between rewards and entitlements is, however, not clear-cut and absolute. For membership in society and in specified social groups are "statuses" which involve the performance of certain roles, and entitlements may thus be interpreted as rewards in exchange for such role performance, rather than simply as rights by virtue of membership.

"Constraints" may be viewed as "negative rewards" or "negative entitlements," since they take the form of specific or general limitations on the level of rights. They are an essential aspect of rights distribution, since they define the limits of the rights distributed to individuals and social groups as rewards or entitlements. In this context one should remember that rights and freedoms in any society can never be unlimited or absolute. Zoning laws which limit the rights of land owners, taxation which defines limits on income, wealth, and wealth transmission, and fines, jail terms, and other forms of penalties, are illustrations of constraints. Like most other rights, constraints tend to be distributed unequally in most societies.

An important aspect of rights distribution is the differentiation between rights distributed directly, in kind, such as land, public education, and health services, and rights distributed indirectly in the form of money, either through market mechanisms or through governmental income transfers. Money is a convenient "right-equivalent" which can be transformed with relative ease, at the owner's discretion, into a broad range of equivalent resources, goods, and services. It can also be stored and accumulated into capital and serve thus as a basis for future rights and delayed claims to goods and services. Rights in the form of money can also be transmitted easily through gifts and through inheritance. Income and holdings of capital expressed in units of money are also convenient, though only very rough, measures of the levels of rights of individuals and groups in modern capitalist societies.

The distribution of rights in a society, and the criteria underlying this distribution, are, no doubt, most significant issues of social policy development. For no other factor seems to have a stronger, direct impact on the circumstances of living of individuals and groups than the nature and scope of their rights with respect to control over material and symbolic resources, goods, and services.

The key processes of social policy have been discussed here as if they were separate sets of societal activities, which they definitely are not. As already indicated, these processes are linked with each other in many ways and their influence over the common domain of social policies is the result of their continuous interaction. Thus, the processes of resource development and resource distribution require input of human labor; yet sustained input of human labor depends on the generation and distribution of life-sustaining resources, goods, and services, and on some form of organization, including the division of the total work load into separate, manageable tasks, the recruitment and assignment of individuals to these tasks, and their preparation and motivation for performing their assigned roles.

One of the most crucial issues in this context seems to be that the relationship between a society's processes of rights distribution and its processes of status allocation is not fixed forever, but is subject to change. Policy variations concerning the linkage of rights to statuses are reflected in varying degrees of interdependence between these two processes, and social policy systems could actually be classified along a continuum ranging from nearly complete independence to nearly complete dependence between them.

Differences of status among members of a society are an essential aspect of the task organization once division of labor is adopted in the course of societal evolution. However, inequalities of rights are, logically, not an essential consequence of task related differences of status. Most societies have, however, adopted inequality of rights as an apparent essential corollary of the principle of division of labor, and have institutionalized inequality of rewards for different statuses. This fact is reflected in a high correlation between rights and statuses. It is, of course, entirely feasible, from a theoretical point of view, to distribute rights equally among all members of a society, by means of universal entitlements, irrespective of the different statuses they occupy. Such a principle of rights distribution would be reflected in independence between rights and statuses. Obviously, any intermediate level of linkage between these two key processes of social policies is theoretically feasible, and can be designed in practice.

The relatively high correlation between rights distribution and status allocation, which is a dominant characteristic of most present-day societies, including several socialist societies, is usually rationalized and justified by reference to incentives and human motivation. It is claimed, in axiomatic fashion, that in order to recruit personnel for the diversity of statuses in society, prospective incumbents must be attracted through incentives built into the reward system. While this may be a correct description of current human behavior, it leaves several important issues unresolved. The descriptive statement that human beings are motivated to accept certain statuses by means of reward-incentives does not explain the dynamics underlying this behavioral response pattern, nor does it answer the question whether this response pattern is biologically determined and, thus, the only possible behavioral mode.

Without digressing into a thorough examination of human motivation, it seems nevertheless necessary to comment on this issue, since it is related to one important proposition inherent in the conceptualization of social policy developed here, namely, that the linkage between the processes of rights distribution and status allocation is subject to significant variability as a major avenue for social policy change.

Biological, psychological, and sociological research indicate that human motivation is a function of biologically given factors and socially learned tendencies. The relative importance of these two sets of factors is not known, but there seems to be little question that learned tendencies are a powerful force of human behavior. Based on these considerations, it seems that existing patterns of motivation and of response to incentives reflect existing patterns of socialization, and that variations in these existing socialization patterns could produce over time different motivational attitudes and response patterns. One is thus led to conclude that the patterns of human motivation used to justify the structured inequalities in the distribution of rights in most existing societies are not fixed by nature, but are open to modification by means of variations in processes of socialization. The view that man responds primarily to the profit motive is not necessarily a correct indication of mankind's social and cultural potential.[5]

A DEFINITION OF SOCIAL POLICIES

Having identified the general domain of all social policies and the key processes through which they operate, it is now possible to suggest a formal, universally valid definition, and a simple diagram of the conceptual model developed here:

Social policies are principles or courses of action designed to influence

1. *the overall quality of life in a society;*
2. *the circumstances of living of individuals and groups in that society; and*
3. *the nature of intra-societal relationships among individuals, groups, and society as a whole.*

Social policies operate through the following key processes and their manifold interrelations:

1. *the development of material and symbolic, life-sustaining and life-enhancing resources, goods, and services;*
2. *the allocation of individuals and groups to specific statuses within the total array of societal tasks and functions, involving corresponding roles, and prerogatives intrinsic to these roles; and*
3. *the distribution to individuals and groups of specific rights to material and symbolic, life-sustaining and life-enhancing resources, goods, and services through general and specific entitlements, task or status specific rewards, and general and specific constraints.*

Social policies tend to, but need not, be codified in formal legal instruments. All extant social policies of a given society constitute an interrelated, yet not necessarily internally, logically consistent, social policy system, which is, at any point in time, in a state of "dynamic equilibrium."

Chart 2.1 is an attempt to represent in visual form the relationships implicit in this formal definition.

CHART 2.1. A CONCEPTUAL MODEL OF SOCIAL POLICIES*

DYNAMIC ELEMENTS: *Key Processes or Variables*	CORE: *Common Domain or Focus*
1. development of life-sustaining and life-enhancing, material and symbolic resources, goods, and services	1. overall quality of life in society
2. "division of labor" or allocation of statuses within the totality of societal tasks and functions, involving roles and prerogatives	2. circumstances of living of individuals and groups
3. distribution of rights to resources, goods, and services through entitlements, rewards, and constraints	3. nature of intra-societal relationships among individuals, groups, and society as a whole

* The dynamic elements and the core components of the model interact with each other in multiple and circular ways.

THE FORCE FIELD AFFECTING THE EVOLUTION OF SOCIAL POLICIES

The processes of resource development, status allocation, and rights distribution, which the conceptual model identifies as the key mechanisms of all social policies, are themselves subject to the influence of certain natural and societal forces. The physical and biological characteristics of a society's natural environment are limiting factors with respect to the development and distribution of life-sustaining resources. Man's own biological and basic psychological properties affect his capacities and his motivation, his interaction with other men and the organization of his work, and hence, indirectly, the key processes of resource development and rights distribution.

Societal forces affecting the evolution of social policies are traceable to man's collective response to the universal characteristics of the human condition sketched above. An early development along the evolutionary path seems to have been the emergence of division of labor as an organizing principle for the tasks that had to be performed in pursuit of survival. Sex, age, physical and intellectual characteristics are likely to have been important factors in this context. Division of labor eventually led to task-specialization and to the perpetuation of linkages between specific tasks and certain individuals and groups. The tendency to perpetuate such linkages probably became one important source of the development of systems of social stratification. A critical next step in terms of social policy evolution in many, but not all, human societies seems to have been the emergence of the principle of unequal rewards for the performance of different tasks, or the incumbency of different statuses, and, hence, unequal rights for members of different social strata. These developments led to efforts on the part of more privileged individuals and groups to perpetuate the material and symbolic advantages accruing to them as a result of such patterned inequalities in the allocation of statuses and the distribution of rights. Inequalities in rewards also enabled the more privileged individuals and social strata to accumulate surplus resources which in turn led to the development of property rights, including the inter-generational transmission of wealth, and of rights inherent in it.

The emergence of these principles and tendencies, the interplay between them, and reactions to them on the part of competing interest groups within societies, seem to constitute major dynamics of the evolutionary, and at times revolutionary, development of human societies and their social policies. Social policies may thus be viewed as dynamic expressions of the evolving structures of, and conflicts within, societies, since they derive from these structures and conflicts, and in turn, support the structures and spur the conflicts. Once initiated, the processes of societal evolution, and the parallel processes of social policy evolution, continue as a result of ceaseless conflicts of interest among individuals and social groups who control different levels of resources, and who differ consequently in rights and power. The processes of social policy evolution are also affected by, and in turn affect, a society's stage of development in the cultural, economic, and technological spheres; its size and its level of institutional differentiation and complexity; its interaction with extra-societal forces; and its values, beliefs, customs, and traditions.

The quality and quantity of the resources, goods, and services a society generates, and the manner in which it organizes its manpower and its productive processes seem primarily affected by its stage of development in cultural, economic, and technological spheres, its size, and its level of institutional differentiation and complexity. The distribution of rights and the allocation of statuses, on the other hand, seem to be affected primarily by inter-group conflicts, and therefore, by the size and organizational structure of competing groups, and by the relative power, or command over resources these groups have secured in the past. Past inequalities in the distribution of rights and the allocation of statuses tend thus to perpetuate themselves, since individuals and groups who have achieved control over disproportionately large shares of a society's resources, and over more desirable and influential positions in its status system, are in an advantageous power position to assure the continuation of these inequalities and perhaps even to increase them in their favor. Also, institutionalized legal and political systems of societies tend to reflect the status quo of power relations among competing interest groups. They are therefore unlikely to upset the dynamic equilibrium prevailing among these groups, and the structured inequalities which are sustained by the established patterns of developmental, allocative, and distributional processes.

Of considerable importance among the forces influencing a society's key processes of social policies, are its multi-faceted personal, cultural, economic, and political interactions with other societies. The significance of these interactions has increased throughout human history as their scope widened and their quality intensified due to worldwide population growth, territorial expansion of societies, and technological developments, especially in land, sea, and air transportation, and in worldwide communications.

VALUES AND SOCIAL POLICIES

The dominant beliefs, values, and ideologies of a society, and the customs and traditions derived from them, exert a significant influence on all decisions concerning the three key processes of social policies. Consequently, any specific configuration of these key processes and the resulting systems of social policies tend to reflect the dominant value positions of a society concerning such policy relevant dimensions as individualism — collectivism, competition — cooperation, inequality — equality, etc. A society's dominant beliefs, values, and ideologies appear thus to constitute crucial constraining variables which limit the malleability of its processes of resource development, status allocation, and rights distribution, and of the social policies derived from these processes. Thus a society which stresses individualism, pursuit of self-interest, and competitiveness, and which has come to consider inequality of circumstances of living and of rights as a "natural" order of human existence, will tend to preserve structured inequalities through its processes of status allocation and rights distribution, while a society which stresses collective values and cooperation and which is truly committed to the notion that all men are intrinsically of equal worth, will tend to develop a system of social policies which assures to all its members equal access to all statuses, and equal rights to material and symbolic, life-sustaining and life-enhancing resources, goods, and services.

While dwelling briefly on the central importance of beliefs, values, and ideologies for social policy analysis and development, it should be noted that public discussion of social policies in the United States tends to neglect these crucial variables. Instead, major, and often exclusive, emphasis tends to be placed on technical matters and on means, while the goals and values which the policies are to attain are pushed to the background. These comments should not be misunderstood. Technical matters are indeed important, and alternative means need to be evaluated in terms of effectiveness and efficiency. However, unless goals and values are clear, and are constantly kept in mind as main criteria for policy evaluation and development, the examination of means and of technologies may be of limited utility.

Though beliefs, values, ideologies, customs, and traditions are not fixed forever in any human society, changing them is usually not a simple matter. The beliefs, values, and ideologies of societies tend to be shaped and guarded by cultural and political elites recruited, mainly, from among the more powerful and privileged strata. Not unexpectedly, these beliefs, values, and ideologies seem, therefore, to reflect and support the interests of these more powerful and privileged social groups. It should be noted, however, that some members of cultural and political elites are recruited from less privileged strata and may thus represent their interests. Also, some members of elites who were recruited from among more privileged social groups are not necessarily committed forever to the narrowly conceived, short-range interests of their groups of origin. Cultural elites are capable of developing, and frequently will develop, comprehensive, broadly-based, long-range conceptions of societal interests. There is consequently always a potential for change in the beliefs, values, and ideologies of societies, and in the social policies, the malleability of which seems limited by them.

It needs to be emphasized in this context that significant changes in a society's system of social policies are not likely to occur without thorough changes in its dominant beliefs, values, and ideologies. Because of this, violent or non-violent revolutions which merely shift the balance of power among competing social groups, but do not modify the dominant value premises of society, are unlikely to be followed by significant changes in the key processes of social policies. Rather, they tend to develop systems of social policies similar in basic principles and dimensions to the ones existing before the revolutions.

CHART 2.2. NATURAL AND SOCIETAL FORCES LIMITING, INFLUENCING, AND INTERACTING WITH THE KEY PROCESSES AND GENERAL DOMAIN OF SOCIAL POLICIES.

A. LIMITING CONDITIONS	B. INTRA-AND INTER-SOCIETAL FORCE FIELD	C. CONSTRAINING VARIABLES	SOCIAL POLICIES	
			Key Processes	Common Domain
1. Physical and biological properties of a society's natural setting	1. Intra-societal interest group conflicts	Beliefs	1. Resource development	1. Overall quality of life
2. Biological and basic psychological properties of man	2. Society's stage of development in cultural, economic, and technological spheres	Values Ideologies	2. Status allocation	2. Circumstances of living of individuals and groups
	3. Size and institutional differentiation or complexity of society	Customs Traditions	3. Rights distribution	3. Intra-societal human relations
	4. Personal, cultural, economic, and political interaction with extra-societal forces			

Note: The forces represented in this diagram do not exert their influence merely in a linear progression from left to right, but interact with each other in multiple and circular ways.

SUMMARY

The conceptual model of social policies which has been developed in this chapter and the various forces, the multiple interactions of which with the key processes of social policies have been discussed, are represented schematically in Chart 2.2. Awareness of the complex and multifaceted inter-relations among these forces is essential to the analysis of social policies, to the development of alternative social policies, and to social and political action aimed at changing the established balance of power among competing interest groups in a society as reflected in its existing system of social policies. Approaches to social policy analysis and synthesis and to social and political action based on such awareness are explored throughout the remainder of this book.

CHAPTER THREE

A Framework for Analysis and Synthesis of Social Policies

INTRODUCTION

In this chapter a framework for systematic analysis of existing or newly proposed social policies, and for development of alternative policies, is derived from the conceptual model presented in the preceding chapter. The framework is designed for use by legislative, administrative, and judicial branches of government at all levels; political parties and other social action and interest groups throughout all segments of society; communications media; and scholars concerned with social issues. The framework should facilitate attainment of the following separate, but related, objectives of policy analysis and synthesis.

The first objective seems to be to gain understanding of the issues that constitute the focus of a specific social policy or social policy cluster which is being analyzed or developed. This involves exploration of the nature, scope, and distribution of these issues, and of causal theories concerning underlying dynamics.

A second objective is to discern the chain of substantive effects resulting, or expected to result, from the implementation of a given social policy, including intended and unintended, short and long-range effects. This involves explication of policy objectives with respect to the focal issues, of value premises underlying these objectives, and of hypotheses guiding the strategies and provisions of a policy. It also involves specifications concerning the size, distribution, and relevant characteristics of target populations, and determination of the extent to which actual effects of a policy match, or are expected to match, its objectives. Once the substantive effects of a policy have been clarified, implications for the structure of society and for the entire system of social policies can be discerned, in terms of changes in the key processes, and the common domain, of social policies. This requires also exploration of the field of forces within which a policy originated, and within which its implementation is to take place, for understanding the interaction between a policy and the social environment seems essential to predicting the policy's eventual consequences.

A third objective of policy analysis is to generate alternative policies aimed at the same or at different objectives concerning the focal issues. Each alternative policy is to be examined, and different policies can then be compared and evaluated, in terms of social policy relevant value premises, attainment of specified policy objectives, implications for social structure and the policy system as a whole, unintended effects, and overall costs and benefits.

The framework presented here is geared to the attainment of the foregoing analytic objectives. Section A corresponds to the first objective, sections B through D to the second objective, and section E to the third objective. It should be noted that an analysis grows more complex as the number of objectives increases, and analysts may therefore decide that for certain purposes, and in certain settings, a policy analysis should be limited to the first two objectives, or merely parts thereof. Whenever it is decided to limit the scope of analysis of a specific policy, appropriate sections of the analytic framework can be used independently of other sections.

The proposed framework consists of a standard set of foci to be utilized in the study of given policies. The set of foci is standardized in order to facilitate systematic coverage of aspects deemed relevant to the understanding of social policies and their consequences for a society. The framework is intended to guide the work of policy analysts toward these relevant analytic foci, the utilization of which is expected to reduce differences in factual findings and predictions among different analysts studying the same policy, since such differences seem often due to differences in the scope of issues explored.

Social policies vary in content, scope, and objectives. Hence the extent to which the several foci of the framework are relevant in the analysis of any given policy will vary. Some foci may be of little or no relevance to certain policies and may consequently be omitted in the analysis. Since the foci differ in many ways, different analytic techniques will be appropriate for different foci. It should also be noted that a certain measure of overlapping is unavoidable among the sections and foci of the framework since these sections and foci examine given policies from different perspectives and on different levels of analysis.

The quality and reliability of available data, and the validity of specialized indicators, are likely to vary with respect to the foci of the framework. Moreover, it is possible that reliable data cannot be obtained, and that valid indicators are not available or cannot be developed, with respect to certain foci. Such negative findings concerning the data base of certain foci are, however, in themselves, important information, since in developing predictions with the help of the framework one needs to be aware of the scope of what cannot be known presently.

Before a given social policy can be analyzed with the aid of the framework, its provisions should be specified. If the policy has already been enacted into law, administrative regulations and judicial decisions concerning it should be taken into consideration along with the language of the law. If a policy proposal rather than an already enacted policy is being analyzed, specificity concerning operational aspects of the proposed policy should be provided to strengthen the reliability of analysis and predictions.

The framework is presented below in Chart 3.1, and its sections and foci are then discussed in detail.

CHART 3.1. FRAMEWORK FOR SOCIAL POLICY ANALYSIS
AND SYNTHESIS

SECTION A: ISSUES DEALT WITH BY THE POLICY

1. Nature, scope, and distribution of the issues
2. Causal theory(ies) or hypothesis(es) concerning the dynamics of the issues

SECTION B: OBJECTIVES, VALUE PREMISES, THEORETICAL POSITIONS, TARGET SEGMENTS, AND SUBSTANTIVE EFFECTS OF THE POLICY

1. Policy objectives
2. Value premises and ideological orientations underlying the policy objectives
3. Theory(ies) or hypothesis (es) underlying the strategy and the substantive provisions of the policy.

SECTION B (*Continued*)

4. Target segment(s) of society — those at whom the policy is aimed:
   a) Ecological, demographic, biological, psychological, social, economic, political, and cultural characteristics
   b) Numerical size of relevant sub-groups and of entire target segment(s) projected over time
5. Short- and long-range effects of the policy on target and nontarget segment(s) of the society in ecological, demographic, biological, psychological, social, economic, political, and cultural spheres
   a) Intended effects and extent of attainment of policy objectives
   b) Unintended effects
   c) Overall costs and benefits

SECTION C: IMPLICATIONS OF THE POLICY FOR THE KEY PROCESSES AND THE COMMON DOMAIN OF SOCIAL POLICIES

1. Changes in the development of life-sustaining and life-enhancing, material and symbolic resources, goods, and services
   a) qualitative changes
   b) quantitative changes
   c) changes in priorities
2. Changes in the allocation of individuals and groups, to specific statuses within the total array of societal tasks and functions
   a) Development of new statuses, roles, and prerogatives
   b) Strengthening and protection of existing statuses, roles, and prerogatives
   c) Elimination of existing statuses, roles, and prerogatives
   d) Changes in the criteria and procedures for selection and assignment of individuals and groups to statuses
3. Changes in the distribution of rights to individuals and groups
   a) Changes in the quality and quantity of general and specific entitlements, status-specific rewards, and general and specific constraints
   b) Changes in the proportion of rights distributed as general or specific entitlements and as status-specific rewards respectively, or in the extent to which the distribution of rights is linked to the allocation of statuses
   c) Changes in the proportion of rights distributed directly, in kind, e.g., public provisions and services, and rights distributed indirectly, as "right equivalents," purchasing power or money
   d) Changes in the specifications of a minimum level of rights for all members and groups of society, e.g., "official poverty line," or "fixed percentage of per capita income," and in the extent to which the distribution of rights assures coverage of such a minimum level

SECTION C (*Continued*)

    e) Changes in the relative distribution of rights throughout society, or in the degree of inequality of rights among individuals and groups

4. Consequences of changes in resource development, status allocation, and rights distribution for

    a) the overall quality of life in society, and

    b) the circumstances of living of individuals and groups, as noted in measurements and perceptions of ecological, demographic, biological, psychological, social, economic, political, and cultural spheres

    c) the nature of intra-societal human relations among individuals, groups, and society as a whole

SECTION D. INTERACTION EFFECTS BETWEEN THE POLICY AND FORCES SURROUNDING ITS DEVELOPMENT AND IMPLEMENTATION

1. History of the policy's development and implementation, including legislative, administrative, and judicial aspects

2. Political forces in society promoting or resisting the policy prior to, and following, its enactment — their type, size, organizational structure, resources, overall strength, extent of interest, value premises, and ideological orientations

3. Physical and biological properties of society's natural setting, and biological and basic psychological properties of its members

4. Relevant other social policies

5. Relevant foreign policies and extra-societal forces

6. Society's stage of development in cultural, economic, and technological spheres

7. Society's size and institutional differentiation or complexity

8. Society's beliefs, values, ideologies, customs and traditions

9. Conclusions and predictions

SECTION E: DEVELOPMENT OF ALTERNATIVE SOCIAL POLICIES; COMPARISON AND EVALUATION

1. Specification of alternative social policies:

    a) aimed at the same policy objectives, but involving alternative policy measures

    b) aimed at different policy objectives concerning the same policy issues

2. Comparison and evaluation:
each alternative social policy should be analyzed in accordance with the framework, and compared throughout this analysis with the original policy and other alternative policies.

INTERPRETATION OF THE FRAMEWORK

The main sections of the framework are designed to elicit answers to five basic questions concerning a policy:

A — Which of the many domains of concern to a society constitute the focus for this policy?

B — How would the policy affect this domain in substantive terms?

C — How would society as a whole be affected by the substantive consequence of the policy?

D — What effects may be expected from the interaction of the policy with various forces within and outside the society?

E — What alternative policies could be designed to achieve the same or different policy objectives concerning the specified domain?

A — Both policy analysis and policy development should begin with the identification and exploration of the issues to be dealt with by given policies. The use of the term "issues" rather than "problems" in this context may require clarification, since social policies are usually considered to be measures for the solution or amelioration of specific social problems. According to the conception presented here, however, social policies are not merely societal responses to perceived problems, but constitute a system of man-designed principles for shaping the quality of life, the circumstances of living, and the human relations within society. Consequently, while many social policies are indeed designed to solve or reduce specified, perceived social problems, such as poverty, many others deal with issues which are not necessarily perceived as social problems, such as the provision of education, the maintenance of health, etc. It seems therefore indicated to denote the general focus of social policies not as "problems," but as "issues." Obviously, this latter term includes also the notion of "problems."

Two related propositions are implied in the title of the first section of the analytic framework. One is that each social policy does have specific, identifiable foci — the issue or issues with which it deals. The other is that the various issues with which specific social policies deal are all components of the general domain of social policies. The purpose of the first section of the analytic framework then is to identify and examine the specific issues dealt with by a policy as basis for the analysis of this policy and for the development of alternative policies. Such identification and examination involves two sets of questions, one set on a descriptive level and the other on an analytic-dynamic level.

A-1 — The manner in which given issues are to be identified and described will depend to a considerable extent on their intrinsic nature and on the state of established knowledge concerning them. In general, issues should be identified and described within the context of the key processes and the general domain of social policies, rather than in terms of specific provisions of given policies. For discrete social policies frequently deal with issues in a fragmented, but not in a comprehensive way. Thus, a given policy may make provisions for retirement income for a specific occupational group, e.g., railroad employees. The issue with which this policy deals should be defined as "retirement income maintenance," or perhaps even more comprehensively as "rights distribution through income maintenance," rather than as "railroad retirement income." Broad definitions of issues make it possible to examine and evaluate the effectiveness of policies in relation to generic societal functions instead of merely in their own limited and fragmented terms. Broad definitions of issues also facilitate the development of alternative policies. It can be seen from these comments that the way policy issues are defined is crucial for the entire analytic process. Care should therefore be taken to avoid definitions which are likely to limit policy analysis and development of alternative policies to the same assumptions and patterns of reasoning which led to the formulation of earlier policies.

One further caveat with respect to the proper identification of issues concerns the fact that policies may at times deal with covert issues rather than merely with overt ones. Thus, public assistance policies may deal overtly with income maintenance for economically deprived segments of a population but may, at the same time, deal covertly with the supply of cheap, unskilled manpower to a "secondary" labor market.[1]

Descriptions of policy issues should identify and clarify major relevant variables concerning the issues. If indicated, a classification or typology of the issues should be developed, problem areas should be specified, and the background and history of the issues should be reviewed. The scope and social significance of issues should be assessed in general terms, and, if appropriate, also in terms of prevalence and incidence rates throughout society, as well as relative prevalence and incidence rates among relevant sub-groups of society.

A-2 — Policy analysis and policy development require not only descriptive knowledge of issues but also insights into their underlying dynamics. Such insights can usually be derived from theories or hypotheses concerning the configuration of forces involved in the issues.

This focus of social policy analysis and development involves, accordingly, a critical review of relevant scientific writings aimed at ascertaining the existing state, and the validity, of applicable theory.

B — The second section of the framework focuses on the objectives of a given policy with respect to the issues it deals with, social policy relevant value premises underlying these objectives, theoretical positions underlying the strategy and provisions of the policy, and the substantive effects of the policy on target and other segments of the population.

B-1 — The objectives of social policies constitute key criteria for the evaluation of their social significance and the anlysis of their effectiveness. Objectives of policies need, therefore, be explicated as clearly as possible. The importance of specification of objectives for policy analysis and development is widely recognized but, nevertheless, such specifications are often neglected in practice. One reason for this seems to be the tendency of many policy analysts to be more concerned with the technical aspects, or means, of a policy than with its objectives. Technical aspects of policy implementation are, of course, important, and alternative means need to be evaluated and compared in terms of their respective effectiveness and efficiency. However, unless objectives have been explicated, and are kept in mind constantly as significant yardsticks for policy evaluation, the examination of means and of technical aspects is likely to be of questionable utility.

One consequence of the dominant interest of many analysts in policy means is the tendency to substitute technical means for social goals. Thus, for instance, "constructing houses" may come to be viewed as a policy objective, replacing the socially more appropriate objective of "housing people." Constructing houses is, no doubt, an important means toward the objective of housing people. However, when this means is elevated to the level of an objective in its own right, its pursuit may, under certain conditions, produce adverse consequences for the policy objective of "housing people." This has actually happened in the United States when several decades of public housing, slum clearance, and highway construction policies resulted in a net decrease of adequate housing for the population. This is not the place to explore the fascinating process of social policy goal displacement and the social forces underlying it. The process is mentioned here merely in order to alert policy analysts to its existence, and to the importance of distinguishing clearly between social policy objectives and social policy means when attempting to explicate the former.

One further difficulty concerning the identification of social policy objectives is the distinction between overt and covert objectives. This distinction corresponds to the one made above between overt and covert issues dealt with by policies. Overt objectives tend to be expressed in the preambles of official policy documents, while covert objectives can only be inferred from provisions in the operational sections of such documents, or from administrative regulations and practices, and subsequent court decisions during the implementation state of a given policy. Frequently overt and covert objectives are in conflict with each other, and awareness of such built-in conflicts is, therefore, important in analyzing the consequences of a policy. It may be noted that policy means designed originally for the achievement of overt policy objectives are occasionally transformed into covert policy objectives by way of the earlier mentioned substitution process. Thus, policies aimed at the elimination of hunger in the United States gradually shifted their primary emphasis toward subsidizing agricultural production and disposing agricultural surpluses.

B-2 — Next to be examined in social policy analysis and development are social policy relevant value premises implicit in the overt and covert policy objectives which have been identified for a given policy. Clarification of these value premises is likely to encounter difficulties similar to those discussed above in connection with the specification of policy objectives. Values underlying overtly expressed objectives are likely to be openly stated or clearly implied in these objectives. On the other hand, values which underlie covert objectives will have to be inferred in the same way that these objectives are inferred, namely, on the basis of detailed aspects of the policy and the manner of its implementation. Once the two sets of values have been discerned, the extent of conflict between them, as well as of possible conflict between them and the general value orientation of society, needs to be assessed.

Clarification of value premises underlying the objectives of given social policies, and of the extent to which these value premises may be in conflict with a society's dominant value premises, is of crucial importance for social policy analysis and development since these dominant value premises act as constraining forces with respect to the malleability of social policy systems. Knowing the value premises inherent in a policy seems, therefore, to be a prerequisite for predicting the manner of its implementation and its actual consequences for society.

At any point in time a society upholds many different values. The extent to which these different values influence social policies varies widely. Some values exert considerable influence on the policy system while the influence of others may be negligible. For purposes of social policy analysis consideration should be given mainly to value dimensions which are most likely to affect attitudes, decisions, and actions concerning resource development, status allocation, and rights distribution. These value dimensions are denoted here as social policy relevant value dimensions. Obviously, judgment is involved in selecting these dimensions, but few analysts will question the policy relevance of such dimensions as equality-inequality, cooperation-competition, collective or public interest-rugged individualism. It thus seems appropriate to examine the value premises of given policies in relation to these specific value dimensions.

B-3 — Once the objectives and value premises of a policy are clarified, theories or hypotheses underlying its strategy and its concrete provisions should be made explicit, and their scientific validity should be examined. The extent to which the strategy and the concrete provisions of social policies are derived from theory is likely to vary from policy to policy. Some policies may not involve any theories or hypotheses. Others may have been intentionally designed in accordance with specific theories, while still others may not have been designed in accordance with theory, but may nevertheless reflect certain theoretical positions in their strategy and concrete provisions. Whatever the extent and nature of the theoretical underpinning of a given policy may be, the analysis should bring it to light. Furthermore, the analysis should also clarify whether the theories that underlie the strategy and the provisions of a given policy are compatible with the theories that explain the dynamics of the issue with which this policy is expected to deal. These latter theories, it will be recalled, are to be explored under the first section of the framework.

A few illustrations may aid in clarifying the connection between social theory and social policy. Social science offers several theories to explain the phenomenon of poverty. One theory views poverty as resulting from a unique, deviant sub-culture — the "culture of poverty" — which supposedly is handed down from generation to generation. Another theory interprets poverty as the result of environmental reality factors, such as economic depressions and extended unemployment, and adaptation to these factors on the part of population segments exposed to them for some time. A third theory explains poverty as the result of socially structured and legitimated inequalities with respect to the allocation of statuses and the distribution of rights in a society. Social policy measures aimed at combating poverty can be devised in accordance with each of these theories. Educational approaches such as "Headstart," "Upward-bound," and various work training and work experience programs are anti-poverty policies derived primarily from the "culture of poverty" theory. Income maintenance programs, work guarantee programs, and minimum wage laws reflect the "environmental reality" poverty theory; and anti-discrimination policies, and other policies eliminating obstructions to equal access to all social statuses and rights, reflect the poverty theory of "socially structured and legitimated inequality."

While compatibility between the theory explaining the dynamics of a policy issue, and the theory underlying the strategy and concrete provisions of that policy, seems to be an essential condition of policy effectiveness, it is not a sufficient condition to assure such effectiveness, since both theories may be invalid, or since policy objectives may be set at an inadequate level. Such inadequacies in the level of policy objectives may in turn reflect the value premises underlying these objectives. It can be seen, thus, that policy objectives, value premises underlying them, and theoretical positions concerning the strategy and provisions of a policy, have to be examined as interacting variables which affect policy outcomes jointly, rather than singly as independent forces.

B-4 — In theory every social policy affects every member of a given society to some extent. For purposes of social policy analysis and development not all effects are of equal significance, however. Every social policy tends to be aimed primarily at specific groups of a society who constitute the "target segment(s)" for the intended effects of the policy. The remainder of the population, "the non-target segment," is likely to be subject to indirect effects, most of which may be unintended, and some of which may be of limited significance only. No doubt, this division of a population into target and non-target segments, and of policy effects into intended and unintended ones, is a somewhat arbitrary dichotomization. It seems, however, to be a useful device for social policy analysis, provided analysts do not interpret these divisions as valid representations of reality but merely as schematic approximations.

Before the effects of a given social policy can be explored the characteristics of target segments within a society must be investigated with respect to the following policy relevant spheres: ecological, demographic, biological, psychological, social, economic, political, and cultural. The more complete and reliable the information obtained in each of these spheres, the more reliable can be the analysis of the policy and the prediction of its effects. In gathering information on the target segments in these spheres analysts should proceed from general toward specific levels, but should avoid specificity beyond a level expected to be utilized in the analysis. The optimum scope of information concerning the several spheres, and the optimum level of specificity, will also depend on the nature of the issue dealt with by the policy, the policy objectives, the policy strategy and provisions, and the theoretical position underlying the strategy and provisions.

Besides describing relevant characteristics of target segments of the population, their numerical size, as well as the size of appropriate subgroups among them, should be clarified, both in absolute terms and relative to the size of the entire population. Furthermore, projections into the future of these absolute and relative numerical sizes should be calculated as a basis for predicting long-range consequences of a given social policy. Published census data and, when indicated, special compilations of raw census data, available from the Bureau of the Census, are the best source for this type of information in most instances.

B-5 — The final focus of the second section of the framework calls for an examination of the chain of effects set in motion by a given social policy throughout the target and non-target segments of society. In this examination analysts should review first the intended effects of a policy, the "policy objectives," and the extent to which these intended effects actually occur. However, not less important than the review of intended effects and the degree of their realization is a search for the possible occurrence and scope of unintended and unanticipated effects of a policy. Both types of effects may occur in the spheres of population characteristics mentioned above. Obviously, not every single policy will have noticeable effects in all these spheres. However, checking each sphere for possible effects will reduce the probability of errors due to oversight.

Once the intended and unintended effects of a policy have been established, they should be examined in terms of their overall costs and benefits. This examination should discern not only economic costs and benefits, but also social costs and benefits, although it may be much more difficult to estimate the latter. The translation of policy effects into cost-benefit terms is important as a basis for comparing alternative policies dealing with the same policy issue with respect to their relative effectiveness and efficiency.

C — The third section of the framework raises what seems to be the most significant questions about specific policies in terms of social policy analysis and synthesis. This section is based on the conceptual model of social policies and is designed to explore the effects of specific social policies on the structure and dynamics of society as a whole by discerning the extent to which the substantive consequences of these policies result in modifications of the key processes and the common domain of all social policies. More specifically, this section of the framework focuses on the identification of possible changes, due to given policies, in the societal key processes of resource development, status allocation, and rights distribution; and consequent changes in the overall quality of life throughout a society, in the circumstances of living of individuals and groups in that society, and in all intra-societal human relations. Several questions need to be explored in relation to each of the key processes and the several aspects of the common domain of social policies.

C-1 — Changes with respect to the development of resources, goods, and services may be qualitative, quantitative, or both. Either change may also reflect changes in the existing system of societal priorities.

Qualitative changes may involve changes in the types of goods and services developed, such as shifts from privately purchased to publicly provided health care, from production of large to that of compact automobiles, or from production of automobiles for private transportation to that of buses and other vehicles for public transportation. Qualitative changes may, however, consist merely of modifications of the same type of goods or services, such as the addition of safety and pollution control devices to the existing type of automobiles, or the shift from privately purchased medical treatment in the patient's home to the same kind of treatment in the physician's office. Qualitative changes may finally involve the development of entirely new resources, goods, and services (or disservices) and the discontinuance of existing ones, such as the spreading of computerized population data blanks, and the elimination of weekend mail deliveries, respectively.

Qualitative changes in the development of resources, goods, and services are usually accompanied also by quantitative changes, since the introduction of innovative or modified products is likely to be reflected in overall changes in the scope of production. The reverse is true less frequently, though shifts toward mass production of goods and services, and other technological changes in production, tend to involve, quite often, qualitative changes of the goods or services produced. It may be noted in this context that the level of technological development of a society is a very important factor with respect to qualitative and quantitative aspects of resource development.

Changes in priorities concerning the development of resources, goods, and services tend to reflect changes in the balance of power and influence of various interest groups, and changes in the dominant value premises of a society. Recent widespread efforts in the United States to shift national resources away from defense functions toward the satisfaction of basic human needs and the preservation of the natural environment, are one illustration of intra-societal struggle over priorities with regard to the development of resources, goods, and services.

C-2 — The processes of status allocation within a society can be affected and changed by social policies in several ways. Policies may establish new statuses with corresponding roles and prerogatives, such as the creation of a professional army in a society which previously had no army at all or one based on universal military service. Policies may also eliminate existing statuses, such as the abolition of slavery or the abolition of a monarchy. Policies may also assure the perpetuation of existing statuses by strengthening them and protecting their exclusiveness. Policies licensing professional practice, business, and other types of activities fulfill this purpose.

The most significant area for policy development and change concerning status systems are the criteria and procedures which a society uses in the selection, preparation, and assignment of individuals and groups to specific statuses within the overall system of societal tasks and functions. Access to all statuses may be completely open on an equal basis for all members of a society, as in an "ideal," egalitarian democracy, or it may be almost completely determined by inheritance, as in a caste system. In between these extremes there are many intermediate types of status allocation, when access to statuses is neither completely predetermined — "ascribed," nor completely open and equal — "achieved." Policies dealing with inheritance, socialization, education, manpower training, discriminatory practices, age and sex roles, etc., are all relevant to this very crucial issue, and modifications of such policies are likely to be reflected in changes in the criteria and procedures of status allocation.

C-3 — The analysis of the effects of specific social policies on the distribution of rights in a society begins with the discernment of qualitative and quantitative changes in general and specific entitlements, status-specific rewards, and general and specific constraints. Illustrations of such changes are the establishment of a comprehensive, national health service, financed through general revenue, for all members of society, or for a specific age group — a general or specific entitlement respectively; changes in the level of minimum wages or in the compensation of government officials — status specific rewards; and changes in the rates and specific provisions of the income tax — general and specific constraints respectively.

Next to be examined are the consequences of such absolute changes in rights distribution for the ratio of rights distributed as entitlements to rights distributed as rewards. Were a society to establish a system of free food distribution or an annual demogrant system as general entitlements for all its members, the ratio of entitlements to status-specific rewards would be changed radically in favor of the former. Such social policies would result also in a significant reduction of the extent to which the distribution of rights would be linked to the allocation of statuses.

One other social policy relevant ratio which may be affected by overall changes in the distribution of rights is that of rights distributed directly, in kind, e.g., publicly supplied provisions and services, to rights distributed indirectly in the form of right-equivalents, such as money or coupons, which the owner may transform into a variety of rights subject to certain rules. Using the foregoing illustrations, a system of free food distribution would increase the proportion of rights distributed in kind, while an annual demogrant would increase the proportion of rights distributed in the form of right-equivalents or purchasing power.

A society's changing concepts and specifications of the levels of minimum rights which it guarantees to all its members is an important aspect of its system of rights distribution. The specifications of such levels, and changes in these specifications over time, are therefore, important social policies. These specifications have taken different forms throughout history. Major formal policy instruments such as the Magna Charta, the U. S. Constitution, and the Bill of Rights defined basic levels of civil and political rights. The Common Law, judicial determinations, and administrative regulations, such as official eligibility standards for public assistance, are other forms of specifying levels of minimum rights. A more recent administrative method of such specifications are "official poverty lines" developed in the United States by the Social Security Administration.[2] Social policies, however, do not merely specify the levels, nature, and scope of minimal rights, but also determine the extent to which coverage of these levels is to be provided in practice. This latter function of social policies is perhaps even more significant for the actual distribution of rights in a society than the formal designation of the minimum levels. Obviously, social policy analysis and development need to be concerned with both aspects, the specifications and the extent of coverage.

The final aspect concerning the distribution of rights in a society which needs to be examined in the analysis and development of social policies is its effects on the relative distribution of all kinds of rights throughout a population, or on the degree of inequality with respect to such rights among individuals and various relevant groups in society. The questions to be examined in this context are whether, and to what extent, given policies change existing relative distributions of various kinds of rights to concrete and symbolic, life-sustaining and life-enhancing resources, goods, and services, be they in kind or in the form of money income, wealth, and prestige, or in the form of civil and political rights. Laws, regulations, and court decisions dealing with discrimination, voting rights, public services, taxes, income from salaries, wages, rents, interest, and transfers are all illustrations of policies which may affect the relative distribution of rights throughout a society.

It should be noted that the five items of the framework concerning policy effects on the distribution of rights are closely related to each other. Unless there is some absolute, qualitative or quantitative change in one or more of the rights distribution mechanisms, there can be no corresponding change in the ratios of distributive mechanisms, and of the types of rights which are being distributed, in the extent of coverage of specified minimum levels of rights, and in the relative distribution of all kinds of rights among individuals and relevant groups in society. Therefore, if analysis of a policy indicates zero change with respect to qualitative and quantitative changes in entitlements, rewards, and constraints (item C-3-a of the framework), then real change will be zero on all other rights distribution items with the possible exception of a change in the formal specification of levels of minimal rights, but not in their actual coverage.

C-4 — With the discernment of effects of specific policies on the distribution of rights in society the analysis of their effects on the three key processes of social policies is complete. The next focus in this section deals with consequences of changes in the key processes for the overall quality of life in society, the circumstances of living of individuals and groups, and intra-societal human relations — the common domain of social policies.

Social policies can affect the overall quality of life and the circumstances of living of individuals and groups in one or more of eight related spheres. These spheres, it should be noted, are the same as the ones used in Section B, items 4 and 5, for describing the characteristics of target segments of populations and the chain of substantive effects of policies on target and non-target segments. Information obtained at that stage of an analysis is being used here with a social-structural perspective. Clearly, not every policy affects the quality of life and the circumstances of living of individuals and groups in all eight spheres.

Nevertheless, each sphere should be examined for possible effects in the analysis of every policy, so as not to overlook less noticeable effects.

In discerning policy effects on the quality of life and the circumstances of living, a distinction needs to be made between effects observable on objective indicators and effects reflected through subjective perceptions. Illustrations of objective indicators of the various spheres are: pollution levels, patterns of settlement, highways, housing, and parks — ecologic; population density, rates of births, deaths, marriages, divorces, and immigration — demographic; infant mortality, morbidity rates, and diet levels — biologic; incidence of mental illness — psychologic; rates of social participation, social alienation, and social deviance — social; levels of production, inventories, distribution of goods and services, distribution of income and wealth, employment rates, and cost of living — economic; type of governance, citizen participation, civil and political rights, administrative and judicial patterns — political; science, education, religion, recreation, art, literature, and music — cultural. Some objective indicators may reflect both the overall quality of life and the circumstances of living, while others may reflect one or the other of these components of the common domain of social policies.[3]

Measures of subjective perceptions of the overall quality of life and of the circumstances of living are usually not readily available and policy analysis may presently have to proceed without such measures, unless special surveys are conducted, or appropriate data happen to be available from relevant surveys. When special surveys are conducted to explore subjective perceptions of the quality of life and of the circumstances of living, they should elicit from representative samples of the population expressions of feelings, attitudes, and opinions concerning the several spheres before and after the implementation of specific social policies. Responses of individuals obtained by such surveys can be aggregated into quantitative measures of subjective perceptions. Eventually such surveys should be carried out at regular time intervals by governments and findings should be published in standardized form along with statistics on selected objective indicators of the various spheres of the quality of life and the circumstances of living.

A clarifying comment seems indicated here concerning the difference between the concepts "quality of life" and "circumstances of living." The former term refers to phenomena on an aggregate level as encountered by society as a whole or by large segments of it. The latter term, on the other hand, refers to specific living conditions of individuals and of social groups. Obviously, the two concepts are related, yet they refer to different aspects and levels of the same reality.

The final item in Section C examines effects of social policies on the nature of intra-societal human relations among individuals, groups, and society as a whole. While objective changes in the key processes of social policies and in the quality of life and circumstances of living can be observed and often measured directly, changes in intra-societal relationships traceable to observed changes in the key processes may be less noticeable, especially when the changes in the key processes are merely minor. Nevertheless, it seems important to discern these changes in human relations. Some of these changes will be on the level of formal, institutionalized relations between statuses, such as changes in doctor-patient relations upon the establishment of a national health service, or changes in relations between employers and employees once social policies establish and enforce recognition of labor unions as bargaining agents. Other changes may be more subtle, such as changes in informal and formal intra-familial relations upon the introduction of such income maintenance schemes as children's allowances, mothers' wages, retirement benefits, negative income taxes, or universal demogrants.

A useful approach toward detecting the nature of changes in intra-societal human relations involves, as a first step, identification of sets of intra-societal relations which are likely to be affected by specific social policies. Systematic review of the various statuses and status clusters involved in these policies will facilitate identification of the sets whose institutional and informal relations may be changed. Once these sets are identified it should be possible to discern the nature of the changes in their relations.

D — The fourth section of the framework carries the analysis of social policies to the level of the force field represented in Figure 2 of the preceding chapter. The purpose of analysis at this level is to study the effects of interactions between specific policies and a variety of forces within and outside a society, which surround the development and implementation of social policies.

D-1 — In preparation for studying these interactions the history of specific policies should be reviewed. Special attention is to be given, whenever applicable, to legislative, administrative, and judicial aspects which are likely to suggest clues to subsequent developments of policies. Information gathered for Section A, when analyzing issues dealt with by specific social policies, is likely to be relevant to the historical review.

D-2 — The second item of this section is actually part of the historical review. Yet, because of the importance of political forces for the development of social policies, they should be examined separately, in spite of the fact that this may involve some repetitions. Not all political forces in a society are, however, relevant to the analysis of every social policy. Only those political forces should be examined here which were involved in the evolution of specific policies, or which are likely to become involved in it in the future. A set of dimensions is suggested in the framework for the description of political forces. These dimensions are considered relevant to understanding the impact of political forces on social policy evolution and implementation.

D-3 — Next to be considered in the analysis of specific social policies are their interactions with the limiting aspects of a society's natural environment, its physical and biological properties, as well as man's own biological and basic psychological makeup. The importance of these interactions can be grasped by studying differences in the evolution of social policies among nomadic societies living on the fringes of deserts, and among sedentary societies inhabiting the fertile valleys of major rivers. Man's biological and basic psychological characteristics are relevant to social policy analysis since they give rise to specific behavioral and motivational response patterns. Assumptions as to the nature and dynamics of these response patterns tend to influence the design of social policies. Thus, for instance, work incentive features in income maintenance policies, and tax reduction features as incentives to philanthropic gifts or capital investments, reflect certain assumptions concerning human behavior and motivational response patterns implicit in the notion of "rational, economic man" who acts in the marketplace to maximize his profit and his perceived self-interest.

It should be noted in this context that while man's basic psychological characteristics reveal usually a high degree of continuity and stability, they are nevertheless subject to variations under the influence of different societal configurations or different social policies. This plasticity of man's psychological characteristics is revealed in the development of human beings who are transplanted in infancy from one societal context to a vastly different one. Behavioral and motivational responses should therefore not be regarded as constant, unchangeable factors in the analysis and development of social policies. Biological properties of man and of his natural environment, on the other hand, seem to be less plastic than his psychological characteristics, and the physical properties of the natural environment tend to be most resistant to change through human intervention. These differences in plasticity of physical, biological, and psychological forces need to be kept in mind when examining their interactions with man-designed social policies.

D-4 and 5 — Interactions between specific social policies and relevant other social policies, and foreign policies, of a society constitute the next foci for analysis. From a theoretical perspective every social policy interacts to a certain extent with every other social and foreign policy. From a practical perspective, however, analysis needs to be limited to interactions with policies, and policy clusters, which are likely to result in significant rather than in minor effects. The selection of these relevant policies and policy clusters, unavoidably, involves subjective judgments. Policies which deal with the same and with related societal issues should certainly always be considered. Beyond that it seems also important to trace the impact of specific policies on the overall flow of resources in a society and, therefore, on policies dealing with that flow, such as tax, tariff, and trade policies. Time and other resources at the command of a policy analyst will usually set reality limits on the extent to which these foci can be pursued.

It should be stressed here that interactions between social and foreign policies are not always considered adequately in the analysis of social policies, although, especially during periods of foreign wars, foreign policies exert considerable, manifold influences over priority decisions concerning intra-societal resource development, manpower allocation, and rights distribution. And, in turn, social policies exert similarly important influences over foreign trade and other aspects of foreign policy, such as economic aid, capital investments, cultural relations, territorial expansion, migration, and war and peace. Examining effects of actual and potential interactions between specific social policies and relevant foreign policies is, therefore, as important an aspect of social policy analysis and development as the study of interactions among the various social policies of a society.

D-6 and 7 — Further sets of interactions to be examined in this phase of an analysis are those between specific social policies and a society's stage of development in cultural, economic, and technological spheres; its size, and its level of institutional differentiation or complexity. It is known in a general way, that societies at different stages of overall development, of different sizes, and organized along different principles, will generate different systems of social policies, and that different social policy systems will, in turn, support different modes of overall development, different patterns of population growth or decline, and different types of societal organization. Specific configurations of these interactions are, however, less well understood, and are not always taken into account in social policy analysis and development. Disregarding these interactions has again and again resulted in major unintended and unexpected consequences of specific social policies. A well-known illustration of this is the invention, and subsequent evolution, of the automobile, and the complex sequence of social policies which this invention stimulated and influenced. Interaction effects between this invention and these policies on the one hand, and many aspects of life in the United States and in foreign countries on the other, have gradually revolutionized the overall quality of life, the circumstances of living, and the nature of human relations on an unprecedented and unexpected scale. Had the attention of policy makers been focused on these multi-faceted interactions at the time when social policies were formulated, which subsequently became important factors in the evolution of the automobile, many undesirable side effects of the unrestrained development of the automobile could, perhaps, have been prevented.

D-8 — A final set of interactions to be studied are those between specific social policies and the beliefs, values, ideologies, customs, and traditions of a society. Information relevant to the exploration of these interactions was obtained earlier in connection with item 2 of section B, but should be reexamined at this stage of an analysis in relation to other forces surrounding the development and implementation of social policies. It is important to clarify in this context whether the value premises of specific social policies are internally consistent with one another, and whether they are compatible with, or in conflict with, the dominant beliefs, values, and ideologies of society, especially with regard to the social policy relevant value dimensions identified earlier, namely, equality-inequality, cooperation-competition, and collective or public interest-narrow self-interest or rugged individualism. Since a society's dominant beliefs, values, ideologies, customs, and traditions exert constraining influences on the malleability and evolution of its entire system of social policies, it seems essential to be aware of differences and interaction effects concerning these variables, between specific social policies and the entire social policy system, as a prerequisite for estimating the fate of these policies in the course of their implementation.

D-9 — It needs to be stressed that the substantive items of section D of the framework are closely interrelated since they all focus on interactions between specific social policies and various sets of forces within and beyond the same society. They are thus dealing with one and the same question from different perspectives. It seems, therefore, important to go through the analysis of all the substantive items of this section before predicting the probable fate of specific social policies, rather than attempting such predictions on the basis of information gathered in relation to merely one or some of the items.

E — The analysis of specific social policies is completed with section D of the framework. The final section moves beyond the analysis of specific social policies to the development and study of alternative policies, and then to the systematic comparison of these various social policies, in terms of specified evaluative criteria. The development and study of alternative social policies is perhaps the most important aspect of policy analysis, and thus the most constructive use to which the framework may be put. For ancient social problems which have defied solution when attacked through conventional, incremental policy strategies, may yield to innovative approaches involving significant restructuring of the key processes of social policies, the existing configurations of which maintain the alienating status quo and sustain its social problems.

E-1 — In general, the development of alternative social policies involves determination of the nature and scope of changes which need to be made in the key policy processes of resource development, status allocation, and rights distribution in order to attain selected policy objectives in the common domain of social policies. These changes are then transformed into substantive program elements which are incorporated into the newly generated policies. It should be reemphasized in this respect that specified policy objectives depend for their realization on specific configurations of these key processes, and that unless these specific configurations are attained by means of appropriate modifications of the key processes, the objectives can simply not be realized.

More specifically, development of alternative social policies involves one or the other of two approaches, or combinations of these approaches. The first approach is concerned mainly with assuring effectiveness and increasing efficiency in relation to constant policy objectives. Alternative policies developed along this path are unlikely to result in significant social-structural breakthroughs or major modifications of the key processes of social policies. They will merely increase the probability that specified policy objectives are indeed achieved, that resources are not wasted in the process, and that undesirable side effects are minimized. An illustration of policy alternatives of this type would be different policies aimed at the identical objective of closing the official "poverty gap." Closing the poverty gap involves transferring income from groups in the population with incomes above the official "poverty line" to groups with incomes below that line in amounts sufficient to close the income gap for all persons whose income is below the poverty line. A number of approaches are available to achieve this objective. Income could be transferred through "negative income taxes" involving work incentive features at varying levels, and administered through different procedures; through "universal demogrants" at, or above, the level of the poverty line, distributed to all members of society, with surplus income recouped through various provisions in the tax laws; through a combination of measures including increases in minimum wages, creation of public service and other jobs, extending social security to currently not covered groups of the population, and increasing minimum social security payments to the poverty level. Obviously, several other policies could be devised to close the poverty gap. Analysis by means of relevant sections of the framework would indicate the extent to which each approach achieved the specified objective of eliminating the poverty gap, what other consequences would occur, and what overall societal costs and benefits would be involved. All these alternative policies would, however, accept, by implication, the closing of the poverty gap as an appropriate policy objective in relation to the underlying policy issue of income distribution.

The second approach to the development of alternative social policies begins with questions concerning the appropriateness of given policy objectives with respect to the issues to be dealt with by these policies. If existing objectives do not seem suitable, alternative, more suitable ones are specified, and policies corresponding to these alternative objectives are then generated. Thus, in relation to the issue of income distribution discussed above, questions could be raised concerning the appropriateness of the objective of eliminating the poverty gap. Such an objective might be considered inappropriate by some policy analysts as it could, in their view, undermine motivation to work and to support oneself and one's family, and lead to a general decline of individual responsibility. Proponents of such views might suggest, as alternative policy objectives, (1) closing merely a portion, e.g., one half, of the poverty gap in order to protect poor individuals and families against extreme hardships while maintaining pressures on them to seek employment; or (2) closing the poverty gap only for groups in the population who are not expected to support themselves by working, such as children, the aged, the disabled, and the handicapped.

Other analysts might view the objective of closing the poverty gap as inadequate since its redistributive effects may seem to them insignificant in terms of equalizing rights and opportunities throughout society, and since, even as a minimum standard of living, the poverty level would be judged by them to be totally inadequate and inhumane. Proponents of these latter views might suggest, as an alternative policy objective concerning the issue of income distribution, to close the income gap up to an objectively measured standard of decent living, such as the Bureau of Labor Statistics' "low" standard of living which is nearly twice the amount of the official "poverty line." It is clear from these illustrations that the selection of policy objectives tends to be influenced by value premises, ideological positions, and theoretical assumptions of different policy analysts, and that such selections are therefore based only partly on objectively established facts.

It should be noted that value premises, ideological positions, and theoretical assumptions concerning human behavior and motivation influence not only the selection of policy objectives but also the selection of policy means. Illustrations of this would be differences in the scope of work incentive features, and in mechanisms for verifying resources of recipients and establishing eligibility, among alternative income maintenance policies geared to the identical policy objective of eliminating the poverty gap. Another illustration would be the choice between "selective" approaches, such as the negative income tax, and "universal" approaches, such as mothers' wages and children's allowances, as means for closing the poverty gap. Selective approaches would maximize the economic value of efficiency, while universal approaches would sacrifice economic efficiency to the value of social integration.[4]

E-2 — Alternative policies developed at this stage of an analysis, be they aimed at attaining originally selected policy objectives or newly suggested alternative objectives, should be analyzed in accordance with relevant foci in sections B through D of the framework, and compared throughout this analysis with the original policy and other alternative policies. These comparisons and evaluations constitute the summation of a policy analysis, and should answer the following questions:

— What values would be maximized by the original and the alternative social policies in terms of social policy relevant value dimensions?
— What are the objectives of the different social policies with reference to the issues dealt with by them, and how effective would each policy be in realizing its respective objectives?

— What would be the impact of these different policies on the structure of a society, the key processes of social policies, and the entire system of social policies?

— What unintended side effects could be expected from the several policies?

— And, finally, what would be the overall benefits and overall real costs to society as a whole of every one of these policies?

SUMMARY

To conclude the discussion of the framework for the analysis and synthesis of social policies, several general observations seem indicated. First of all, it needs to be reemphasized that the framework is not meant to yield automatic solutions to policy questions. It is definitely not designed as a substitute for informed and critical human intellect, but merely as an important aid to it. The more thoroughly policy analysts understand the complex dynamics of their society and the substantive issues dealt with by specific policies, the more useful could the framework be in their work.

Few policy analysts can be expected to have sufficiently mastered all the relevant scholarly disciplines dealing with societal dynamics and substantive policy issues such as biology, ecology, demography, psychology, sociology, anthropology, economics, political science, etc. It would appear, therefore, that in order to achieve optimal results with the aid of the framework, policy analyses should, preferably, be carried out by multi-disciplinary teams rather than by individual analysts working independently. Such teams, because of the collective competence of their members, will be skilled in identifying and utilizing the types of data needed to carry out complete policy analyses, and they will know where and how these data can be secured efficiently. Moreover, teams of policy analysts working under the auspices of government bureaus, policy institutes in and outside universities, or of citizens' organizations, could develop and maintain permanent files of relevant series of data, instant availability of which would greatly facilitate and accelerate the systematic analysis and development of social policies.

While, then, the implementation of comprehensive, valid, and reliable policy analyses requires considerable resources because of the complex nature and scope of the task, it is nevertheless possible to utilize the framework in a flexible manner on a lesser scale of effort and investment. This can be done by individual analysts or by small ad hoc teams working outside well equipped organizations. Such less complete analyses may often be sufficient for purposes of initial orientation concerning specific policies or policy clusters. Abbreviated analyses should utilize the five general questions listed on page 36, each of which corresponds to one section of the framework. From these general questions analysts could proceed to deal with the first-order (numbered) items of relevant sections of the framework, by-passing the second-order (lettered) sub-items. The reliability of shortened analyses will not be as high as that of complete analyses, and interpretations, conclusions, and predictions based on them will have a wider margin of error. Yet, nevertheless, there are likely to be many instances when such shortened analyses will be all that is required, and when it would even be wasteful to carry out more comprehensive analyses.

One further general comment concerns differences in the use of the framework in the analysis of existing or already specified policies, and in the development of new ones. In either case, it is important to start with a study of the issues to be dealt with by a policy — section A of the framework. However, when analyzing an existing or specified policy the remaining sections of the framework are followed in proper sequence from B through E, while in developing new policies work on section A is followed by sections E, B, C and D, in that order. Also, when generating new policies it is important to develop specific statements of the provisions of the proposed policies before proceeding with sections B through D of the framework. Without such specific policy statements the analysis could not be carried out properly.

The foregoing somewhat abstract and technical discussion of the framework and its utilization in the analysis and synthesis of social policies has probably left several unanswered questions in the minds of readers. These questions, it is hoped, will be clarified in the next chapter through an illustration of the application of the framework in the analysis and development of one specific social policy. This illustrative analysis was carried out by one analyst working by himself, and it is, therefore, not as comprehensive, thorough, and reliable in all respects as it could and should be, were it undertaken, as recommended, by a multi-disciplinary team, competent in all relevant social and life sciences. Shortcomings of the following policy analysis reflect thus limitations of the analyst's competence, but not of the method, and are, therefore, not expected to thwart the purpose of the illustration, which is to further clarify the analytic approach, rather than to fully analyze one specific social policy.

AN ILLUSTRATION
OF SOCIAL POLICY ANALYSIS AND SYNTHESIS

CHAPTER FOUR

Mothers' Wages, Children's Allowances, Parents' Wages — Analysis and Synthesis of a Social Policy Cluster

The use of the framework for social policy analysis and synthesis is illustrated in this chapter in a discussion of a social policy proposal involving mothers' wages and children's allowances referred to hereafter for brevity as "Mothers' Wages Policy." This proposal was developed and published several years ago as a contribution to the public debate on eliminating, or at least reducing the scope of, poverty in the United States.[1] The proposal is outlined below and is then subjected to analysis in accordance with the framework.

THE PROPOSAL

The policy proposal of "Mothers' Wages" derives from the following premises. Childbearing and child rearing are not merely private and familial functions but are also societal functions and "investments" since they assure the continuity and survival of a society. These functions are usually performed by families as "agents" of society. But society as a whole, having, supposedly, a very real interest in the optimal development of every newly born citizen, should share responsibility for his rearing and socialization. Efforts and energy invested, and work performed, toward these objectives, should be considered components of the Gross National Product. Society should, therefore, compensate mothers who choose, or are obliged, to stay out of, or to disengage themselves partly or completely from, the labor market, in order to engage in child care.

American society tends to be ambiguous in defining the scope of parental and societal roles and responsibilities for the rearing of children. It would seem, however, quite consistent with nineteenth- and twentieth-century social and legal developments concerning the status and rights of children, to accept the rearing of the next generation as a societal function and responsibility, and to recognize the rights of mothers — and of fathers under certain circumstances — to be compensated adequately for their efforts. Indeed, the unpleasant truth needs to be faced that unless society compensates mothers for their partly voluntary, partly forced withdrawal from the labor market, and for the assumption of the complex tasks of childbearing and rearing, it is actually exploiting the biological role of women as a basis for the recruitment of "child care slave labor."

American society has gradually come to accept responsibility for childrearing tasks and for the socialization function whenever children enter institutionalized settings. No one would any longer question the appropriateness and legitimacy of compensating teachers, child-care workers, and foster parents for efforts on behalf of children assigned to their care, although, especially with regard to foster parents, the compensation is sometimes provided reluctantly and is often minimal or merely symbolic.

In view of these considerations, the policy provides for society to pay wages to every mother and to every expectant mother for as long as childbearing and childrearing tasks keep her outside the labor market, by choice or by necessity. Such wages should be fixed by federal law, should correspond at least to the prevailing minimum wage established by the Fair Labor Standards Act, and should be paid for eight hours a day, seven days a week, and fifty-two weeks a year to mothers engaged in no other gainful work. A mother's wage should vary in relation to the extent to which she chooses to participate in the labor market. Thus, mothers who undertook part-time employment or self-employment should receive wages on a prorated basis. Mothers who engaged in full-time employment should, however, receive 25 percent of full mothers' wages to compensate for the fact that maternal childrearing involves around-the-clock, 365-days-a-year, stand-by responsibilities.

A mother's wage should not vary with the number of her children since it is paid as compensation for staying outside the labor market and for investment of effort in a societal function. However, in accordance with this policy, mothers' wages should be linked to a system of adequate children's allowances payable on behalf of all minors, to assure larger incomes for larger family groups.

The sole criteria for receiving mothers' wages and for determining their amount are the status of motherhood or expectant motherhood and the extent of a mother's participation in the labor force. Accordingly, marital status, ownership of property, support from husbands, or income from other sources would be disregarded in determining a mother's right to the wage. However, since mothers' wages constitute income, the income tax system would assure recoupment of progressively larger portions of mothers' wages from families with other sources of income, and thus the net amount of mothers' wages would decrease as the total resources of a family increased. Children's allowances, too, would be subject to income tax for the same reasons as mothers' wages.

Mothers' wages would also be subject to social security deductions in order to assure to mothers the same social security benefits for which other members of the work force are eligible, such as old age, survivors, disability, and health insurance (OASDHI).

Mothers' wages as conceived by the policy are a compensation related to a specified societal event and context, namely, disengagement from the labor market because of motherhood or maternity. This conceptualization places mothers' wages within the social security model and the program should therefore be administered by the Social Security Administration. To obtain her wages a mother or expectant mother would register her claim at the nearest Social Security office giving the necessary simple information concerning herself, her children, and her employment status. Wages would be paid to her as long as she remained eligible and provided the Social Security office with the required, relevant information. Such limited data as would be required could be provided routinely on the back of signed paychecks. Information furnished by a mother would be considered valid, subject merely to random checks, and no special eligibility investigations would be necessary. Provisions would also be made for due process review and appeal procedures concerning administrative eligibility decisions. Children's allowances would also be administered in the same simple manner. Both mothers' wages and children's allowances would be financed entirely from general revenue derived from appropriate, progressive reform of the federal tax system.

ANALYSIS

A. ISSUES DEALT WITH BY THE POLICY

1. Nature, scope, and distribution of the issues: The "Mothers' Wages" policy deals with the following related societal issues:

   a. the status and rights of women;
   b. the rights of children;
   c. the societal definition of work;
   d. the redistribution of rights through transfer of purchasing power.

Throughout the evolution of human societies the access of women to statuses, and their share of concrete and symbolic rights, has been influenced by their biological role in childbearing. This influence is reflected in socially structured inequalities between males and females which usually took the form of narrowing the scope of statuses and rights open to women, and of assigning them to specialized statuses involving limited rights. These institutional limitations on the status options of women led frequently to various kinds of overt and covert exploitation and discrimination. The special statuses and rights of women as women tend to be independent of other criteria of social stratification such as age, ethnicity, intellectual potential, educational and occupational achievement, wealth, etc. Because of this, inequality of statuses and rights between the sexes can usually be discerned within any social group, stratum, or class, although there are variations in these inequalities among the different social groups and during different stages of social, cultural, economic, and technological development.

Women in the United States at the present time continue to be subjected to rather widespread exploitation and discrimination, in spite of recent trends toward more equality between the sexes with respect to statuses and rights, especially among more privileged social strata. One important source of discriminatory practices against women is the traditional societal expectation for mothers to assume primary responsibility for the care of their own children. This expectation tends to limit considerably the freedom of women to choose and enter other statuses. Moreover, it also tends to deprive them of equal access to goods and services, since the tasks of caring for one's own children are excluded from the societal and economic definition of "work," and mothers are consequently not entitled to rewards for their child-caring responsibilities. Mothers who own no personal wealth from savings, gifts, or inheritance, and who lack occupational skills and opportunities for "gainful" employment or self-employment, in which they engage in addition to caring for their children, have thus to depend on their husbands for their rights and those of their children. Within the existing social order such mothers have few options indeed, when the income of their husbands is inadequate, when husbands fail to support them, or when they have no husbands. In such circumstances they are forced to work in unskilled, poorly paid jobs, frequently under alienating working conditions, to seek aid from relatives and friends, or, as a last resort, to subsist on grossly inadequate public assistance grants. Neither of these options is satisfactory as they tend to result in adverse consequences for the mothers and their children.

The rights of children are in the United States linked closely to the statuses and rights of their parents. However, the scope of rights to which children are entitled as children, and which society is ready to guarantee, e.g., public education, has been increasing steadily since earlier times when the circumstances and authority of parents determined the rights of their children with hardly a challenge by society. Recent years have seen important legal and judicial developments toward strengthening the social and civil rights of children. Implied in this issue are such conceptual questions as whether children are the "property" of their parents, or whether they "belong" to society, whether they have specifiable civil and social rights and, hence, whether society has specific obligations to assure these rights, and, if so, what are the rights of children, and what is the extent of societal obligations toward them.

The way a society defines the concept "work" has important consequences for the circumstances of living of individuals and their relations to each other, especially when rewards for the performance of work roles constitute a major mechanism for distributing rights to individuals. By excluding certain functions and contexts from the social and economic definition of work persons assigned to these functions are deprived of economic rewards. Also, by defining certain functions and contexts as "voluntary work," symbolic and psychologic rewards are substituted for economic ones, which is merely another mechanism for economic exploitation. It should be noted in this context that women are constantly urged to engage in "voluntary work." Business executives who entertain prospective customers are "working," and so are professional ball players who are throwing balls, but volunteers who "entertain" patients in a hospital, tutors of "slow learning" children in schools, and women who clean their family's home, prepare meals and care for children are "not working." These brief comments on the issue of defining the concept of "work" illustrate the essentially social nature and dynamics of this definitional process and, hence, the relevance of this issue for social policy analysis and development.

The final issue identified above as being dealt with by the mothers' wages policy is the redistribution of rights through transfer of purchasing power. In a capitalistic economy individual purchasing power is an important means for securing one's rights to goods and services, since many essential and other goods and services must be purchased in the open market. Consequently, one obvious approach toward redistributing, and reducing inequalities of, rights in such an economy is to transfer purchasing power from groups in the population whose purchasing power is above the mean to groups whose purchasing power is below the mean. Different techniques are available to carry out such transfers, each having their own strengths, weaknesses, and side effects. It should be noted in this respect that the specific transfer technique selected may be less important than the aggregate amounts of purchasing power involved in the transfer, the resulting shape of the distribution of purchasing power in the population, and the characteristics of the population segments affected by the transfers.

The four issues reviewed above with which the mothers' wages policy is expected to deal are reflected in many aspects of life throughout all strata of society. All women at some points in their lives experience the sex-linked tendencies of the processes of status allocation and rights distribution. Similarly, all children are affected by the manner in which their rights are determined, be it on the basis of the statuses and rights of their parents, on the basis of universal societal arrangements, or, as is the present situation, on the basis of some combination of these factors. The societal definition of the concept of work concerns every individual in a society in which work constitutes a major source of personal rights, and of equal relevance and importance is the shape of the distribution of rights throughout society, and modifications of that distribution by way of transfers of purchasing power.

While then these four issues affect directly or indirectly the lives of nearly every individual in society, the problematic aspects inherent in them are especially detrimental for groups in the population who are subjected to severe, absolute or relative deprivation as a result of other interacting criteria of social stratification, such as age, race, education, etc. Thus the discriminatory and exploitative tendencies toward women, the lack of adequate societal provisions for children, the societal definition of work, and the unequal distribution of rights have relatively minor adverse effects on women and children in privileged social strata, while their effects are extremely destructive for families and individuals in the lowest fifth of the income distribution, and nearly as destructive for those in the next to the lowest fifth.

2. *Causal theories or hypotheses concerning the dynamics of the issues:*
Sex-linked differences and inequalities concerning the allocation of statuses and the distribution of rights seem to be a result of similar societal dynamics as other socially structured inequalities among individuals and groups.[2] Their specific origin was, obviously, the biological difference between the sexes, which was utilized during early stages of societal evolution as an important criterion for the division of labor. As these early, nature-linked arrangements were elaborated socially into stable cultural patterns and taboos, male dominance, and its corollary, subjugation and exploitation of females, became institutionalized in human societies. Socialization over countless generations resulted in widespread identification of men and women with the socially determined range of sex roles, and, hence, fairly general acceptance of constraints in the allocation of statuses and the distribution of rights. It should not be overlooked, however, that throughout history many women and some men have questioned, and occasionally revolted against, traditional patterns of sex-linked limitations on statuses and rights, and as a result traditional constraints were gradually reduced, especially during the twentieth century.

Socially structured limitations of the rights of children are another social pattern derived from biological conditions. The rights of children are usually linked closely to the statuses and rights of their parents. Human infants are utterly dependent on their mothers and, indirectly, their fathers. Children, at least during their early years, lack physical strength, social skills, and awareness, and their ability to survive unaided is consequently limited. This bio-psycho-social imbalance between adults and children constitutes the source of various forms of protection, domination, and exploitation of children by their parents, who are the adults closest to them in biological, psychological, and social terms. In many societies, especially those who adopted private property as one major princple of social organization, children came to be viewed as the "property" as well as the responsibility of their parents. They were, in fact, an economic asset and a means toward enhancing family power. It is only in recent centuries that Western societies began to view children as "citizens" in their own rights who are entitled to a growing measure of protection by society against excessive parental power and exploitation, and against economic exploitation by agricultural, commercial, and industrial enterprises. The notion that children were individuals in their own rights, rather than merely possessions of their parents, gradually led to the concept of a societal obligation to assure the rights of all children, and to limit the extent to which their rights are determined by the statuses, rights, and authority of their parents.

The societal definition of work seems rooted in the principles and values which underlie a society's overall organization and, more specifically, the organization of its economy. In a general "socio-economic" sense "work" includes all activities presumed to contribute to a society's existence and survival, that is, activities involved in the production and distribution of all life-sustaining and life-enhancing goods and services, as well as ritualistic activities. Participation in "work" at appropriate stages during the life cycle is the usual basis for an individual's claim to a share in his society's manifold resources. The foregoing generic definition of work tends to undergo modifications in relation to the social contexts in which activities are performed. Thus, for instance, services performed within a family group by wives for husbands and vice versa, by parents for minor children, by adult children for aged parents, by any individual for a sick or handicapped relative, etc., are usually excluded from the generic socio-economic definition of work and are defined instead as "duties," intrinsic to specific personal statuses and social relationships. Such familial duties do not entitle individuals performing them to specific economic rewards but to certain "reciprocal duties" and societal recognition. Failure to perform such status-intrinsic duties tends to result in severe social sanctions. Socially structured relationships involve often inequalities of statuses, rights, and power and in such situations the redefinition of work as reciprocal duty may be merely a rationalization for covert exploitation of individuals whose personal status is less powerful by those whose status is more powerful. While the redefinition of "work" as "duty" may result in exploitation even in situations when reciprocity functions well, severe exploitation is usually unavoidable when individuals are expected to perform status-linked duties in spite of breakdowns of reciprocity systems. Child care performed by mothers in fatherless families is one illustration of this type of situation. The mother's activity continues to be defined as "duty" which entitles her to certain reciprocal duties from an absent or nonexistent man, but not to specific economic rewards as would be the case if society defined child care as work. The societal context of "reciprocal duty," as well as the earlier mentioned context of "voluntary work," both of which are used to obtain "free labor," support the hypothesis that societal definitions of work serve to bias the distribution of rights in society in favor of more powerful statuses and groups by depriving less powerful ones of economic rewards for role performance.

Significant inequalities in the distribution of income, wealth, and all other forms of rights among individuals and groups seem to result from several principles which were institutionalized by many societies during early stages of their development, and from a set of values which emerged simultaneously with these principles, interacted with them, and reinforced them.[3] Foremost among these principles are: provision of unequal rewards for performance of different roles; accumulation of private property of land and of other forms of durable wealth out of savings from surplus rewards; intergenerational transmission of privately controlled property as inheritance, and, hence, amassing of family wealth and economic and political power. These principles and the corresponding values of individualism, competition, and inequality have shaped, and continue to maintain, the social order and the economic system of many societies. In modern times these principles and values led to the development of "free-market-capitalism," an economic system in which production is organized primarily to maximize profit for capital owned and controlled by individual entrepreneurs or corporations, rather than to maximize the common good of all individuals and groups in society. Major inequalities in the distribution of income and wealth, and of all other life-sustaining and life-enhancing, concrete and symbolic goods and services, seem to be intrinsic consequences of the principles and values mentioned above, and of social orders and economic systems derived from them. In spite of the inevitability of such inequalities, it is possible to obtain minor shifts in the distribution of rights and in the dimensions of inequality without thoroughly changing these principles and values, and the social orders and economic systems which they sustain. Such marginal, incremental changes do, in fact, occur constantly as a result of conflicts and negotiations among interest groups who compete with each other in the political arena. However, major reductions of extant inequalities in the distribution of rights through significant transfers of purchasing power, and through other appropriate structural measures, cannot materialize, unless a society constrains the uninhibited operation of the foregoing principles and values, and develops a social order and economic system based on alternative principles and on alternative values of collectivism, cooperation, and equality.

B. OBJECTIVES, VALUE PREMISES, THEORETICAL POSITIONS, TARGET SEGMENTS, AND SUBSTANTIVE EFFECTS OF THE POLICY

1. Policy objectives:

a. to assure women caring for their children a minimum level of rights and economic independence in the form of purchasing power transferred to them as wages out of the national income; hence, to assure women the right to obtain goods and services in the market without having to engage in "gainful employment or self-employment" other than caring for their children. This objective involves also widening the options of mothers by eliminating the threat of economic sanctions which under existing social policies forces them to accept employment on unfavorable terms even when they prefer to care for their children. Finally, this objective involves freeing mothers from economic dependency on husbands, or on other related and unrelated individuals.

b. to assure minor children the opportunity to be cared for by their mothers with society assuming the cost of such care whenever mothers provide it, and, further, to assure children a minimum level of economic rights in the form of purchasing power — children's allowances — transferred on their behalf from the national income.

c. to redefine child care provided by mothers to their own children as "work" which entitles women performing it to social and economic rewards in the same manner as incumbents of many other statuses are rewarded for the performance of their roles.

d. to redistribute rights in society by reducing inequalities of purchasing power affecting families with children.

e. to assure fathers the same rights as are assured mothers under this policy, whenever special circumstances in a family require fathers to assume the care of their children.

2. Value premises and ideological orientation underlying the policy objectives: The objectives pursued by the mothers' wages policy involve a weakening of the primacy of values upholding individualism and inequality, and a corresponding shift toward values stressing collective responsibility and equality of rights. These changes in value premises are reflected in societal assumption of a larger share of responsibility for the care of children, in a lessening of opportunities for economic exploitation of women, and in significant reductions in the dimensions of inequality of purchasing power. It should be noted that these shifts in value premises constitute a major departure from dominant beliefs, values, customs, and traditions with respect to child care, motherhood, parental rights and responsibilities, and economic relations. Because of this the mothers' wages policy is likely to en-counter resistance prior to adoption and, if adopted, in the course of its implementation.

While then the mothers' wages policy involves important shifts in overt value premises, it involves also continuity with regard to covert values of discrimination against women in the allocation of statuses. This is reflected in the fact that the policy strengthens the rights of women who care for their own children without, at the same time, opening access of women to all statuses. Also, the fact that the policy is directed primarily at mothers, and only marginally at fathers, reveals the underlying bias against equality of rights for both sexes.

3. *Theories or hypotheses underlying the strategies and substantive provisions of the policy:* The strategies and substantive provisions of the mothers' wages policy are derived mainly from theoretical premises similar to those discussed above in connection with the dynamics of the issues dealt with by this policy.[4] It was shown there that socio-economic deprivation of mothers and children was largely a result of discriminatory and exploitative societal practices patterned around bio-logical phenomena. The strategies and provisions of the mothers' wages policy are designed to counteract these practices. Thus, defining child care as a joint responsibility of parents and society would reduce the extent to which the rights of children are determined primarily by the statuses, rights, and authority of their parents. And assumption by society of the cost of maternal child care, and provision of children's allowances would be concrete expressions of increased societal com-mitment to assure the rights of all children. Similarly, defining child care performed by mothers as "work," paying wages for it out of national income, and including mothers in the Social Security system would significantly reduce the scope of established patterns of social discrimination against, and economic exploitation of, women. Further-more, transferring sizable amounts of purchasing power from high income segments of the population to segments whose income is below the median, through mothers' wages, social security benefits, and children's allowances, as well as through appropriate corresponding modifications of the income tax system, would effectively reduce major inequalities in the shape of the rights distribution.

One further theoretical premise implicit in the strategies and pro-visions of this policy is that income transfers such as children's allow-ances which utilize the principle of "universal entitlement," are pre-ferable to income transfers such as "Negative Income Taxes" which utilize the principle of "selectivity based on need." Universal entitle-ment is assumed to be more conducive to societal cohesiveness and solidarity than selectivity, since all individuals within a specified social category, such as children, are treated equally with respect to the transfer process, irrespective of their economic circumstances. Universal entitlements avoid also the controversial issue of "work incentives" since they are paid independently of other income. Selectivity on the other hand is often considered to be more efficient in economic terms, since income transfers are channeled only to individuals within categories defined by economic need. It should be noted, however, that the net economic effect of income transfers can be designed to be roughly equal in both approaches by means of suitable adjustments of income tax provisions.[5]

Finally, theoretical premises underlying the proposed levels of mothers' wages and children's allowances need to be made explicit. The federally established minimum wage has been suggested as standard rate for mothers' wages, and $50 per month in 1970 dollars as the standard children's allowance for the following reasons. Firstly, the proposed rate for mothers' wages reflects a societal position, that the social and economic value of child care performed by mothers is not less than that of other tasks for which the government establishes a minimum wage floor. Secondly, as shown by the following calculations, these rates for mothers' wages and children's allowances would bring about significant reductions of income inequalities between men and women, and among families with children, and would greatly reduce social and economic deprivation among these families. The minimum wage at the 1970 level of $1.60 per hour paid for eight hours a day, 365 days a year would give mothers a personal annual income of $4672. This is nearly half the 1970 median family income of $9870, more than twice the 1970 median income of women of $2240, yet only 70 percent of the 1970 median income of men of $6670.[6] Such a wage combined with a children's allowance of $50 per month would provide a fatherless family of four with an annual income of $6472, which is nearly two-thirds of the 1970 median family income of $9870, or 92 percent of $6960, the lower level budget for an urban family of four as measured by the Bureau of Labor Statistics in the spring of 1970.[7] The U. S. economy seems capable to sustain income transfers at the suggested levels, since the redistributive potential of an economy is reflected in the mean income, which tends to be higher than the median, the statistic used in the foregoing argument. Since the suggested transfer rate would not bring the income of all families up to the median, the redistributive potential within the economy would not be exceeded.

The foregoing arguments are relevant also to a related aspect of the mothers' wages policy. This is the choice of a uniform rate of mothers' wages rather than of a differential wage scale based on different levels of opportunity costs, or potential earnings, which mothers forego when engaging in child care instead of in employment outside their homes. A uniform rate of mothers' wages is considered conducive to the reduction of inequalities of rights among families with children, whereas a differential wage scale would counteract this policy objective. Furthermore, a uniform rate of mothers' wages symbolizes a societal position according to which the value of child care is deemed equal for all children, irrespective of variations in the occupational skills and earning potential of mothers who provide the care.

4. *Target segments of society:* Since the mothers' wages policy deals with the rights of women and children through redistribution of purchasing power both vertically, between income strata, and horizontally within income strata, it is bound to affect the circumstances of living of all individuals and segments of society. Its specific target, however, are mothers and children, or families with children, especially those whose annual income falls within the lower half of the income distribution. The following figures derived from publications of the U. S. Bureau of the Census indicate the numerical size of the target segments of the policy. In 1969 the U. S. population included 70.8 million children under age 18 in 29.8 million families. About one-half of these families with children under age 18 had annual incomes under $10,000. This latter segment of slightly over fifteen million families constitutes the primary target of the mothers' wages policy. This group of families is classified by income steps in Table 4.1 below.

TABLE 4.1.   TOTAL MONEY INCOME OF FAMILIES WITH CHILDREN UNDER AGE 18 — 1969*

INCOME	NUMBER OF FAMILIES	NUMBER OF FAMILIES CUMULATIVE
under $3000	2,040,000	2,040,000
$3000-$4999	2,560,000	4,600,000
$5000-$6999	3,600,000	8,200,000
$7000-$9999	6,957,000	15,157,000
$10,000 and over	14,664,000	29,821,000

*Source: U. S. Department of Commerce, Bureau of the Census, *Consumer Income, Current Population Reports,* Series P-60, No. 75, December 14, 1970, Table 14, p. 29.

To grasp the full meaning of the income distribution shown in this table, it should be realized that nearly 3.5 million families, including

10.5 million children under age 18, were classified in 1970 as "poor" in accordance with poverty criteria established by the U. S. government. For a nonfarm family of four the official poverty threshold was $3968 in 1970.[8] Of these 3.5 million poor families with children under age 18 about 1.7 million were headed by women and about 1.8 million were headed by men. Nearly 2.6 million families among those in "poverty" were by the end of 1970 on the rolls of the "Aid to Families with Dependent Children" program. These AFDC families had a total of 9.7 million individuals, 7.1 million of whom were children.[9] Furthermore, the number of children under age 18 in families whose income in 1970 was below the "near-poverty" level, was 14.6 million, over one-fifth of all children under age 18 in the United States.[10] The "near-poverty" level is defined as 125 percent of the official poverty level. Thus the near-poverty threshold for a nonfarm family of four was $4960 in 1970.

The foregoing discussion of family income indicates that the target segments of the mothers' wages policy include poor, marginally poor, and working or lower middle class families with children under age 18. It is important to note here that the target segments of this policy do *not* include families without children under age 18 and "unrelated individuals." Consequently, nearly 1.8 million families without children under age 18 and over 5 million unrelated individuals who together constituted 33.7 percent of all persons classified as poor in 1970, are not included in the target segments.[11] These poor families and individuals who are outside the scope of the mothers' wages policy are mainly retired older men and women, as well as unemployed, underemployed, or marginally employed individuals of all ages. Families without children under age 18 and unrelated individuals among the near-poor and the working or lower middle class are also not included in the target segments of the mothers' wages policy and would therefore not derive direct benefits from it.

The income criterion used here to identify the target segments of the mothers' wages policy reveals also several other characteristics of the target population which tend to be associated with poverty and low income. The target population, though distributed all over the nation in rural and urban areas, is more highly concentrated in inner cities and in economically depressed and less developed regions of the country. Families belonging to the target segments tend to be subject to higher rates of physical and emotional illness, social and psychological deviance, and family breakdown than families with children under age 18 in the upper half of the income distribution. Also among target segment families, educational achievement and occupational levels tend to be lower, unemployment rates tend to be higher, quality of housing and neighborhoods tends to be lower, and levels of social involvement and participation tend to be lower.

Families belonging to racial minorities are significantly overrepresented among the target segments of the mothers' wages policy. While less than 12 percent of all families with children under age 18 in the United States are black, one-third of all poor families with children under age 18 are black. Also, while about 8 percent of white families with children under age 18 were officially classified as poor in 1970, about 34 percent of black families with children under age 18 were so classified. Furthermore, 10 percent of white children under age 18 as against 40 percent of black children under age 18 were poor.[12] And finally, 74 percent of black families as against 48 percent of white families had incomes under $10,000 in 1970.[13]

Families headed by women are also significantly overrepresented among the target segments of the mothers' wages policy. While 10 percent of all families with children under age 18 were headed by women in 1969,[14] 47 percent of all poor families with children under age 18 and 61 percent of black poor families with children under age 18 were headed by women.[15] Families among the target segments, and especially among the poor, and even more so among the black poor, also tend to have more children under age 18 than all families with children in the United States. Thus, while in 1969 about 18 percent of all families with children under age 18 in the nation had 4 or more children, 35 percent of poor families with children under age 18 and 46 percent of poor black families with children under age 18 had that many children. Conversely, while 63 percent of all families with children under age 18 had 1 or 2 children, 47 percent of all poor, and 38 percent of poor black families with children under age 18 had 1 or 2 children.[16]

The numerical size and major characteristics of the above sketched target segments of the mothers' wages policy have remained fairly constant relative to the entire U. S. population over the past 25 years. This stability of relative size is not likely to change unless social policies are developed and implemented which will bring about significant redistribution of purchasing power among the entire population. The foregoing conclusion concerning the magnitude of the target segments seems inescapable since the target segments are defined primarily in terms of family income strata, and characteristics associated with these strata, and since the general shape of the income distribution of the U. S. population has remained essentially unchanged since the end of World War II.[17] The only long-term changes to be expected in the future in the absolute size of the target segments, assuming no real changes in social policy, are, therefore, changes due to the natural increase of the population. In addition to this certain short run variations should be expected in the relative magnitude of target segments as a result of fluctuations in aggregate economic activity, and the impact of this activity on employment rates, wage levels, and the cost of goods and services as well as a result of constantly occurring marginal, incremental modifications of the social policy system.[18]

5. *Short and long range effects:* When implemented the mothers' wages policy would result in the attainment of the several objectives specified above,[19] provided federal tax and other economic measures will be amended so as not to counteract the overall redistributive purposes of this policy. The transfer income of mothers from full time mothers' wages would be $4672 per year in accordance with the 1971 minimum wage level. This amount is more than twice the 1970 non-farm poverty threshold for unrelated women of $1935, and even slightly more than the 1970 nonfarm poverty threshold for female-headed, 5 person households of $4639.[20] When, as specified in the policy, mothers' wages are linked with a $600 a year children's allowance per child in 1970 constant dollars, the total transfer income of families with children under age 18 would exceed the 1970 nonfarm poverty and near-poverty thresholds for female-headed families with any number of children. Table 4.2 below demonstrates these circumstances by showing the excess of transfer income for different family sizes over corresponding poverty and near-poverty thresholds.

Table 4.2 suggests several important observations. Firstly, no female-headed family consisting of mothers and children under age 18 would have to live on an income below the near-poverty threshold once the mothers' wages policy is implemented. However, the combined transfer income of mothers' wages and children's allowances would be less than the 1970 median family income of $9870, as long as a mother had fewer than 9 children under age 18. Clearly, also, the federally financed program of "Aid to Families with Dependent Children," or the expanded, yet inadequate, "Family Assistance Program," if enacted, as well as supplementary, state financed programs of general assistance for families and children would no longer be needed. The table also reveals that mothers and children would not be lifted merely out of conditions of severe poverty, but they would have sizable amounts of purchasing power beyond the official near-poverty levels. While this margin of purchasing power beyond the near-poverty

TABLE 4.2 MOTHERS' WAGES AND CHILDREN'S ALLOWANCES COMPARED WITH 1970 NONFARM POVERTY AND NEAR-POVERTY THRESHOLDS FOR FEMALE-HEADED HOUSEHOLD.

SIZE OF FAMILY UNIT	MOTHERS' WAGES	CHIL-DREN'S ALLOW-ANCE	TOTAL TRANSFER INCOME	POVERTY THRESH-OLD*	EXCESS OVER POVERTY THRESH-OLD	NEAR-POVERTY THRESH-OLD*	EXCESS OVER NEAR-POVERTY THRESH-OLD
Mother, 1 child	4672	600	5272	2522	2750	3153	2119
Mother, 2 children	4672	1200	5872	3003	2869	3754	2118
Mother, 3 children	4672	1800	6472	3948	2524	4935	1537
Mother, 4 children	4672	2400	7072	4639	2433	5799	1273
Mother, 5 children	4672	3000	7672	5220	2452	6525	1147
Mother, 6 children	4672	3600	8272	6317	1955	7896	376

*Source: U.S. Department of Commerce, Bureau of the Census, *Consumer Income, Current Population Reports,* Series P-60, No. 77, May 7, 1971, Table No. 6, p. 6.

threshold would decrease gradually with family size, economics of scale can be expected to compensate to a certain extent for this gradual decrease of purchasing power.

Mothers in female-headed or male-headed families with children under age 18 are not likely to engage in part or full time employment outside their homes unless such employment would markedly improve the overall economic and psycho-social situation of a family. It seems consequently safe to assume that families with children under age 18 would be assured at least the level of purchasing power resulting from the combined full time mothers' wages and children's allowances to which they would be entitled. Any income earned by fathers and/or husbands, as well as by children, would of course improve the overall economic circumstances of families with children under age 18 beyond the levels guaranteed by mothers' wages and children's allowances.

Before continuing the exploration of the multiple effects of the mothers' wages policy it seems necessary at this point to present an estimate of the magnitude and incidence of the aggregate transfer of purchasing power pursuant to this policy. Yet prior to considering such an estimate, a caveat seems in order which is that a transfer of purchasing power among consumption units, and segments of a society, is not to be equated with a real economic cost in a societal sense, al-though such transfers may involve considerable "costs" in the form of taxes paid by various individuals, business firms, and segments of society. A transfer of purchasing power merely means that claims to the totality of goods and services produced by a society are being re-shuffled or redistributed. As a result of this redistribution, the rates at which different individuals and segments of society can participate in the consumption of goods and services are readjusted, and pre-transfer consumption patterns are transformed into new post-transfer patterns. Ultimately redistribution of purchasing power may lead to modifications of aggregate production, consumption, savings, and in-vestment of capital and work effort, and in this way real economic costs and/or gains may result from the transfers. The extent to which such costs and gains will actually materialize following the transfer of purchasing power depends on many other policies pursued by a society including fiscal, monetary, wage, price, interest, and foreign trade measures. The important thing to keep in mind, however, is that the magnitude of the transfer of purchasing power is not, in itself, a direct measure of real economic costs or gains.

In 1970 the U. S. population included about 29 million mothers with children under age 18 and about 71 million children. If all these mothers were to collect mothers' wages the aggregate wage at mini-mum wage rates prevailing in 1970 would be $135.5 billion. The aggre-gate transfer amount for children's allowances for the same year would be $42.6 billion and the combined amount for both these transfer programs would be $178.1 billion.

About 10 million mothers participated in the work force during 1970 and would have been entitled only to fractions of full mothers' wages in proportion of their work force participation. Some mothers — and no one knows how many — would, of course, withdraw from employment outside their homes once a mothers' wage policy is im-plemented. It seems safe to assume that mothers whose purchasing power would not increase noticeably as a result of employment out-side their homes would withdraw from such employment. Few mothers work year-round in full-time employment, and most working mothers are employed in low-level jobs which offer low wages and limited job satisfaction. Less than 10 percent of working mothers earn more than $5000 per year[21] and it thus seems that 9 out of 10, or about 9 million mothers, are likely to withdraw from the work force once a mothers' wages policy is introduced. These considerations suggest that the ag-gregate transfer amount for mothers' wages would be reduced by about $3.5 billion as a consequence of work force participation by mothers, and the total amount needed to carry out the transfer programs of mothers' wages and children's allowances in 1970 would thus have been close to $175 billion.

Since mothers' wages and children's allowances would be paid on a universal basis to all mothers and children irrespective of economic position, nearly half the aggregate transfer, or $85 billion, would be paid to mothers and children in families whose annual income is above the median of the national income distribution. These "horizontal" transfers among income units in the upper half of the distribution would involve mainly transfers from childless households to families with children under age 18, and would reduce existing inequalities in per capita purchasing power within the more affluent segments of the population.

About $90 billion of the total transfer amount would go to mothers and children in families whose income is below the median of the income distribution. This amount, which is less than 10 percent of current Gross National Product, represents the extent of real "vertical" transfers from the affluent segments of society to currently poor, near-poor, and working or lower middle class families with children under age 18. Some horizontal transfers would also occur within the lower half of the income distribution from childless households to families with children under age 18, and would reduce inequalities within that segment of the population.

In connection with the estimate of the magnitude of vertical transfers of purchasing power, consideration should be given to fiscal implications of phasing out existing vertical transfer programs, and of using amounts budgeted for these programs for the mothers' wages policy. Between $5 and $6 billion would be available from the AFDC program, federal food programs, and state operated general assistance programs. Should the federal Family Assistance Program be enacted another $5 billion would be available. Furthermore, a broad range of programs aimed at aiding poor and near-poor families which are now operated by the Office of Economic Opportunity and by the U. S. Departments of Health, Education, and Welfare; Housing and Urban Development; Labor; and Agriculture could also be gradually phased out, and funds appropriated for these programs could then be used to offset new appropriations for the mothers' wages policy. The scope of new revenue for vertical transfers pursuant to the mothers' wages policy could thus be reduced to under $80 billion.

Financing the total income transfers of the mothers' wages policy would require major adjustments and reforms of the nation's tax system. Several comments seem indicated in this context. First of all, mothers' wages and children's allowances would be subject to income tax in order to reduce progressively the transfer amounts retained by families with other sources, and varying amounts, of income. Secondly, existing income tax deductions for children, wives, and husbands would have to be eliminated since their effects on after-tax purchasing power are regressive and thus in conflict with the redistributive objectives of mothers' wages and children's allowances. Thirdly, many special provisions in the tax laws which now favor selected interest groups such as oil companies, real estate enterprises, and individual home owners would have to be eliminated, and in this way the annual tax yield under present tax rates could be increased by about $50 billion.[22] Finally, the entire federal tax system would have to be overhauled, amended, and reformed in order to generate the revenue flow necessary for the vertical and horizontal transfers involved in the mothers' wages policy, and in order to eliminate from the existing provisions all regressive tendencies which counteract the principles and values of the new policy.

Transfer payments of the magnitude indicated here, if financed through a consistently progressive tax system, would result in significant changes in the existing shape of the income or rights distribution in society. The socio-economic distance between high-income groups and low-income families with children under age 18 would be narrowed considerably, and the proposed policy would thus have a decisive impact, over time, not only on absolute poverty, but also on relative poverty and bio-psycho-social deprivation. It may thus be expected that various biological, psychological, social, and cultural correlates of poverty and low-income life in American society would gradually decrease in scope and intensity. It is not suggested here that such destructive phenomena as delinquency, crime, family breakdown, mental illness and retardation, psycho-social alienation, drug addiction, deterioration of neighborhoods, and a variety of physical ailments would disappear as soon as the economic roots of poverty are eradicated. It is submitted, though, that progress in overcoming these phenomena is possible only when economic deprivation is no longer permitted to exist in an affluent society, and that, therefore, social policies involving significant reductions in income inequalities constitute essential, though not sufficient, measures for controlling and eventually preventing these dysfunctional phenomena.

Having reviewed effects of the mothers' wages policy in general terms, several more specific observations seem now indicated. The work force participation response of mothers is one important aspect which has already been referred to. It was suggested that most working mothers, 9 out of 10, would probably withdraw from employment outside their homes since such employment provides them presently with fewer benefits than mothers' wages would. This response of mothers could lead to wage increases and general improvements of working conditions in service occupations and in many industrial jobs now filled by women. It could also lead to reduced unemployment and better working conditions for men and for women who are not engaged in rearing their children, and in reduction of poverty among unrelated individuals and couples without children whose poverty would not be directly ameliorated by the income transfers of the mothers' wages policy. A further consequence could be accelerated development of automation and cybernation which is now often held back because of the availability of cheap labor. Gradual price increases for certain goods and services could result from the foregoing changes in the work force and the price of labor, but increased efficiency in methods of production due to increases in automation and cybernation would counteract the pressures from higher cost of labor. Furthermore, overall economic activity would be stimulated considerably as the consumption potential of the population for basic goods and services would expand. This increase in economic activity would in turn yield additional taxes for local, state, and federal governments which could lead to overall improvements in public services.

Critics of children's allowances and also of mothers' wages expect an increase in the birthrate to follow the introduction of such programs. Evidence from many countries, including Canada, England, and France, who have had similar programs on a smaller scale for many years, does not support this assumption.[23] Human behavior concerning fertility is the resultant of a complex set of forces, the interactions of which are so far insufficiently understood. Economic factors are certainly important elements of this set of forces. However the relationship between economics and fertility is not a linear one. While it is probably true that some families are more likely to have children as their ability to provide for them adequately increases with income, it is also true that escape from poverty has usually been followed by decreases in fertility of formerly poverty stricken social strata along with overall changes in attitudes and life style of these strata. The assumption that mothers and families are going to have more children simply in order to obtain additional mothers' wages and children's allowances seems to derive from an over-simplification of complex psycho-social processes, especially in view of the fact that wages and allowances per child do not cover the cost of supporting an additional child. It may be of interest in this context to point to a significant decrease in birthrates among recipients of AFDC in New York City following the legalization of abortions in New York State and increased availability of family planning services to participants of the AFDC program.[24]

The mothers' wages policy is also expected to affect the self-image of mothers and fathers, the relations of women and men, and, consequently, family life and all aspects of child development. Freeing mothers from total economic dependence on their husbands is apt to result in more meaningful intra-familial relations. Mothers would be more equal as partners in a marriage and more equally respected as members of society once their work would be remunerative economically and rewarded with social prestige, both in their homes and in the labor market, where they could no longer be severely exploited. While fewer marriages may be contracted, and fewer marriages would continue merely for economic reasons, once mothers' wages are instituted, couples who married and remained together would probably lead a more harmonious family life than many an American family does now. With economic elements receding in importance as far as family relations are concerned, human relations would become the dominant force f . maintaining family life and keeping families together. Increased harmony in intra-familial relations should have positive effects on the overall functioning of family members in and outside the home.

Along with changes in the role of mothers, the roles of husbands and fathers would also undergo changes. Fathers and husbands would be valued in their families for their human qualities and not primarily as economic providers. Such a change may not be easy for many men who were socialized into a specific pattern of the male and father role. Some men are likely to resent the change and so may also some women. These negative reactions by men as well as by women would seem to be understandable consequences of attitudes which evolved over countless generations. These reactions may lead to conflicts and separations in some families during early stages of the implementation of the mothers' wages policy. In the long run though, positive reactions are likely to outweigh by far such negative ones, and family relations are expected to improve over time to a considerable degree.

Economic security and gradual improvements in the quality of family life will in turn enhance physical, intellectual, educational, social, and emotional aspects of child life and child development among the main target segments of the mothers' wages policy. In this sense the policy can be viewed as a long-range societal investment in human capital.

Some individuals, families, and business firms whose wealth and earnings would be subject to higher taxes following introduction of the mothers' wages policy, might view this policy as damaging to their interests, and might reduce their work efforts, savings, and investments when additional income would, in their judgment, yield too little additional benefits. Some persons might even choose to emigrate while some might attempt to reduce their tax liabilities in various ways. Other members of higher income strata may, however, be more favorably disposed toward the mothers' wages policy, and may cooperate in its implementation upon realizing the dynamics of human interdependence in society, and the likelihood that direct and immediate benefits which their higher taxes provided for low income families with children would eventually lead to indirect, comprehensive, and long-range benefits for all members and segments of society. It would seem that chances for cooperation of upper income strata could be enhanced by emphasizing, in promoting the mothers' wages policy, its long-range potential for serving the interests of all groups in society, rather than merely the important short run benefits for the policy's target segments.

The overall benefits and costs of the mothers' wages policy can now be summarized:

Benefits

— Elimination of poverty and near-poverty for families with children under age 18, a total of about 17 million individuals out of 25.5 million poor persons in 1970;
— Increase in purchasing power of all families with children under age 18 whose income is now below the median family income as a result of a $90 billion vertical transfer of purchasing power from the upper half of the national income distribution;
— Reduction of inequalities in per capita purchasing power of families with children under age 18 throughout the population by way of horizontal transfers from households without children under age 18;
— Overall stimulation of economic activity to meet increased demand for basic goods and services. Related to this reduction of unemployment and of poverty among able-bodied unrelated persons and couples without children under age 18 who would not benefit directly from mothers' wages and children's allowances. Unemployment among men and women without children under age 18 would also decrease as a result of reduced work force participation of mothers;
— Increase in tax revenue of local, state, and federal governments derived from transfer income and increased economic activity.

These additional taxes could support more and better public services;

— Wage increases and improvements in working conditions in un-skilled and marginal jobs formerly filled by poor mothers;
— Acceleration in the development of automation and cybernation to counteract shortages of cheap labor;
— Development of a more equitable and more consistently pro-gressive system of taxation without special benefits for powerful interest groups;
— Improvement in the self-image and the social prestige of mothers along with marked improvement in their social rights and eco-nomic circumstances;
— Shifts in the role of fathers and husbands in the family from economic control toward sharing as equals in a more meaningful relationship;
— Improvement in the human quality of family life, and in relations between men and women;
— Improvement in economic, biological, emotional, intellectual, social, and cultural aspects of child life and child development throughout all social strata but especially among poor, near-poor, and working or lower middle class families;
— Increased societal responsibility for the economic security and general well-being of children;
— Over time, reduction of incidence and prevalence of physical and mental illness, mental retardation, and of various forms of devi-ance in social and psychological functioning;
— Over time, improvement in the quality of housing, neighborhoods, and public services;
— Entitlement to social security benefits for women on the basis of maternal child care work;
— Phasing out of AFDC, and several other extant public welfare programs resulting in savings of over $10 billion.

Costs

— An annual transfer flow of $175 billion of purchasing power gen-erated through marked increases in progressive taxation on indi-viduals and groups in the upper half of the income distribution. Nearly half of this transfer would be circulated horizontally among households in the upper half of the income distribution, while the rest would be transferred vertically to poor, near poor, and working or lower middle class families with children under age 18;

— Loss of cheap labor of about 9 million mothers;
— Increases in the price of labor, and the cost of production and, related to this, increases in the price of some goods and services;
— Loss of economic control of wives by husbands;
— Increases in taxation and corresponding reductions in consumption and profits of individuals and business enterprises. Related to this possible decreases in work effort, savings, and investments;
— Significant reductions of economic inequalities and, related to this, gradual reductions in social prestige and privileges of upper income strata.

A review of these benefits and costs suggests that anticipated benefits of the mothers' wages policy outweigh by far its perceived costs when humanistic, public interest, and egalitarian criteria are applied. Clearly, this is a value judgment and different conclusions could be reached by applying different criteria. It should also be noted that many elements, e.g., the increase of wages for marginal jobs, can be viewed as a benefit as well as a cost, depending on one's value premises. However, even within the humanistic, public interest, and egalitarian value premises one could question whether the mothers' wages policy represents the most effective and efficient use of this sizable amount of transfer funds. In other words, since even an affluent society is faced with limitations of resources, questions of opportunity costs must be considered. It thus could be asked whether the same amount of transfer funds should be used to yield an adequate income for all poor persons rather than primarily for families with children under age 18. Or whether, perhaps, some of these transfer funds should preferably be channeled into ecological rehabilitation programs, aid to poor and developing nations, or some other, not less critical, societal need. These essentially evaluative questions belong, however, to the final section of an analysis. They are mentioned at this point merely to illustrate the proposition that social policies cannot be evaluated properly in terms of their intrinsic benefits and costs, but need to be examined in relation to the entire policy system of a society.

C. IMPLICATIONS OF THE POLICY FOR THE KEY PROCESSES AND THE COMMON DOMAIN OF SOCIAL POLICIES

1. *Changes in the development of resources, goods, and services:* The mothers' wages policy is not aimed directly at the development of resources, goods, and services. However, vertical transfers of significant amounts of purchasing power from higher to lower income

groups of the population, and consequent stimulation of economic activity and comprehensive changes in the consumption patterns of former low income households, would result in marked qualitative and quantitative changes in the development of goods and services by private and public sources.

In general the direction of these changes would be away from the production of less essential and luxury-type goods and services which are consumed primarily by upper income households, toward the production of more basic necessities including homes, home-furnishings, durable goods, clothing, and health care services. Improvements in economic circumstances and life styles of former low income groups, and related increases in tax payments to local and state governments, would result in increased pressures for equalization of the quality and quantity of public services. These demands and newly available revenue would in time bring about the development of better schools, transportation, sanitation, fire and police services, and ecological and neighborhood rehabilitation.

Priority decisions affecting development of these new patterns of resources would be mediated, as in the past, through the operation of the market and the political system. The difference with respect to these decision mechanisms following the introduction of the mothers' wages policy would be that formerly poor and low income households would now share more equally in economic and political power, and would thus have a better chance to register their preferences, and to influence the eventual outcome of decisions.

It should be noted here that implementation of the mothers' wages policy may slow down the development of one important, yet controversial, service resource which for a variety of reasons has attracted in recent years considerable interest from many different groups. This service resource encompasses various types of child care services such as group and family day care facilities, nursery schools, early childhood education programs, etc.[25] A wide range of benefits and costs are assumed to be associated with these services, depending on variations in quality and objectives. The common element intrinsic to all these services is a shift of child care functions away from mothers. It seems that demand for such services by mothers and by the public would decrease, and motivation to promote their development would lessen, when mothers could care for their own children without being penalized economically, socially, and psychologically.

2. *Changes in the allocation of individuals and groups to statuses:* The mothers' wages policy is also not aimed directly at bringing about

major changes in the way individuals and groups in society are "allocated" to statuses. However, while the direct impact of the policy on status allocation would not be very significant, the indirect, long-term impact could be considerable.

One direct consequence of the mothers' wages policy for the status system would be the redefinition of maternal child care as socially recognized work, for which mothers would receive concrete and symbolic rewards in the form of purchasing power, social security benefits, and a measure of social prestige. This redefinition would strengthen the status "mother," and would afford mothers increased protection against forced allocation to undesirable statuses in service and industrial occupations which tend to offer low rewards in purchasing power, prestige, and job satisfaction.

Another direct consequence of the policy for the status system would be the strengthening and protection of the status "child," by increasing societal responsibility for the economic security of children, and by assuring children the right to be cared for by their own parents whenever mothers or fathers wish to provide such care, with society assuming the cost of "labor" involved.

The mothers' wages policy would also eliminate certain existing statuses, namely those of clients and administrators, of "AFDC" and other public assistance programs. Over time, as various extant programs for aiding poor families would be phased out, the statuses of clients and administrators of these programs would also be eliminated.

The policy would also modify the statuses of "father" and "husband." The power and control inherent in these statuses at present because of economic dynamics would be reduced, and social and psychological aspects in relation to other family members which are also inherent in these statuses would be enhanced. Also, under certain circumstances, such as the absence of mothers from a family, the status of "father" would be broadened to encompass the child care role and prerogatives intrinsic to that redefined role.

It should be stressed here that the mothers' wages policy would not bring about significant changes in extant criteria and procedures by which women gain access to the wide range of statuses in society. In a certain sense the policy may even strengthen the traditional, strong linkage between the child care role and biological motherhood, and may thus decelerate progress toward equal access for women to all statuses in society.

Indirect, long-term effects of the mothers' wages policy on the allocation of statuses would be mediated through the reductions it would bring about in inequalities of economic circumstances, educational opportunities, and life styles. Access to many valued statuses in society tends to depend on extended educational preparation, yet educational opportunities are at present not available to all children on an equal basis. Economic circumstances of families appear to be important determinants of the educational opportunities of their children and, hence, of the occupational options and eventual social statuses of adults. Reductions of major economic inequalities through social policies such as the mothers' wages would, therefore, over time reduce inequalities of educational opportunities and would in this way gradually reduce existing obstacles to equal access to all statuses for individuals from former low income families.

3. *Changes in the distribution of rights to individuals and groups:* The major, direct thrust of the mothers' wages policy is obviously aimed at changing the distribution of rights as it affects mothers and children in general, and, more specifically, currently poor, near-poor, and lower income families with children under age 18. The policy would also directly modify the shape of the distribution of rights throughout society.

The most important change due to the policy would be a status-specific reward for mothers who choose to care for their children. While at present such mothers may receive no direct economic rewards from society other than public assistance in the form of means-tested relief, they would receive socially financed wages and social security benefits once the mothers' wages policy is implemented. Children under age 18, too, would be recipients of a new specific entitlement, a children's allowance, which in itself would guarantee them minimal economic security and which, in combination with their mothers' societal wages would assure them the right to an adequate standard of living. Besides, as indicated above, children would also gain the right to be cared for by their mothers or fathers, depending on family choices and circumstances.

Along with the new rights for mothers and children the policy involves a set of corresponding new constraints through progressive tax reforms, affecting primarily segments in the population whose income is above the median. In aggregate terms, about 10 per cent of total national income would be shifted from the 50 percent of the population who now obtain about 75 percent of all income to the other half of the population who now obtain merely 25 percent of all income. The policy would therefore result in a new income ratio between the two halves of the population, and a related new pattern of rights.

The new ratio would be approximately 65 to 35 of national income instead of 75 to 25.

The mothers' wages policy would result also in a minor shift among the two distributive mechanisms of status-specific rewards and general or specific entitlements. As a result of the children's allowance about $43 billion, or approximately 4 percent of 1970 G.N.P., would be distributed as a universal entitlement to all members of society under age 18, independent of any work performed by the recipients. Mothers' wages themselves, it should be noted, are not a universal entitlement, but a status-specific reward for "work" performed by mothers, and thus would fit more closely the more conventional pattern of rights distribution in American society, namely, rewards for work.

The new rights pursuant to the mothers' wages policy would be distributed entirely in the form of purchasing power, that is as "rights-equivalents." However, to the extent that a portion of this purchasing power will be absorbed by local and state taxation, it will be transformed into, and distributed "in kind" as, public services primarily for groups in the population who receive at present inferior and inadequate public services.

The mothers' wages policy would establish new definitions of minimal economic rights for mothers and fathers caring for their children as well as for all children. These minimal levels of rights would be set sufficiently high so as to assure an adequate standard of living for all families with children under age 18. The minimal level of mothers' wages would be linked to the minimum federal wage and the level of children's allowances would be linked to the value of the 1970 dollar. In this way the new minimum levels would have to be adjusted automatically as minimum wages are readjusted throughout the economy and as the value of the dollar would change with inflation or, perhaps, deflation. The relative position of families with children under age 18 would thus be assured within the overall rights distribution of society. Coverage of the designated new minimal economic rights would be provided for in law through authorization of annual open-ended appropriations, and through corresponding, progressive modifications of the federal tax system.

In summarizing the various changes in the distribution of rights, it is evident that the mothers' wages policy would result in significant shifts in the relative distribution of purchasing power from affluent to low income segments of the population, and hence in marked reduction of inequalities of many rights which are associated with purchasing power. It should be reemphasized, however, in this context that the redistribution of purchasing power and of related rights under this policy would *not* benefit directly low income families without children under age 18, and low income unrelated individuals. Some of these families and individuals, namely those of working age, would probably benefit from the indirect effects of the redistribution of purchasing power, the growth in economic activity and manpower shortages in unskilled and semi-skilled jobs. However, others, and this includes mainly poor and near-poor, aged and disabled couples and individuals, would receive neither direct nor indirect benefits. On the contrary, the inequalities of purchasing power and of related rights suffered now by these segments of the population would probably increase in relative terms, unless special, vertical transfer programs are developed and enacted which would eliminate poverty and near-poverty for aging and disabled members of society who would otherwise constitute a "new underclass."

Finally, in discussing the effects of the mothers' wages policy on the overall distribution of rights it needs to be reemphasized that, while strengthening considerably the economic security of mothers, it would have only limited effects on the more complex issues of equalizing the rights of women to those of men in terms of access to statuses in society.

4. Consequences of changes in resource development, status allocation, and rights distribution for the overall quality of life in society, the circumstances of living of individuals and groups, and the nature of intra-societal human relations: Precise answers to questions implied in this focus of the analysis are not possible since sufficient knowledge concerning many relevant variables is not available. Yet in spite of this, it seems possible to anticipate certain, likely, societal developments should the mothers' wages policy be adopted.

In examining consequences of the mothers' wages policy for the common domain of social policies in all relevant spheres, three major segments of society need to be considered. These are (1) the primary target segment of the policy, namely, families with children under age 18, especially those whose income is below the national median; (2) low income households without children under age 18, consisting mainly of aged, handicapped, and disabled couples and unrelated individuals; and (3) upper income families and unrelated individuals.

Economic sphere. The most important change in circumstances of living from which many other constructive changes would gradually emanate would be a major improvement in the economic situation of several million families with children under age 18, who are now living in conditions of poverty, near-poverty, and low income, and who tend to experience feelings of insecurity, frustration, and alienation. The assurance of economic security at an adequate level for these families would set in motion a process of social rehabilitation and reconstruction, the effects of which would reach into many spheres of their lives, as well as the lives of other groups in society.

No seriously adverse economic consequences are likely to result for population segments who would pay higher taxes than now to generate the transfer funds needed for implementation of the mothers' wages policy, since the estimated tax increase would be less than 10 percent of their aggregate income. Their wealth and after-tax income would still exceed by far the wealth and income of the recipients of the transfers, and no major decline in their standards of living is likely to occur. While then the financial costs borne by the more affluent segments of the population would not cause them real economic damage and serious disadvantage, they would benefit from the subtle consequences of the mothers' wages policy for the overall quality of life in society in the various spheres of societal existence discussed below. The aggregate effect over time of these various benefits would be a less divided, less alienated, and less pathological, and a more humane and better integrated society.

Households without children, consisting mainly of aged, handicapped, and disabled persons would derive no immediate direct economic benefits from the mothers' wages policy, and would initially even experience a decline in their circumstances of living in relative terms, since they would be the only population segment left without adequate income. These households include less than 10 percent of the entire population. Their being left behind when all other low income groups would achieve considerable progress would pose serious questions of equity, would lead to intensive political pressures, and would probably before long result in the development of income transfer policies geared to their special circumstances. It should be noted in this context that public attitudes toward elderly, handicapped, and disabled persons tend to be less rejecting than toward younger, able-bodied, poor persons. It thus seems that while this segment of the population would derive no immediate economic benefits from the mothers' wages policy, and while it would even experience initially more severe relative social deprivation, its chances to benefit over time from the far-reaching social changes stimulated by this policy seem considerable.

Biological. Early consequences of the new economic strength of formerly deprived families would probably occur in spheres of concrete,
primary human needs such as nutrition and physical health. Qualitative
and quantitative deficiencies in nutrition are now an important source
of morbidity and mortality among low income segments of the population. An adequate diet made possible by an adequate income would
soon be reflected in improvements in the health of expectant mothers
and newborn infants, in lower rates of infant mortality and of consti-
tutionally determined physical and mental deficiencies, in heightened
resistance to a variety of pathogenic influences throughout the life
cycle, and, hence, in an all around healthier population. Along with
an adequate nutrition former low income families would also be able
to secure a more equitable share of health care and medical services,
even if no progress were made toward a long overdue, comprehensive
reorganization of the nation's health care system.

Improvements in the diet of present low income segments of the
population would have no adverse effects on upper income groups since
proper food is certainly available in sufficient quantity in the United
States. Increased food consumption might even improve the conditions of the farming sector of the economy. Improvements in the
general state of health of poor families is also an improvement in the
overall quality of life in society and would thus indirectly benefit all
members of society.

Increasing the share of low income families in medical care may
result in reductions of the quantity and quality of these services for
other population segments, unless the entire health care system of the
nation is reorganized. Chances are good that movement toward such
a reorganization would accelerate once demands for health care, and
political pressures supporting these demands, are broadened throughout society. It should be noted here that because of the existence of
"Medicare" within the Social Security system, the elderly segment of
the population would not be affected adversely to a significant extent
by improvements in medical services for families with children.

Demographic. Demographic consequences are linked closely to biological and economic ones. Improvements in the physical health of
mothers and infants, and of poor families in general, would over time
affect survival rates and thus population size and the age distribution
of the population. "Economic incentives" may initially cause increases
in the birthrate, yet, since economic improvements would also lead
to improvements in education, and through it to shifts in attitudes concerning life styles and the number of children women desire to raise,

such initial increases would soon be compensated by subsequent decreases. The net effect of the mothers' wages policy, over time, on population size and age distribution seems therefore to be negligible.

Ecologic. Substantial improvements of economic conditions of low income families would gradually be reflected in improvements in the quality and quantity of housing, the patterns of settlement and land use, the quality of neighborhoods, and the quality, quantity, and distribution of public services, including public education. In view of the current depressed state of housing and neighborhoods, and of all public services in low income areas, improvements in this complex sphere of human needs would take considerable time. Furthermore, if the supply of housing and land, and the rehabilitation of neighborhoods were left to "self regulation" by the "market," without adequate public initiative, controls, and planning, progress would be spotty, and large amounts of newly transferred purchasing power would be transformed into profits of private real estate, construction, and other enterprises, rather than into ecologic improvements. These last comments illustrate the interdependence of social policies and, hence, the importance of striving for coordinated and consistent changes throughout the social policy system, rather than for piecemeal changes of single, narrowly circumscribed policies. For without coordination and consistency among separate social policies, objectives achieved by one policy could be nullified by contrasting tendencies of other policies.

It is obvious that ecologic changes would benefit entire communities and regions and not just former low income families who would be the primary beneficiaries. For changes of ecologic dimensions certainly involve changes in the overall quality of life in society.

Psychological and social. Improvements spurred by economic gains of low income families in such concrete spheres as nutrition, health, housing, neighborhoods, and public services would eventually lead to improvements in psychological and social functioning. The now prevailing sense of insecurity, mistrust, and alienation would gradually give way to a sense of security, trust, and solidarity. The self-image of inadequacy of many low income individuals which is shaped by a reality of frustrating experiences and failures would be replaced by one of adequacy shaped by a different reality of more positive experiences and successes. Over time these psychosocial changes would be reflected in lower prevalence of mental illness and emotional stress, in more constructive and satisfying intra and extra familial relations, in more effective social functioning in primary groups and in other social contexts, and in a gradual decrease of juvenile delinquency and adult crime, to the extent that these socially deviant acts are rooted in hostility against, and alienation from, a frustrating social order. Similarly, there would also be a decrease in alcoholism, drug use, and drug addiction, as there would be less individual need, and less peer group pressure, to escape from reality.

Here again it should be noted that these psychological and social consequences for the circumstances of living of former low income families would stimulate far-reaching improvements in the overall quality of life, and would thus greatly benefit all segments of society.

Cultural and political. Economic, ecologic, psychologic, social, and educational changes would over time result also in marked changes in life styles, in attitudes, in family and personal aspirations, in cultural orientations, and in recreational interests of former low income families. Simultaneously, as a result of increasing consciousness of their changing circumstances of living, of their generally inreased rights, and, especially, of their newly gained economic strength and related political power potential, these families would become more involved in community affairs, in voluntary associations, and in informal and formal political processes on the local level and beyond. The content and direction of these new family and personal aspirations, attitudes, cultural orientations, and political activities, would, of course, be influenced by the total societal context prevailing at the time the mothers' wages policy would be implemented, and especially by developments concerning society's system of beliefs and values.

From a social structural perspective it would seem that changes in the several spheres of the circumstances of living discussed so far would result in significant transformations of American society. Existing multidimensional divisions in life experiences and life styles among segments of the population who differ in income, education, occupation, neighborhoods, and ethnicity would be smoothed along with the flattening of the shape of the income distribution. This process would be reflected in a gradual bridging of existing gaps between the various ethnic groups, especially between the white majority and the several non-white minorities, between inner city dwellers and suburbanites, between rural and urban populations, between the several geographic regions, between blue and white collar workers, etc.

Intra-societal human relations. While a wide range of intra-societal human relations would be affected by the changes in the key processes

of social policies implicit in the mothers' wage policy, several specific sets of relations would undergo significant modifications. These specific sets are relations between men and women in general, and, more specifically, between husbands and wives, relations between parents and children, and relations between women and their actual or prospective employers.

Changes in relations between men and women in general and, more specifically, between husbands and wives, would derive from the new social and economic rights of women which would free them from economic control and exploitation by men. At present, only a minority of women can expect to be economically independent throughout their adult lives. They are now especially disadvantaged when they have children. Awareness of these circumstances by both sexes tends to affect in subtle and, at times, not so subtle ways, relations between men and women prior to, and subsequent to, marriage.

While with the implementation of the mothers' wages policy women would not gain full equality in terms of access to statuses in society, they could, nevertheless, expect a fairly adequate personal income throughout life: from employment when not bearing and rearing children, from mothers' wages during periods of pregnancy and child rearing, and from earned social security benefits during periods of unemployment and retirement. Women would thus no longer have to fear economic dependency and would be in a better position to relate to men on a freer and more equal basis. Men, too, would be well aware of this changed context, and would gradually learn to relate to women in a more egalitarian and humane manner. Male-female relations would more likely be based on mutual attraction and respect, rooted in personal qualities, as they would be over-shadowed by economic considerations to a far lesser extent than they are now. The quality of relations between the sexes is thus likely to become more balanced, more secure, more satisfying, and relatively free from elements of coercion.

Not only women and mothers would be economically more secure than they are now, once the mother's wages policy would be implemented, but also all families with children under age 18 would be assured sufficient income, and would no longer be threatened by the depressing consequences, or prospects, of actual or potential poverty. Awareness of these changed circumstances would be reflected in a new sense of economic security which, in turn, would enhance the quality of all intra-familial relations, between husbands and wives, as well as between parents and children. It needs hardly be pointed out in this context that strains and worries of life in poverty and near-poverty, and its multi-faceted destructive correlates, tend to be important factors of family breakdown. Elimination of these strains and prevention of related feelings of insecurity and self-doubt would contribute to the development of stronger and healthier mutual relations among family members.

The relations of children to parents would also be affected by changes in the sources from which families obtain their economic support and by changes in the relative shares of fathers, mothers, and children in providing a family's economic support. At present fathers are considered in most families as the dominant source of economic support, although many mothers and children participate in earning their families' livelihood. The dominant position of fathers in this respect affects the father and mother images in the perception of family members and determines qualitative and quantitative aspects of the children's interaction with their parents, and the parents' interaction with each other. Fathers are considered in many families the final authority with regard to major decisions. Also, because of their economic and occupational responsibilities, fathers tend to be away from the home for much of the day, and they are thus experienced as less familiar and more distant and powerful in social and psychological terms.

Under the mothers' wages policy the work of mothers would become a steady and secure source of family income and children too would be recipients of regular, unconditional allowances from society. These important shifts in the economic resources of families would lead to corresponding shifts in structural and psychological elements of intra-familial relations. The role of fathers would no longer be as dominant as now. Parents in many families would carry a fairly equal share as economic providers and, consequently, as decision makers concerning family affairs. The images of fathers and mothers would undergo corresponding changes in their own and in their children's perceptions, and these changes, in turn, would be reflected in modifications in the relations and interactions of parents and children.

Since children, too, would be a source of income for families, it may be assumed that they would gain a larger measure of independence than they now enjoy, and a larger share in decisions affecting them directly. These economic and structural changes, too, would be reflected in intra-familial relations and in patterns of family interaction.

The trends discussed here concerning family economics and family relations could also lead to an increase in the number, the rate, and the general societal acceptance of single parent families since mothers, and also fathers, would be able to support and care for children without a second parent. The development of the single parent family into a socially sanctioned alternative family type would have important consequences for child development and for parent-child relations in such families.

Finally, with the assumption by society of increased responsibility for the support and the care of children, the relations of children and families to society as a whole would undergo subtle modifications, since society would over time develop a growing interest in protecting the quality of care children receive in their families.

One further specific set of human relations to be considered are relations between women, especially mothers, and actual or prospective employers. Under existing circumstances the bargaining position and power of most women and mothers in the labor market is weak and they are consequently frequently subjected to severe exploitation. Women are often forced to choose either to undertake poorly paid, undesirable, and unsatisfying work, while neglecting the care of their children, or to exist with their children on an utterly inadequate and demeaning public assistance grant. With such limited options open to them, many women and mothers are likely to feel powerless and alienated in the employment relationship.

The economic rights mothers would be assured under the mothers' wages policy would significantly change the bargaining position of women in the labor market, and, hence, their relations to actual and prospective employers. Employment relationships would no longer have as coercive and alienating a quality as now, because women would have a more genuine choice to accept or reject a position, and, therefore, a real opportunity to negotiate the terms of their employment. Women could no longer be subjected to rude exploitation by employers who would have to relate to them in a humane manner if they wanted to keep them on the job. Employers would have to respect the rights of women, to consider their personal needs and interests, and to improve their working conditions and wages if they wanted to induce them to accept, and to stay with, offered positions. While the mothers' wages policy would protect primarily mothers by offering them an alternative to employment in the market, the effects of the policy would reach all working women since the withdrawal of many mothers from work would result in labor shortages, and the bargaining position and power of all women who were ready to fill vacant jobs would consequently be considerably strengthened.

In concluding the discussion of consequences of the mothers' wages policy for intra-societal human relations it should be noted that the gradual bridging of divisions and gaps among many diverse sub-segments of society which was mentioned above[26] would be reflected in significant changes in relations among members of these sub-segments. These changes in relations would parallel a series of developments beginning with income transfers from higher to lower income segments of the population, and involving reduction in economic distance between these segments, reductions in major differences of life styles, attitudes, and aspirations, and, ultimately, reduction in social distance. Throughout the stages of this process the self-image and the consciousness of members of social segments affected by it would undergo changes, and along with these changes would occur corresponding changes in the relations of individuals and groups to other individuals and groups in their own, and in other, social segments, as well as in the relations of the several social segments to each other and to society as a whole. In general, these changes in the quality of human relations among individuals and sub-segments of society would involve a gradual decrease in hierarchical, and a corresponding increase in egalitarian elements.

D. INTERACTION EFFECTS BETWEEN THE POLICY AND FORCES SURROUNDING ITS DEVELOPMENT AND IMPLEMENTATION

1. *History of the policy:* The mothers' wages policy, except for the children's allowance component, is an innovative social policy which, so far, has received little attention in the public policy arena in the United States. The proposal was circulated by its author to political leaders and organizations during the 1968 presidential campaign. The press reported the proposal after it was published in a professional journal in 1968 and presented at the National Conference on Social Welfare in 1969.[27] The policy was not adopted by any social action group, and since neither its author nor any one else engaged in further attempts to publicize and promote it, it faded from public attention shortly after its initial publication.

While the mothers' wages proposal aroused little interest in the United States, it should be noted that several European countries have for some time implemented policies involving similar principles. In France mothers who care for their children, and who are not employed outside their homes, receive special supplements to family allowances.[28] And in Hungary mothers of children under age 3 are entitled to special allowances in order to encourage them to care for their own children instead of participating in the work force.[29]

In spite of the European experience mothers' wages are still a new and essentially untried social policy. Children's allowances, on the other hand, have an extended history in Europe, as well as in Canada, Australia, and New Zealand, and in several African, Asian and South American countries. They have been widely used in both capitalist and socialist societies.[30] The United States is actually the only modern industrial society which has never utilized a "direct," universal children's allowance.

The purpose of children's allowances has remained unchanged since they were introduced in Europe early in this century. This purpose is to promote the well-being of children by publicly subsidizing the cost of rearing them. The purpose is achieved through governmental payments of allowances to families on behalf of every eligible child. These transfer payments are designed to reduce vertical inequalities of income among families with children belonging to different income strata, as well as horizontal inequalities of per capita purchasing power among families of different sizes belonging to the same income strata. The amounts of children's allowances are the same for all children of a specified age, in families of a specified size, irrespective of total family income. However, after-tax amounts of allowances are adjusted through progressive tax rates of graduated income taxes, so that allowances decrease as the size of total family income increases.

A review of the history of children's allowances reveals considerable differences, among societies using this policy, concerning such variables as size of allowances relative to per capita income and to total family income, number of children per family for whom allowances are payable, age range of children included in the program, administrative procedures, financing, etc. Although there has been controversy in many societies concerning various aspects of children's allowances, few countries abolished this policy after having established it. In general, the overall experience with children's allowances has not been unfavorable. Fears, respectively hopes, that children's allowances would stimulate increases in the birthrate did not materialize to any significant extent. In many instances, however, children's allowances failed to attain their objectives since the size of allowances tended to be relatively small, and since allowances frequently did not keep up with increases in the cost of living.

While the United States never adopted a children's allowance policy in the usual meaning of this term, it instituted, nevertheless, a similar policy involving tax-free exemptions for dependent children through the income tax system. One usually unnoticed aspect of this "indirect children's allowance" is that its cash value increases, rather than decreases, as total family income increases. To comprehend this paradox feature one needs to consider savings resulting from non-payment of taxes on tax-free exemptions of equal size, for taxpayers whose total income places them into income brackets taxed at different rates. Thus a taxpayer with a small income who pays tax at a rate of 14 percent would save $14 for every $100 of tax-free exemptions from his income. To such a low income family the value of a $750 tax-free exemption per child would be $105. On the other hand, a wealthy taxpayer whose income would place him in a 50 percent tax bracket would save $50 for every $100 of tax-free exemptions from his income. To such a family the value of the same $750 tax-free exemptions per child would be $375, or nearly four times as much as for the former family.

During the 1960s several individuals and organizations attempted to promote adoption of a "direct" children's allowance in the United States.[31] These efforts coincided with mounting public interest in eliminating poverty and reforming the welfare system which was generally viewed as utterly unsatisfactory. Interest in the children's allowance concept was shared for some time by several government departments, and in 1968 the Office of Economic Opportunity and the Department of Health, Education, and Welfare were about to sponsor a large scale experiment to explore the effects of children's allowances.[32] This experiment was designed to parallel an earlier initiated study which explored the effects of "negative income taxes." Implementation of the children's allowance experiment was, however, cancelled when the government adopted in 1969 the "Family Assistance Plan," a derivative of the negative income tax, as its answer to poverty and to the welfare crisis, and thereupon decided against launching experiments designed to test alternative approaches to the income maintenance policy it had selected.[33] These developments seem to have led to the shelving of efforts to provide a children's allowance policy in the United States, at least for the time being.

2. Political forces in society promoting or resisting the policy: Since the mothers' wages policy has never been actively promoted in the political arena in the United States potential support for, or resistance to it, can only be estimated roughly on the basis of theoretical considerations. In general one may expect that population segments who would benefit, were the policy implemented, would tend to support it, while segments whose perceived interests would be adversely affected would be more likely to oppose it. Segments whose circumstances remained essentially unchanged would tend to be neutral, or, depending on their value premises, would sympathize with supporters or opponents of the policy.

The foregoing general assumptions involve, however, several difficulties, if one wants to estimate expected political responses to a policy. One major difficulty is that determining what constitutes "benefits" or "disbenefits," and what is one's "interest," is not a simple, objective process, but depends on the criteria one uses, and on such complex factors as "objective facts," subjective perceptions, nature and scope of available information and interpretation concerning a policy, and one's values and beliefs. The manner in which, and by whom, a policy is promoted and interpreted is likely to affect perceptions of, and attitudes and reactions toward it, on the part of individuals and social groups. These variables would therefore have to be considered along with factual aspects concerning a policy.

Another difficulty in anticipating support for, or resistance to, a policy is that such political decisions involve strategic and tactical considerations which go beyond the mere evaluation of a policy on its merits. A policy involving a set of benefits may, when enacted into law, prevent enactment of another policy involving more extensive benefits. Because of this, potential beneficiaries of the former policy may choose to oppose it, and may hold out for enactment of an alternative policy. Similarly, groups whose interests would be adversely affected by a policy may decide to support it nevertheless, so as to forestall enactment of policies they consider even less desirable.

Finally to be mentioned in the context of estimating likely responses to a policy is the fact that some individuals and groups may support or resist a policy on the basis of abstract principles and long-range benefits or disbenefits, rather than on the basis of concrete and immediate benefits or disbenefits. Such criteria for choosing among policies could be viewed, however, as extensions of the "benefit" and "interest" criteria, since correspondence between a policy and one's principles, as well as anticipated long-range benefits irrespective of short run costs, constitute, nevertheless, "benefits."

The foregoing considerations suggest that political alignments for or against the mothers' wages policy would depend to a considerable extent on the societal context prevailing at the time some political action group decided to promote this policy, and on the manner in which it would go about it. With these caveats in mind the following estimates may be ventured.

When promoted by a humanistic movement, and interpreted constructively as serving the underlying interests of society as a whole, support for the mothers' wages policy can be expected from many and diverse segments of society. However, in spite of such an emphasis, considerable opposition to the policy should also be expected. Strong support for the policy would come from families with children whose total income is below the national median, be they poor or near-poor, headed by men or by women, white or non-white, urban, suburban or rural, and whether the family-head is working, unemployed, or unable to work. These families would, of course, be the primary beneficiaries of the policy, and most of them would receive considerable amounts of transfer funds, were it enacted. Unless alternative income transfer policies offering higher benefits or more satisfactory terms were promoted simultaneously these families would have few substantive, strategic, or tactical reasons for opposing the mothers' wages policy.

One important political asset of the policy should be noted here. This is the fact that the mothers' wages policy could unite poor, near-poor, and working or lower middle class families with children into one unified political force sharing a common interest, since all these families would benefit directly and immediately from the implementation of this policy. Working or lower middle class families would, therefore, not be forced into conflict and competition with poor and near-poor families, the typical context surrounding "selective" welfare, and anti-poverty, policies which involve direct means tests.

It should not be assumed, however, that there would be no opposition at all to the mothers' wages policy from individuals and groups among the policy's primary target segments. Some opposition can be expected on "moral," "philosophical," or "religious" principles to such aspects of the policy as "paying for motherhood," "paying for sex-relations" and for "having out-of-wedlock children," and "giving rights to women." Chances are that some groups in the population who would oppose the policy, as it would not serve their perceived interests, would mask their materialistically motivated opposition in moral, philosophical and religious arguments, in order to stimulate resistance to the policy among its potential beneficiaries.

Furthermore, many individuals and groups among the low income population who would not benefit directly and immediately from implementation of the mothers' wages policy, such as aged, handicapped, and disabled persons living in households without children under age 18, are likely to object to the policy on substantive grounds, unless it was amended to assure appropriate transfer benefits for them as well.

Women's rights groups, and especially the intellectual, middle class leaders of that movement, are likely to respond to the mothers' wages policy in an ambivalent manner. They might favor some aspects of the policy such as children's allowances and enhanced economic rights for women. However, they are likely to be critical of the fact that the policy fails to assure women equality of access to statuses, and that it may strengthen the ties between women and child care and home-making roles.

Major opposition to the mothers' wages policy is likely to come from individuals and organized economic interest groups among upper income segments and among owners of great wealth. Their main objections would focus on the relatively large scope of income transfers involved in the policy; large, that is, in terms of conventional social policies concerning income transfers to the poor, near-poor, and other low income groups. A shift of about 10 percent of national income from the upper to the lower half of the income distribution would seem to many of this group as a radical and unwise measure which could threaten the very "stability" of the national economy, and the survival of society and the social order to which they have become accustomed.

It may be expected that some economists, and political and other social scientists, would supply technical arguments to opponents of the mothers' wages policy from among upper income and wealth strata, since these scientists, too, might consider the scope of the transfers as excessively large, unconventional, untested, and a serious threat to the existing economic and social system. They might advocate experiments to study the effects of the policy before implementing it. It may be of interest to note in this context that experimentation to study effects of a policy prior to its implementation has never been recommended by social scientists when government transfers and subsidies to upper income groups are involved, such as oil depletion allowances, major tax cuts for industry, loan guarantees to failing corporations, and subsidies to shipping, air transport, and other powerful interest groups.

Some economists would be opposed to the mothers' wages policy also because it utilizes the principle of "universality" rather than "selectivity" with regard to transfers of purchasing power. The principle of universality, it will be recalled, is considered by many economists as an inefficient approach to filling income gaps of low income segments of the population.

Other economists and social scientists may take a more positive, though not uncritical, stance toward the mothers' wages policy as they would recognize the overall, long-range, social, and economic benefits inherent in it, and as they might not be committed to the preservation of the social status quo and the principles of the free enterprise system.

Not all individuals and groups among upper income and wealth segments of the population would oppose the mothers' wages policy. Some might favor it because they endorsed the children's allowance concept and the horizontal transfers involved in it. Others might support the policy because they identified with its principles and philosophy. In this connection it should not be overlooked that many middle and upper class persons tend to support liberal, progressive, and even radical political causes and movements, and are thus likely to support policies which would promote social justice and the general human welfare even if in the short run these policies would result in material losses for them. Still others among these upper income groups would recognize the long-range, economic, and social benefits which would result from the mothers' wages policy for all groups in society, and would support it on this basis.

It does not seem possible to estimate the size, organizational structure, resources, overall strength, level of interest, values, and ideologies of the various groups whose orientations toward the mothers' wages policy were sketched above. These aspects would depend on the nature of the social movement that would spearhead a political thrust advocating the mothers' wages policy, the substantive content, quality, and scope of political and educational activities undertaken by that movement, the general societal context and value orientations at the time these efforts are launched, and, finally, the existence or generation, in the political arena, of alternative social policies addressed to the same policy issues.

3. *Interaction effects between the policy and physical and biological properties of society's natural setting, and biological and basic psychological properties of its members:* Implementation of the mothers' wages policy would encounter no limits or constraints from the natural environment and would hardly be affected by it, since the policy involves no procedures which would be in conflict with natural forces and processes, and also requires no significant increases in resources drawn from the environment, but merely redistribution of claims to these resources. Also, no limits or constraints would be encountered by, and no marked effects would result for, the policy from biological, and intrinsic psychological properties of the population. However, certain deeply ingrained psychological orientations which were acquired through processes of socialization over countless generations, and which involve relatively fixed images concerning parental roles and parent-child relations, could constitute severe blocks to the notion of payment for maternal child care. This deep-seated, powerful, psychologically determined resistance to the acceptance of the mothers' wages policy does, however, not seem unsurmountable, since it is not rooted in human-biological processes, but is acquired through learning in social experience.

As for reverse effects resulting from implementation of the mothers' wages policy for the natural environment, no immediate and direct consequences are likely to ensue. Yet to the extent that this policy could, over time, contribute toward more thoughtful attitudes concerning resource development and utilization, and ecologic issues, as neighborhoods and housing stock are being rehabilitated under the policy's direct impact, it may also contribute, indirectly, to the evolution of less exploitative and more protective approaches toward the natural environment, and may thus enhance chances for its preservation.

Effects of the mothers' wages policy on biological and psychological properties of the population are likely to be significant over time. Expected improvements, due to the policy, in physical and mental health, and, hence, in overall bio-psycho-social functioning of individuals, would increase the ratio of stronger and healthier persons in lower income segments and throughout the population. Such improvements in health and functioning of the population would eventually be transmitted between generations through biological, psychological and social processes.

Were the mothers' wages policy implemented, learned perceptions of parental roles and parent-child relations would also undergo gradual changes, and the modified perceptions would be internalized through early social learning and would also be transmitted between generations. In this way acquired psychological characteristics, which would constitute sources of early resistance to acceptance of the mothers' wages policy, would themselves be modified, over time, under that policy's influence.

4. *Interaction effects between the policy and relevant other social policies:* The most significant effects of the mothers' wages policy are expected in the area of rights distribution throughout society, and, more specifically, the distribution of purchasing power. However, if the objectives of the policy in this area are to be achieved, rather than counteracted, other policies dealing with the distribution of rights and purchasing power would have to be coordinated with the mothers' wages policy. Included among these policies would be policies dealing with taxation, the government's chief tool for constraining individual purchasing power and for generating transfer funds; and policies dealing with social security, public assistance, and general public and social welfare services, tools the government uses for distributing rights through purchasing power and in kind.

Of crucial importance for the "'real" size and effects of mothers' wages and children's allowances would be the incidence of new taxes which would have to be enacted in order to raise the revenue needed for implementing the new policy. The more progressive the incidence of these new taxes would be, the more "on target" would be the effects of the new policy, and the more adequate would be the net amounts of mothers' wages and children's allowances. It would seem appropriate if these new taxes were raised from households with incomes above the median, and if tax rates would rise in an increasingly steeper progression for households in the upper half of the income distribution. It seems indicated, also, to repeal currently existing tax-free exemptions for children, and several other special provisions, the effects of which on tax incidence are regressive. In addition to reforming individual federal income taxes, policies concerning federal taxes on capital gains, corporate income, various forms of wealth, gifts, and inheritances, as well as corresponding state and local taxes, would have to be gradually adjusted so as to conform to the redistributive objectives of the mothers' wages policy. Obviously, these multiple adjustments in tax policies on all levels of government would not be enacted automatically, once the mothers' wages policy is accepted, as each adjustment would involve separate political contests. However, these controversial issues are likely to surface, and would have to be dealt with over time if, and when, the mothers' wages policy is introduced into the political arena.

The existing social security system would also have to undergo modifications in order to conform to the mothers' wages policy, especially as a result of the redefinition of maternal child care as "work." This change in social and political philosophy would bestow on mothers the right to be included in the social security system as contributors and beneficiaries. To finance the new benefits the government, as "employer" of mothers, would have to transfer its share of "payroll deductions" into the social security trust-fund, and it may also be necessary to raise the wage base which would have to be subjected to social security deductions in order to assure the solvency of the trustfund over time. These comments involve the assumption that the existing social security system, which utilizes general insurance principles, would continue to operate. It would, of course, be possible to substitute in its place a more equitable social security system financed through progressively raised general revenue, rather than through regressive payroll deductions.

While effects of the mothers' wages policy on tax policies, and vice versa, would involve intensive political contests, its effects on existing cash, and, in kind, public assistance transfer policies and programs, would be largely automatic. Increases in income of families with children under age 18 from mothers' wages and children's allowances would usually exceed public assistance eligibility standards and would, therefore, cause the phasing out of the following programs, as far as such families are concerned: AFDC or its proposed, more far-reaching, yet inadequate substitutes, the "Family Assistance Program" (FAP) and the "Opportunities for Families Program" (OFF), state general assistance, food stamps and commodity distribution, and "Medicaid." Considerable savings in transfer funds and administrative costs could be realized from the termination of these programs. However, at the same time, large numbers of federal and state civil service employees now engaged in their administration would be displaced from their jobs. This displacement could cause a certain degree of bureaucratic resistance and political controversy unless compensatory measures were designed.

Policies concerning housing, zoning, neighborhood development, urban renewal, and urban, suburban and rural settlement and land use, would also be affected by, and would in turn affect, the mothers' wages policy. Existing public housing policies involve eligibility standards similar to the ones used in public assistance, food, and medical assistance programs, and families with children under age 18 would thus no longer be eligible for public housing. One consequence of this would be that poor and near-poor households without children under age 18 would encounter shorter waiting periods for public housing accommodations. However, this would also mean an increase in residential segregation of aged, handicapped, and disabled persons from the rest of the population.

Another consequence would be that demand for housing by families whose improved economic circumstances would result in loss of eligibility for public housing would cause strong pressures on the housing situation. Merely raising eligibility standards for existing public housing projects would not be an adequate answer to these pressures, since many former low income families with children would no longer be satisfied with the type and quality of housing which is now available to them in housing projects, and would be likely to demand better homes without the connotations and stigma of existing public housing projects. Increased economic and political strength of these families would make it more likely that their demands would be heard, and responded to, in the political arena. This could lead to the phasing out of existing public housing and urban renewal policies, and their gradual replacement by an integrated set of policies concerning housing, zoning, neighborhood development, urban renewal, and urban, suburban, and rural settlement and land use, which would be more in line with newly emergent social, economic, and political realities, and ecologic insights.

It needs hardly be mentioned that resolution of the complex housing and settlement issues which would be raised by enactment of the mother's wages policy would involve intense political strife, the outcome of which may not be as constructive as suggested above. It is not unlikely that solutions of housing and related problems would be left, in "good American tradition," to a large extent, to the vagaries of free enterprise. Adequately integrated policies and programs would not be likely to emerge in this way, and some potential benefits of the mothers' wages policy for target segments of the population and for society as a whole would be unlikely to materialize, since resources needed for their realization would be transformed into profits for private enterprises. In view of the scope and the complexity of the issues involved in this policy cluster, which seem to exceed the scope and complexity of space exploration, planning and guidance by public authorities seems essential, so as to enhance chances for a constructive outcome with maximum benefits for all segments of society.

One further cluster of social policies which would be affected by the mothers' wages policy and would, in turn, affect its implementation, includes policies concerning general public and social welfare services such as public health, sanitation, and safety; public education; employment services and manpower training programs; personal social and rehabilitation services, as well as special social services operated by anti-poverty programs. At present all these services tend to be administered with a built-in, official or unofficial means-test — that is, they are segregated by socio-economic position of consumers.

Some of these services, especially those sponsored by the Office of Economic Opportunity, the Model Cities Administration of the Department of Housing and Urban Development, and the Department of Health, Education, and Welfare, tend to be earmarked for utilization by poor segments of the population, and this special context is reflected in the qualitative aspects of the services. They tend to reflect a "poor house" mentality and milieu, and, though they are supposedly rehabilitative, anti-poverty measures, most consumers continue to be poor while, and after, experiencing these services, official claims to the contrary notwithstanding.

Other services such as public health, sanitation, and safety; employment, manpower training, education, and personal social services, are administered without a formal, official means-test. However, as a result of residential segregation by socio-economic position, members of different socio-economic strata tend to receive segregated public services. Not infrequently, these public services are not only segregated by socio-economic strata, but services in lower income neighborhoods tend to be of lesser quality than those available in areas inhabited by middle, and upper, income strata.

Improvements in socio-economic conditions of families with children, due to mothers' wages and children's allowances, would probably result in the phasing out of policies and special programs administered now for poor families only. It may, however, be more appropriate, instead of terminating such special services as "Headstart," child development and day care programs, manpower training programs, and special educational programs, etc., to continue them selectively within non-stigmatizing contexts, in settings not segregated by socio-economic positions of consumers. For it should be realized in this respect that many special social services are now doomed to failure, not necessarily because of intrinsic philosophical and methodological shortcomings, but since their consumers are left in a state of severe economic deprivation without realistic escape routes. The services simply cannot overcome the structural causes of poverty, as they have not been designed to do so. Once these structural aspects would be dealt with successfully through adequate transfers of purchasing power, as would be the case were the mothers' wages policy implemented, some of the special social services could probably contribute in important ways to the enhancement of human potentialities and the enrichment of life.

It should be noted, however, that demand for certain social services such as child welfare, child protection, child placement including adoptive placements, and day care services would probably decrease were the mothers' wages policy implemented. Presently, many families with children require these services as a direct or indirect consequence of poverty and low income. It seems logical to expect a significant reduction in the need for these child welfare services, as well as for other social services which deal with poverty-related problems of families with children, once severe poverty is successfully eliminated for such families.

With respect to policies governing the administration of general public and social welfare services, implementation of the mothers' wages policy would ensue in intensified political pressures for elimination of all "de facto" means-tests, or segregation by socio-economic position of consumers, and of the discriminatory differences in the quality of these services, which are now associated with residential patterns. The thrust of the mothers' wages policy for overall reductions in social inequalities would certainly be severely inhibited, or even defeated, unless these political pressures for elimination of discriminatory administration of general public services were successful.

Health maintenance and medical care policies are likely to be affected by implementation of the mothers' wages policy in a similar way as policies concerning general public services. It seems even likely that the increase in economic strength and political power of families with children could become an important factor in a political thrust for adoption of a universal, comprehensive, national health maintenance system financed through general revenue, and available to all on an equal basis.

In concluding this review of interaction effects between the mothers' wages policy and relevant other social policies, some comments are also indicated concerning the broad policy issues of the status and rights of women and children. The mothers' wages policy would strengthen social and economic rights of mothers and would protect them, and other women, against coercion in status allocation. However, it would not assure women free choice and equal access to statuses in society. One unintended consequence of enactment of the mothers' wages policy could therefore be a delay in obtaining acceptance of a more comprehensive social policy which would not merely strengthen social and economic rights of mothers but would assure full equality of rights and status allocation to all women.

The mothers' wages policy would also strengthen the social and economic rights of all children by establishing a societal subsidy for their support. However, here, too, an unintended consequence could ensue, as agencies of the state, charged with administering mothers' wages and children's allowances to families with children, could move beyond this original objective toward a more comprehensive objective of influencing the quality of child rearing. This could, under certain circumstances, lead to excessive and undesirable interventions in parent-child relations, especially among less powerful segments of the population.

5. *Interaction effects between the policy and relevant foreign policies and extra-societal forces:* While the mothers' wages policy would have no direct effects on United States foreign policies, and while its implementation would also not be influenced directly by foreign policies and by extra-societal forces, important indirect interaction effects are likely to occur.

The primary context of these interaction effects would be competition for societal resources through appropriations in the federal budget. Implementing the mothers' wages policy would require allocation

of significant portions of the budget for income transfers. Such allocations for a major, innovative social policy seem, however, unlikely as
long as the United States would continue to commit sizable portions
of its national resources to the conduct of overt and covert foreign wars,
and to the preparation for, or prevention of, possible future wars,
through the maintenance of a powerful military defense establishment.
This assumption derives from political rather than from economic realities, as in theory there would be no "real" economic obstacles to implementing income transfers such as those involved in the mothers' wages
policy simultaneously with large-scale defense appropriations. For, as
has already been pointed out,[34] income transfers do not constitute real
economic costs to society, although they tend to be perceived in this
way by groups in society who are required to finance the transfers
through higher taxes. Political consequences of these subjective perceptions of economic realities would present nearly unsurmountable
obstacles to the acceptance of the mothers' wages policy prior to termination of a major foreign war, and prior to significant cuts in defense appropriations.

Major reductions of United States defense budgets would lessen
resistance to the mothers' wages policy not only by freeing necessary
economic resources but also as a result of possible shifts in this nation's
dominant values, which could underlie such reductions in the defense
budget. The existing defense budget reflects a certain national stance
concerning United States relations to the rest of the world community.
One important factor shaping these relations in recent decades has
been efforts to maintain and defend an economically advantageous
position of this country vis-a-vis other nations of the world. It should
be noted in this context that the United States controls about 40 percent of the world's resources, and consumes annually a similar portion
of worldwide production, while its population constitutes less than
6 percent of mankind. United States foreign and defense policies protect and perpetuate this glaring inequality of worldwide resource distribution. In order to do so, the United States defends not merely its
own territory and its worldwide concrete economic interests, but also
the values and ideology of free enterprise capitalism, a major source of
its privileged position, whenever and wherever these values and ideology, and societies supporting them, are threatened by movements or
societies committed to egalitarian and collectivistic values and ideologies. Many past and present international conflicts in which the United
States has become involved were related to this complex, ideological
struggle, as well as to the concrete issue of defending a powerful and
advantageous position. Defense budgets of the United States are

operational expressions of these dual tendencies of its foreign policies, namely, to protect the benefits derived from the unequal distribution of world resources, and to contain societies committed to political and economic value premises which challenge this privileged position and its dominant value premises.

To the extent that reductions of the United States defense budget would derive from a lessening of the tendency to resist with force the spreading of an ideology different from its own, and to the extent that the lessening of such a tendency would derive from increasingly toler- ant attitudes among Americans toward egalitarian and collectivistic philosophies and values in other societies, the United States may gradually become more tolerant, also, toward such philosphies and values among its own citizens, and would thus be more likely to imple- ment policies such as the mothers' wages, which aim to reduce social and economic inequalities within society, and to strengthen egalitarian and collectivistic values in the social order.

In the not too likely case that the mothers' wages policy would gain sufficient support, and be adopted in the United States prior to major changes in foreign and defense policies, this policy would be likely to contribute toward eventual changes in the foreign sphere as well. For implementation of the mothers' wages policy would constitute a considerable departure from extant social policies. Such a change would involve major shifts in the dominant value premises of society, which could not fail to be reflected eventually also in the foreign and defense policies of the United States, and in the quality of its relations to other nations. If significant reduction of inequalities with- in its own country can become a working principle of social policies in the United States, similar efforts in other societies would no longer have to be perceived as a serious threat, and the United States might even adopt a more positive attitude toward the complex issue of redistributing the world's resources more equitably among all na- tions.

Implementation of the mothers' wages policy would enhance the image of the United States abroad. This society is respected for its scientific and technological achievements, but its failure to solve social problems and human conflicts in spite of immense natural wealth and scientific strength is a cause for contempt. Adoption of an innovative social policy which could contribute to the reduction of many seri- ous social ills would be noticed abroad, and would change the exist- ing image of failure in the social domain. The United States could thus regain the moral leadership it earned during its early years, when it committed itself to humanistic principles through its Declaration of Independence and its Bill of Rights.

6. *Interaction effects between the policy and society's stage of development in cultural, economic and technological spheres:* The current stage of economic and technological developments in the United States would place no limits or constraints on the implementation of the mothers' wages policy, nor would this policy adversely affect continued development of the economy and technology. Some obstacles to enactment of the policy would originate, however, in certain features of the prevailing culture, but should the policy be implemented, in spite of these obstacles, its principles and provisions are likely to become over time integral aspects of the culture.

Discussion, earlier in this chapter, of economic features and consequences of the mothers' wages policy indicated that the economy would be stimulated by transfers of purchasing power to low income segments of the population, and that the urgent need of these population segments for basic goods and services and for housing would result in qualitative and quantitative changes in production. These qualitative and quantitative changes in consumer demand, as well as changes, due to the policy, in the size and composition of the work force, would also stimulate technological changes in production processes and would accelerate further development and utilization of automation and cybernation. It thus appears that the economy and technology would not only continue their development without interruption, were the mothers' wages policy enacted, but would be likely to develop along more constructive lines, as the products and achievements of the economy and technology would be shared more widely throughout the population. The mothers' wages policy would thus contribute to the solution of one major shortcoming of the current stage of development of the economy, namely, its failure to perform its distributive function more satisfactorily and equitably.

Obstacles to enactment of the mothers' wages policy related to the current stage of cultural development in the United States would derive from prevailing beliefs, values and traditions concerning the status and rights of women and children in society. These values, beliefs, and traditions would tend to inhibit progress toward increased economic rights for women and children, societal subsidies for child rearing, and redefinition of maternal child rearing as work. However, cultural development and change are continuous processes, and such highly developed, complex, sophisticated and pluralistic cultures as the United States can integrate innovative, and seemingly strange, elements fairly quickly, especially when these elements do not represent total discontinuities with respect to the existing culture. Since the new and unconventional elements of the mothers' wages policy involve conceptual continuities to elements and ideas already accepted in the United States, their integration into the culture is likely to proceed in spite of some ongoing resistance, once sufficient political support could be generated to secure that policy's enactment. Once integrated, the new elements would be likely to stimulate further developments in American culture in the direction of more humanistic and egalitarian socio-cultural patterns.

7. *Interaction effects between the policy and the size and institutional differentiation or complexity of society:* The size of a society's population and territory seems to have no significant effects on the implementation of the mothers' wages policy, once that society is large enough to develop a money and market economy. Nor is that policy expected to have significant, long-range effects on the size of the population, although there could be a temporary increase in the birthrate among former poor and low income families, soon after the policy's enactment, in reaction to the sudden marked increase in their financial resources. Over time, however, as the new policy would become a regular feature of society's distributive mechanisms, and as increased economic resources would be gradually transformed into education and other life-style elements, the initial increase in the birthrate is likely to drop again, and fertility among these families is likely to stabilize at a somewhat lower level than it had been prior to implementation of the mothers' wages policy.

Implementation of the mothers' wages policy requires also a certain level of institutional differentiation or complexity in a society. Thus it would not seem feasible to establish such a policy in a relatively simple agricultural society prior to the development of a money and market economy. However, in as complex a society as the United States, where institutional differentiation has reached a post-industrial level, there would seem to be no institutional obstacles to implementing this policy. The mothers' wages policy, once enacted, would be likely, in turn, to further the processes of institutional differentiation through changes it would induce in the structure of the family and in the roles of parents, and also by strengthening societal participation in, and responsibility for, the child rearing function.

8. *Interaction effects between the policy and society's beliefs, values, ideologies, customs, and traditions:* The value premises and ideological

orientation implicit in the objectives of the mothers' wages policy are, in many ways, incompatible with dominant beliefs, values, ideologies, customs, and traditions of American society at the present time. While this incompatibility is not absolute, and while many linkages and continuities exist between the values implicit in the policy and those dominant in society, the value conflict seems serious enough to generate nearly unsurmountable obstacles to the acceptance of the mothers' wages policy in the foreseeable future, unless, of course, significant shifts were to take place in the dominant value premises and ideological orientation of American society.

In terms of the major policy relevant value dimensions identified in an earlier chapter,[35] the mothers' wages policy reflects different positions from the dominant positions of the extant social policy system of the United States. Thus, while the extant social policy system stresses individualism and competitiveness in pursuit of self-interest and self-support, the mothers' wages policy reflects a more collectivistic and cooperative ideology through such elements as societal wages for maternal child care, and universal children's allowances. By custom and tradition parents, and especially fathers, are now responsible for the livelihood of families, and mothers are expected to care for their children. The circumstances of living of children depend, consequently, to a considerable extent on the individual circumstances and opportunities of their parents. The mothers' wages policy would cause significant departures from these firmly established traditions by requiring society to compensate mothers for their work in caring for children, as well as to subsidize the costs of child support. Were such a policy implemented, the circumstances of living of families would no longer depend nearly exclusively on the individual circumstances, efforts, and opportunities of parents but, at least in part, on measures taken collectively by society as a whole.

The provisions of the mothers' wages policy would conflict not only with long established values and traditions concerning primary parental responsibilities for child care and support, but would also interfere to a considerable extent, with principles of the free enterprise system by protecting mothers against exploitation in low paying, undesirable service and industrial jobs which many women are now forced to fill in order to escape starvation or its only alternative, inadequate and dehumanizing public assistance.

The most significant deviation, however, of the mothers' wages policy from the dominant value premises and ideology of the extant social policy system concerns the dimension of equality vs. inequality.

While the dominant values and ideology uphold and defend social and economic inequalities as an organizing principle of circumstances of living and of all spheres of societal existence, the mothers' wages policy would result in marked reductions of inequalities of rights through redistribution of purchasing power and also through redistribution and readjustments of general public and social services. These egalitarian trends of the policy would seem most objectionable to important segments of American society who are ideologically opposed to the notion that the state should take firm and positive measures to reduce inequalities in the circumstances of living and the social and economic opportunities of members of society. Yet, at the same time, the notion of equality of rights and opportunities for all is not really foreign to American thought, at least not on a philosophical level. For this notion has been expressed again and again as a goal in important past and present public documents and declarations, though it has never been translated into social reality, nor has much use been made of it as a guiding principle for development, and as a yardstick for evaluation, of social policies. The egalitarian ideology of the mothers' wages policy represents, therefore, real continuity in terms of early American ideology, and supporters of the policy could rightfully claim that they promote values which this society has always enunciated and believed in, but so far has failed to live up to.

It should also be noted that the value of collective interest in, and responsibility for, the well-being of all members of a community, as well as the value of cooperation among members of a community in pursuit of the common interest, are by no means new ideas for American society. However, the fate of these values has tended to be similar to that of the value of equality of rights and opportunities. They are considered by political pragmatists to be impractical ideals and, as such, their influence on social and political reality has tended to be limited. The mothers' wages policy would require that these "impractical ideals" be translated into important organizing principles of the social order and, because of this, it would meet strong resistance from powerful segments of society whose perceived interests benefit from adherence to the extant dominant values of pursuit of self-interest, competition, and inequality.

While, then, the mothers' wages policy would deviate in major ways from dominant values, ideologies, and traditions of the extant social policy system, it conforms to them with respect to two important issues, namely, the linkage between motherhood, child care, and homemaking functions, and the emphasis on work as a principal mechanism for the distribution of rights. The policy is expected to increase the proportion of mothers who choose to care for their own children and to reduce the participation of women in the general work force. It should be noted, however, that this reduction would affect primarily less desirable, unskilled occupations, and would probably have minor effects only on technical and professional occupations, which offer women real career opportunities, more desirable working conditions, and higher compensation than mothers' wages. The policy would, therefore, not discourage women from pursuing meaningful careers, but would give them an opportunity for a real choice between caring for their children and engaging in less meaningful, less gratifying, and economically less rewarding occupations. Yet, in spite, or perhaps because, of these features, the mothers' wages policy would slow the movement of women away from child care and homemaking functions into occupations and careers outside their homes.

As for the traditional emphasis on work as the major mechanism for the distribution of rights, the mothers' wages policy would use this value premise in order to legitimate new economic rights for mothers, simply by redefining their traditional roles as "work." It should be noted that this redefinition is not a mere tactical step or political trick. Rather, it is a correction, or revision, of an earlier political process which resulted in the denial of the reality of mothers' work, and which thus constructed a "new reality," one that was more suited to the exploitation of mothers, wives, and women.

In concluding this discussion of the value premises and of the ideological orientation of the mothers' wages policy in relation to dominant societal values, it should also be noted that the values and ideology implicit in the several objectives of this policy are not internally consistent in all respects. The overall ideological thrust of this policy is in the direction of social and economic equality. However, this egalitarian thrust is not followed through consistently with respect to equality of opportunities for women and men concerning the allocation of statuses. As noted above, the mothers' wages policy conforms to the traditional societal bias of steering women into child rearing and homemaking roles. While the policy provides for the possibility that men would occasionally undertake child care roles and be eligible for "mothers wages," this is considered an exceptional, temporary occurrence. The policy does not encourage parents to develop their own, unique, egalitarian patterns for sharing child care responsibilities so that both husbands and wives could also pursue occupational and career interests. Instead, there is a built-in assumption that, in the case of two-parent families, the wife would care for the children and receive mothers' wages, while the husband would pursue a gainful occupation away from home. There are corresponding assumptions that in a female-headed, one-parent family the mother would stay home, care for her children, and draw mothers' wages throughout the years of their childhood, while in a male-headed, one-parent family the father would care for his children and receive mothers' wages on a temporary basis only until he could make alternative arrangements for their care, and return to his occupation away from home. To adhere consistently to an egalitarian ideology with respect to the status and rights of men and women, a policy would have to establish alternative societal child care settings available on a universal basis to all families at their request, and to provide flexible options concerning the payment of child care wages, so that parents would be encouraged to develop their own patterns for sharing child rearing responsibilities and for pursuing career interests while receiving from society "parents wages" rather than mothers' wages.

There is one further aspect of the mothers' wages policy which reflects inconsistency with respect to its egalitarian thrust. This is the fact that the policy aims to improve the circumstances of living of specified population segments only, albeit very large and important ones, rather than of all low income segments. Consequently, in spite of the relatively large scope of aggregate income transfers provided for in this policy, several million households without children under age 18, consisting mainly of aged, handicapped, and disabled persons, would still continue to live in poverty and deprivation after the policy were implemented.

Finally, to avoid misunderstandings, it should also be noted that the mothers' wages policy does not aim to establish equality of social and economic rights for all members of society, but merely to reduce certain existing inequalities. It is thus a major reform policy which would, if enacted, significantly modify social conditions in a humanistic, egalitarian direction, but it is not a radical policy which would restructure the social order and the economic system by eliminating the structural roots and dynamics of inequality, so as to assure equal social and economic rights and opportunities to all.

9. *Conclusions and predictions:* The review of potential interaction effects between the mothers' wages policy and forces within and beyond American society revealed that this innovative policy proposal has never had a political constituency committed to its promotion in the United States, nor has it had a political history in this country. Therefore, "predictions" ought to deal with the questions whether such a constituency is likely to emerge in the political arena in the forsee-

able future, what the composition of such a constituency might be, and what chances, if any, it would have for gaining acceptance for the mothers' wages policy.

Before suggesting answers to these questions it seems important to note that analysis of the mothers' wages policy did not reveal contra-indications or obstacles to its implementation in American society in terms of "real" economic, ecological, biological, demographic, techno-logical, and social-structural factors. The feasibility of implementing this policy is consequently a function of political, ideological, cultural, and psychological factors. In terms of these latter factors the analysis seems to lead to the conclusion that existing political parties and social action organizations would not be eager to adopt the mothers' wages policy in its proposed, comprehensive form, and that, also, no new organization would be likely to emerge in the political arena in the near future, committed to the promotion of this policy.

The foregoing conclusions seem warranted in spite of the fact that considerable political support could be generated for the mothers' wages policy among low income and other segments of the population, in view of the policy's immediate, concrete benefits for low income families with children under age 18, and its potential, long-range, con-structive consequences for society as a whole. Yet, the relatively liberal income transfer provisions of this policy and the value premises im-plicit in it, seem to constitute too marked a deviation from, and too obvious a challenge to, the existing social and economic order of the United States and its underlying political balance, the perceived inter-ests of powerful economic forces, and the firmly established beliefs, values, ideologies, and traditions of the prevailing culture. Hence, the policy would trigger intensive resistance from a broad spectrum of con-servative political forces, were any party or organization bold, ideal-istic, or perhaps naive enough, to inject the mothers' wage policy into the political process of the nation.

The intensive, conservative, political opposition would be likely to derive considerable support from "expert" opinions of civil servants and professionals, many of whom would be critical of selected tech-nical and economic aspects of the mothers' wages policy, such as the principle of "universality" and resulting "inefficiencies" concerning income transfers, as well as the aggregate scope of the transfers, which they would interpret as a threat to the stability of the existing economic system. Such expert opinions would carry considerable weight in politi-cal contests surrounding the mothers' wages policy since they would be viewed as "objective and neutral facts" rather than merely as opin-ions, based on fallible assumptions concerning human behavior and the workings of the economy, assumptions which in turn are derived from the dynamics and the ideology of the established social order and its economic system.

Opposition to the mothers' wages policy would thus be formidable, were a coalition of low income interest groups and liberal and progressive upper and middle class sympathizers sponsoring it on the American political scene. This policy would evoke also little enthusiasm and support from radical social and political action groups who reject the existing American social order, its economic system, and its underlying dominant beliefs, values, ideology, and traditions. For these groups would object to the intrinsic value inconsistencies of the mothers' wages policy and to serious shortcomings in its substantive provisions. They would, therefore, tend not to lend support to a political coalition sponsoring the policy, and would be likely to promote instead alternative policies concerning the issues dealt with by the mothers' wages policy. Such alternative policies would be internally consistent in terms of value premises and ideological orientation, and would aim to reduce, or perhaps even to eliminate, social and economic inequalities for all segments of society rather than for specific population segments only, and would also avoid the built-in, traditional sex bias of the mothers' wages policy.

In summing up these considerations, it seems that, while the mothers' wages policy would constitute one feasible reform for the American social policy system, it is not too likely to attract within the existing political milieu, a pragmatically minded social action coalition, willing to sponsor its adoption, and willing also to invest considerable human and economic resources in a political struggle with only a limited chance of success. Yet, in case such a political coalition were to come into being, and succeeded to overcome its opposition and to gain enactment of the mothers' wages policy, the policy, once it was the law of the land, would generate its own dynamics and would gradually gain wide acceptance as a result of its direct and indirect benefits. The mothers' wages policy would thus become an integral component of the American social policy system and of American culture in the same way in which earlier significant social reform policies, such as "Social Security" and "Medicare," were integrated relatively quickly and easily after overcoming intensive political opposition prior to their enactment.

E. DEVELOPMENT OF ALTERNATIVE SOCIAL POLICIES; COMPARISON AND EVALUATION

Alternative policies to a specific social policy may be designed to achieve the same, or nearly the same, objectives as the ones pursued by the original policy, or to achieve markedly different objectives concerning the same policy issues. Alternative policies of the former type utilize different measures from the ones employed by the original policy, measures which are expected to be more effective, and/or efficient, in attaining the original objectives, but which may, at times, also modify these original objectives. The different measures are often also likely to reflect differences in underlying value premises and ideological orientations. Alternative policies of the second type substitute, by design, different objectives for the objectives of the original policy. These different objectives are usually derived from different value premises and ideological orientations. Obviously, alternative policies of the second type involve also different policy measures geared to the attainment of their different objectives. Two alternative social policies to the mothers' wages policy are presented below, one illustrating an alternative policy of the first type, the other an alternative policy of the second type.

1. Alternative social policies

a. aimed at the same policy objectives, but involving alternative policy measures: The first alternative policy aims to attain, or to approximate, the objectives of the mothers' wages policy[36] more efficiently by substituting the principle of "selectivity" for that of "universality" concerning the payment of mothers' wages and children's allowances. This change would involve (1) limiting eligibility for income transfers, under both provisions, to families with children under age 18, with total current income below the median family income, adjusted for family size, and (2) modifying the amounts of mothers' wages and children's allowances so that the combined income of families, including transfer payments, would in no case exceed the adjusted median income. Other aspects of the original policy would remain on the whole unchanged, with the exception of horizontal income transfers among households with incomes above the median. This specific provision would be eliminated automatically since no income transfers would be made to families with incomes above the adjusted median, irrespective of their size.

This alternative policy establishes also procedures for implementing the means-test implicit in its provisions. The procedures would require potentially eligible families to file a claim for transfer payments and a declaration of income with appropriate local government offices. Claims and declarations would be accepted as valid subject only to random checks, rather than to case by case investigations. The transfer programs would be administered in conjunction with the Internal

Revenue Service. Annual income tax returns could thus be used as supplementary checks on claims and on declarations of income, and as a basis for annual adjustments of accounts for all households, whether or not they had filed claims during the year.

The administrative purpose implicit in this alternative policy is to avoid transferring income to families from whom it would have to be recouped eventually through income taxes, as would be the case were the original policy implemented. In this way efficiency is expected to increase and administrative costs to decrease, while the net aggregate amount of vertical income transfers from population segments with incomes above the adjusted median to families with children under age 18 with total incomes below the adjusted median would be the same as under the original policy. The net amounts of transfer payments received by individual families would also remain essentially unchanged.

b. aimed at different policy objectives concerning the same policy issues: The second alternative policy is designed to modify the objectives of the original mothers' wages policy so as to overcome the built-in sex bias of that policy, which tends to strengthen the traditional ties between motherhood and child care and homemaking roles. This alternative policy would reduce, but not eliminate, the inconsistencies in value premises noted in the analysis of the original mothers' wages policy by instituting additional modifications in the key policy processes of status allocation and rights distribution. As for status allocation, this alternative policy would remove conventional obstacles for women in access to social statuses by enhancing options concerning intra and extra familial child care modalities and by providing in this way real opportunities for mothers to pursue careers outside their homes. With respect to rights distribution this policy would go beyond the original mothers' wages policy by broadening the nature and scope of provisions designed to reduce inequalities of social and economic rights.

To attain these wider objectives the following substantive changes in, and additions to, the provisions of the original mothers' wages policy would be instituted:

— Mothers' wages would be redefined as "parents' wages" or "child care wages." These wages would be payable to mothers and/or fathers on equal terms in relation to the time they would devote to child care work or to gainful employment, respectively. Families with children would thus be encouraged to design their individual "division of labor" within and outside the home. The combined parents' wages of families would in no case exceed the equivalent of one full time wage.

— Publicly financed, comprehensive child care and child development services would be established throughout the country by the federal government in cooperation with state and local governments. The quality of child care and the equality of standards in these public facilities would be ensured through supervision by the federal government. Parents, irrespective of their economic circumstances, would be able to use these facilities at their discretion in accordance with their employment and/or educational schedules. It would, therefore, be necessary to operate some facilities on a 24-hour basis. Special facilities would have to be established for children with exceptional needs, be these needs physical, mental or emotional. Parents would have the right to participate on a decision-making level in the operation of these child care and child development facilities. Provisions would be made for reduction of children's allowances in proportion to the time children would be cared for in public child care facilities. Parents' wages, too, would be reduced when all children of a family would be cared for in child care facilities.

2. Comparison and evaluation

The two alternative policies developed above will now be analyzed in accordance with the standard framework, and will be compared with the mothers' wages policy throughout this analysis. Since the major purpose of this chapter has been to illustrate an approach to social policy analysis and synthesis rather than to explore the mothers' wages policy and alternative policies, and since this purpose seems to have been accomplished already, the analysis and comparison will be conducted in an abbreviated, instead of in a comprehensive manner.[37] Similarities to, and differences from, the mothers' wages policy will be indicated. Material reported in the analysis of the original policy will not be repeated as it can be reviewed under the corresponding items in that analysis. The first alternative policy will be referred to as "selective mothers' wages" policy and the second alternative policy as "parents' wages" policy. Capital letters and Arabic numerals refer to corresponding sections and foci of the standard framework for policy analysis and synthesis.

A — Both alternative policies are designed to deal with the same issues and problems as the original policy.

B-1 — Objectives of the selective mothers' wages policy are nearly identical to those of the original policy though modified by the "selectivity" principle which would eliminate direct benefits for families with children under age 18 with incomes above the adjusted median.

In addition to the objectives of the original policy, the parents' wages policy would aim to eliminate inequalities between wives and husbands, and mothers and fathers, concerning child care responsibilities, and concerning educational, occupational, career, and economic opportunities. This policy would also strengthen societal responsibilities and provisions for child development through the establishment of universal, comprehensive child care services.

B-2 — The underlying value premises and ideological orientation of the selective mothers' wages policy are similar to those of the original policy. However, the egalitarian and collective thrust of the original policy would be blunted under this policy since the entire population would be divided more sharply into recipients and non-recipients of transfer payments. Internal value inconsistencies, as well as continuities with the dominant value premises of American society, which are reflected in the objectives of the original policy, would thus be even more evident in this alternative policy.

The egalitarian and collective value premises of the original policy would be strengthened in the parents' wages policy. This policy would facilitate equality of rights, and of access to intra and extra familial statuses, for husbands and wives, and would strengthen societal responsibilities and provisions to assure more equal opportunities for men, women and children. It would thus overcome some, though not all, of the value inconsistencies of the original policy, and would therefore involve less continuity to the dominant value premises of American society than the mothers' wages policy.

B-3 — The theories and hypotheses underlying the strategies and provisions of the selective mothers' wages policy are essentially identical to those of the original policy except for several additional hypotheses concerning the principle of selectivity. This principle is assumed to maximize the preservation of societal resources, to be equitable and straightforward, and to have no divisive effects on the population. These hypotheses are untested and their validity would seem to depend on many aspects of the total societal context.

The parents' wages policy also involves additional hypotheses to those of the original policy. One further hypothesis is that defining mothers' wages as parents' wages, and making the wages available on equal terms to fathers and mothers, would result in a more egalitarian division of labor within the family, and in more equal opportunities for women in access to statuses outside the family. Another hypothesis is that child development would not be adversely affected, but would be enhanced by shifting many child rearing functions away from the family to public child care facilities. These hypotheses, too, have not been tested sufficiently, and their validity would also seem to depend on many variables of the societal context.

B-4 — The primary target segment of the selective mothers' wages policy would be smaller than that of the original policy since mothers and children in families with incomes above the adjusted median would be excluded from direct benefits.

The primary target segment of the parents' wages policy would be larger than that of the original policy since children from all families, irrespective of social and economic circumstances, would be eligible for services from public child care facilities, and also, because parents' wages and child care services would gradually affect the division of labor in nearly all families with children under age 18.

B-5 — Substantive short and long range effects of the selective mothers' wages policy are expected to match the specified objectives of this policy. These effects would be similar, in all relevant spheres, to the effects of the original policy, with respect to the more limited target segment. However the general societal context surrounding the implementation of this policy, and especially psychological and political dimensions, would differ from the context of the original policy since families with children with incomes above the adjusted median would not receive direct benefits, irrespective of family size. This fact could adversely influence attitudes toward this policy and its beneficiaries. Costs of the selective mothers' wages policy would seem to be less than those of the original policy, since the aggregate amount of transfer payments would be $85 billion less than the amount required for the original policy. This reduction would be reflected in lower tax rates for individuals and business firms and in a smaller scope of new tax measures which would have to be instituted. This reduced need for new taxes would, however, be more apparent than real, since the scope of vertical transfer payments would remain unchanged. The reduction in taxes would merely reflect elimination of that portion of the transfer payments which, under the original policy, would be largely recouped through taxes, and elimination of horizontal transfers from smaller to larger families with incomes above the adjusted median.

Substantive short and long range effects of the parents' wages policy are also expected to match the objectives of that policy. These effects are expected to exceed those of the original policy in terms of significant changes in intra-familial roles, relations, and life styles; patterns of child care and child development; the composition of the work force and the occupational distribution of women, etc. These changes would spread throughout the population and would not be limited to one or another population segment. The parents' wages policy would involve a significant increase in real economic costs compared to the original policy, to finance the establishment and operation of public child care services. Assuming full utilization by eligible children, this increase in real costs could eventually exceed $50 billion per year. The scope of transfer payments for parents' wages and children's allowances would, however, decrease as utilization of child care services would gradually increase. It should be noted, however, that the establishment and operation of these costly facilities is likely to have constructive effects for the economy, the occupational structure of the work force, and for the statuses and rights of mothers, fathers and children. Moreover, children are assumed to derive comprehensive developmental benefits from these services.

C-1 — The selective mothers' wages policy would have similar implications to the original policy for the development of resources, goods, and services.

The parents' wages policy would also have similar implications to the original policy for resource development except for the area of child care services. Whereas the original policy would be likely to reduce demand for the development of child care facilities since government funds would be available for mothers' wages and children's allowances but not for child care services, the parents' wages policy would probably accelerate the establishment of child care services as it would allocate new government resources for this purpose, in addition to making provisions for parents' wages and children's allowances. Demand for these services would be likely to increase once they became available since the parents' wages policy would encourage parents to develop their own patterns of combinations of child care and occupational careers.

C-2 — Effects of the selective mothers' wages policy on status allocation would be similar to those of the original policy, but would be concentrated mainly on families with children in the lower half of the income distribution.

The parents' wages policy would have important, direct effects on the allocation of statuses in addition to the indirect effects it would have in common with the original policy. These direct effects would be reductions in inequalities of intra and extra familial statuses between husbands and wives in families with children upon substitution of parents' wages for mothers' wages, and establishment of public, comprehensive child care services.

C-3 — Effects of the selective mothers' wages policy on the distribution of rights would be similar to the effects of the mothers' wages policy, but concentrated on families with children, with incomes below the median.

Effects of the parents' wages policy on the distribution of rights would go beyond the effects of the original policy. Conventional intra familial inequalities of rights between husbands and wives tend to be rooted in their differential access to statuses. To the extent, therefore, that the parents' wages policy would significantly reduce inequalities of intra and extra familial status allocation for women and men it would result also in corresponding reductions in inequalities of rights between husbands and wives. As for children, this policy would enhance their rights significantly beyond the mothers' wages policy through the establishment of public, comprehensive child care services, which would especially strengthen the rights of children from low income families. It should be noted that shortcomings in the original policy concerning the distribution of rights to poor and low income households without children under age 18 would not be overcome by the parents' wages policy in spite of its stronger egalitarian thrust.

C-4 — Consequences of the selective mothers' wages policy for the circumstances of living and for the overall quality of life would be nearly the same as the consequences of the original policy. Yet while the original policy is expected to facilitate societal integration and a sense of solidarity through the distributive principle of universality, this alternative policy, by substituting the distributive principle of selectivity, could adversely affect tendencies toward integration and solidarity. Effects of the selective mothers' wages policy on intra familial and on employment relations would be the same as the effects of the original policy, but would be limited primarily to the lower half of the income distribution.

Consequences of the parents' wages policy for the circumstances of living and the overall quality of life would exceed the consequences of the original policy. Parents, especially in lower, but also in middle income strata, would be likely to experience new freedoms and new opportunities as conventional patterns concerning access to statuses and rights would gradually change. These new opportunities could generate, also, some stress and anxiety during early stages of adjustment, but are expected to result over time in constructive changes in patterns of family life, characterized by equality, freedom, independence, and mutual respect. The foregoing changes in family milieu, as well as the universal availability of comprehensive child care and child development services are, in turn, expected to provide children with enriching and growth-enhancing experiences. Progress in this sphere would also not be smooth, since establishment and operation of a new, nation-wide service system would encounter many administrative and substantive difficulties. However, the overall trend would be in a positive direction as far as child life and child development are concerned. The many constructive changes expected to result from the parents' wages policy, especially for women and children, and hence for the patterns and quality of family life, would be reflected, eventually, in psychological, social, cultural, and political aspects of local community life and, in time, throughout the entire social structure of the nation. Effects of the parents' wages policy on specific sets of intra-societal human relations between men and women, husbands and wives, parents and children, and women and men and their employers, would also exceed the effects of the original policy because of more thorough changes under the parents' wages policy in the statuses and rights of men, women, and children. The general trend of these changes would be reflected in further reductions of inequalities and hierarchical elements in all these relations.

D-1 — The history of the selective mothers' wages policy is identical to that of the original policy — it has no history except for the children's allowance component, and it has no political support in the United States.

The history of the parents' wages policy is similar to that of the original policy except for the child care services component which has had an extended history and which currently has strong political support in the United States.

D-2 — Political reactions to the selective mothers' wages policy would be similar to reactions to the original policy. However, there is likely to be less resistance from upper income segments of the population because of the reduced scope of total transfer payments, and from government and academic economists because of the shift to the "selectivity" principle. On the other hand, some potential supporters of the original policy among middle income groups may be less ready to support this alternative policy because of its potentially divisive effects, and because of the elimination of horizontal income transfers which, under the original policy, would reduce inequalities of per capita purchasing power among families with children in the upper half of the income distribution.

Reactions to the parents' wages policy would also be similar to reactions to the original policy. However, many opponents of the original policy would be likely to oppose this policy even more intensely because of its increased costs and stronger egalitarian tendencies. On the other hand, women's rights groups, groups interested in the promotion of public child care services, and groups committed to egalitarian ideologies would be more inclined to support this policy than the original policy.

D-3 — Effects of interactions between the selective mothers' wages policy and physical and biological properties of the natural environment, and biological and basic psychological properties of the population, would be nearly the same as effects of such interactions with the original policy.

Effects of interactions between the parents' wages policy and physical and biological properties of the natural environment, and biological and basic psychological properties of the population, would also be similar to effects of such interactions with the original policy. However, psychologically and culturally conditioned resistance to the notions of parents' wages, and equality of access to statuses for women, could be more intense than to the notions of mothers' wages, and of stronger economic rights for mothers and wives. Should the parents' wages policy be adopted in spite of such resistance, experiences of children in public child care facilities could become, over time, important factors in changing psychologically and culturally conditioned attitudes concerning the statuses and rights of women and men.

D-4 — Effects of interactions between the selective mothers' wages policy and relevant other social policies would be similar to effects of such interactions with the original policy. However, because of the reduced scope of transfer payments under the selective mothers' wages policy effects on tax policies would be more limited. Also, since this policy incorporates the principle of selectivity it would be less likely than the original policy to further the elimination of formal and informal means-tests and other divisive features in the administration of public and social services.

Effects of interactions between the parents' wage policy and relevant other social policies would also be similar to effects of such interactions with the original policy. However, because of the cost of child care services the impact of this policy on tax policies would be more extensive. Because of its stronger egalitarian thrust this policy would also be more likely than the original policy to further the elimination of formal and informal means-tests and other divisive features in the administration of public and social services. Another difference of the interaction effects of this policy from those of the original policy would be acceleration rather than deceleration in the development of child care services. Furthermore, contrary to probably unintended effects of the original policy of slowing progress toward equality of rights and access to statuses for women, this policy would accelerate progress toward such equalities. Finally, establishment of public child care services under this policy may increase the risk, noted in the analysis of the original policy, of excessive intervention by public authorities in parent-child relations and in child care provided by parents.

D-5 — Effects of interactions between the selective mothers' wages policy and relevant foreign and defense policies of the United States would be similar to effects of such interactions with the original policy. However, since the amounts of transfer funds required for the implementation of this policy are smaller than the amounts required for implementation of the original policy, chances for implementation of this policy prior to major reductions in defense appropriations seem better than for implementation of the original policy.

Effects of interactions between the parents' wages policy and relevant foreign and defense policies of the United States would also be similar to effects of such interactions with the original policy. However, because of the significantly higher costs of this policy, chances for its implementation prior to major reductions in defense appropriations would be even less than chances for implementation of the original policy. In the unlikely case that this policy would, nevertheless, be implemented prior to major reductions in defense appropriations, and prior to major changes in the underlying premises and thrust of American foreign policies, this policy would be likely to exert a stronger influence than the original policy toward reductions in defense spending and changes in foreign policies because of its stronger humanistic and egalitarian thrust.

D-6 — No significant differences are expected in effects of interactions between society's stage of development in cultural, economic, and technological spheres and each one of the three policies, selective mothers' wages, mothers' wages, and parents' wages. However culturally rooted obstacles to enactment of the parents' wages policy are likely to be more serious than obstacles to enactment of the original and the selective mothers' wages policies since the parents' wages policy is more at variance, with beliefs, values, ideologies, and traditions of the prevailing culture, concerning the status and rights of women and children, and concerning societal involvement in the child rearing function.

D-7 — No differences whatsoever are expected in effects of interactions between the size, and the institutional differentiation, of society, and each one of the three policies, selective mothers' wages, mothers' wages, and parents' wages.

D-8 — The value premises and ideological orientation of the selective mothers' wages policy are similar to those of the original policy, but involve more continuity with the dominant value premises and ideological orientations of American society. Effects of interactions between this policy and dominant beliefs, values, ideologies, customs, and traditions would, however, not differ markedly from effects of such interactions with the original policy.

The parents' wages policy reflects more egalitarian and collective, and less traditional, values concerning the statuses and rights of women and children than the original policy, and involves less continuity with dominant values and ideologies. Interactions between this policy and dominant beliefs, values, ideologies, and traditions of American society would, therefore, generate more intense conflicts and resistance than would result from such interactions with the original policy. It should be noted in this context, however, that, while the parents' wages policy would eliminate one major value inconsistency of the mothers' wages policy, namely, the built-in bias favoring a close linkage between motherhood and child care and homemaking roles, it would not overcome another value inconsistency of the original policy, namely, its failure to eliminate poverty, and to reduce social and economic inequalities, for families and individuals in households without children under age 18.

D-9 — Nearly all conclusions and predictions concerning interaction effects between the original policy and societal forces are relevant also to the selective mothers' wages policy. Chances for promotion and adoption of this policy within the existing political milieu of the United States are only slightly better than chances for adoption of the original policy. The slight difference is due to significantly lower perceived costs of the selective mothers' wages policy, and to its presumably higher efficiency. It should be noted, however, that, while opposition to the selective mothers' wages policy is likely to be less intense than to the original policy, potential support for it does not seem to be any stronger.

Conclusions and predictions concerning the likely fate of the parents' wages policy within the extant context of the American political arena, would have to be even less optimistic than conclusions and predictions concerning the original policy. The stronger, less ambiguous, egalitarian and collective thrust of this policy, its innovative, comprehensive provisions for child care services, and its relatively high costs would generate even more intense political resistance than the original policy. Yet those very same aspects of the parents' wages policy could result in stronger support for it, than for the original policy, from diverse political forces, including women's rights groups, proponents of child care services, and groups committed to egalitarian and collective ideologies. However, such additional potential support would hardly suffice to overcome the strong resistance this policy would be likely to trigger among political forces committed to the preservation of the existing social order and its value premises and ideology, were it promoted in the currently prevailing political milieu of the United States.

SUMMARY

The abbreviated, comparative analysis of the selective mothers' wages and parents' wages policies, and the preceding comprehensive analysis of the mothers' wages policy suggest the following summary.

1. All three policies reflect egalitarian and collective values and are thus at variance with dominant beliefs, values, ideologies, and traditions of the extant social policy system of the United States which stresses individualism, competition, and social and economic inequalities.

While all three policies aim to reduce significantly extant social and economic inequalities, and to strengthen collective responsibility for the well-being of members of society, they vary in the degree of consistency with which they pursue these objectives. The parents' wages policy is most consistent by these criteria, the mothers' wages policy involves several ambiguities and inconsistencies, and the selective mothers' wages policy is the least consistent of the three policies. Conversely, the selective mothers' wages policy is closest to dominant value premises of the extant social policy system, the mothers' wages policy involves several linkages to dominant value premises but is less close to them than the selective mothers' wages policy, and the parents' wages policy seems farthest removed from the dominant values and ideology of the prevailing social policy system.

2. The three policies share a common set of objectives concerning the policy issues of the status and rights of women, the rights of children, the definition of mothers' work, and the redistribution of social and economic rights through the transfer of purchasing power. In addition to the common objectives each policy pursues also separate objectives. All three policies would assure a minimum level of rights and economic independence to mothers in low income families by recognizing and rewarding their contributions to society. All three policies would also protect mothers from serious exploitation in the labor market. Furthermore, the three policies would assure children minimal economic rights as well as the right to maternal care when mothers wish to offer such care. To assure the foregoing rights the three policies would effect a vertical transfer of purchasing power from the upper to the lower half of the income distribution. This transfer of roughly 10 percent of national income would eliminate poverty for all families with children under age 18, reduce social and economic inequalities throughout society, and stimulate the national economy. The mothers' wages and parents' wages policies would involve, also, horizontal income transfers from smaller to larger families throughout the population and would thus also reduce per capita inequalities of purchasing power within socio-economic strata. The parents' wages policy would achieve the additional objectives of reducing inequalities of statuses and rights between wives and husbands within the family, and of reducing inequalities in access to occupational and educational statuses for women throughout society. Furthermore, the parents' wages policy would provide comprehensive public child care and child development services and facilities, and would stimulate the evolution of new patterns of family life and child care. The selective mothers' wages policy would emphasize fiscal efficiency and would limit direct benefits to families with children under age 18 with incomes below the median. The mothers' wages and parents' wages policies are likely to strengthen trends toward societal integration and solidarity while the selective mothers' wages policy could have divisive effects on society as a whole. All three policies are likely to achieve their specified objectives if implemented as proposed. Finally, it should be noted that all three policies would

fail to deal directly with poverty and inequalities of families and individuals in households without children under age 18, households which consist primarily of aged, disabled, and handicapped individuals.

3. The mothers' wages and selective mothers' wages policy could have the unintended effect of slowing progress toward equal rights for women concerning access to occupational and educational statuses as these policies would tend to strengthen the traditional linkage between motherhood and child care and homemaking roles. All three policies, but especially the parents' wages policy, could have the further unintended effect of excessive public intervention in parent-child relations because of growing societal responsibilities for economic support and direct care of children.

4. All three policies would have a major impact on the social structure and on the entire system of social policies. They would cause constructive shifts in the quality and quantity of resources developed in response to changes in demands for goods and services resulting from the sizeable transfers of purchasing power to lower income groups. The parents' wages policy would stimulate nation-wide development of a new resource — public child care facilities and services. As for status allocation, all three policies would result in modifications of intra-familial statuses, and would also improve the access to educational channels into the status system for children from currently poor and low income segments of the population. The parents' wages policy would also remove intra-familial obstacles to equality of status allocation especially for women, and would enhance their chances for occupational and educational equality beyond the family setting. The major impact of the three policies would, however, be in the area of rights distribution as a result of relatively large-scale vertical and, in the case of the mothers' and parents' wages policies, horizontal transfers of purchasing power. In a highly developed money economy such as the United States, purchasing power is perhaps the most valid indicator of an individual's rights, and of his command over resources, goods and services. In these terms the three policies would involve considerable shifts in the existing rights distribution toward less inequalities. About 10% of national income would be shifted to the lower half of the income distribution and all families with children would be assured a minimally adequate income. Under the parents' wages policy children would be assured additional new rights through "in-kind," public child care services. All three policies would also enhance the "entitlement" approach to rights distribution through children's allowances. The selective mothers' wages policy would, however, exclude children in

families with incomes above the median from receiving children's allowances.

The several major modifications in resource development, status allocation, and rights distribution would be reflected in marked changes in the overall quality of life and in the circumstances of living. These changes would involve improvements in ecological, biological, psychological, economic, social, and cultural aspects of living. Finally, human relations within and beyond the family would undergo changes toward more egalitarian and less hierarchical patterns. These changes would be especially marked under the parents' wages policy, less so under the mother's wages policy, and least under the selective mothers' wages policy.

5. The amounts of transfer payments involved in the three policies would be considerable, but "real" economic costs are likely to be limited. The annual income transfers for the selective mothers' wages policy would be approximately $90 billion and for the mothers' and parents' wages policies approximately $175 billion. The parents' wages policy may require, eventually, up to $50 billion per year for the establishment of child care services. However, as the utilization of child care facilities would increase, parents' wages and children's allowances would decrease. The amounts required for child care services would involve real economic costs. Another economic cost of the three policies would be the loss of cheap labor supplied now by poor mothers, and resulting increases in the prices of some goods and services.

As for "benefits," the three policies would eliminate poverty and near-poverty for families with children under age 18. This, in turn, would result in considerable stimulation of the economy, in constructive, qualitative and quantitative changes in production, and in reduction of unemployment. The direct benefits to families with children would thus spread through wider groups of society. The tax structure would become more equitable, the overall yield of tax revenue on local, state, and federal levels would increase, and general public and social services would be improved considerably and distributed more equitably. The development of automation and cybernation in industry and in public services would be accelerated to counteract shortages of cheap labor, and general working conditions would improve.

Benefits of the three policies for family life would include improvements in the self-image and social prestige of mothers along with improvements in their social and economic rights; shifts in the role of fathers and husbands from economic control toward sharing as equals in meaningful human relations; general improvements in the quality of family life, and in relations between women and men; and improvements in economic, biological, emotional, intellectual, social, and cultural aspects of child life and child development, especially in poor, near-poor, and working or lower middle class families. Over time a gradual reduction could be expected in the incidence of physical and mental illness, mental retardation, and various forms of deviance in social and psychological functioning, and a corresponding increase in overall societal integration. Furthermore, there would be gradual improvements in the quality of housing and neighborhoods, and in the patterns of land use and settlement. The foregoing benefits would tend to be more limited in nearly every sphere under the selective mothers' wages policy. On the other hand, under the parents' wages policy there would be additional benefits, namely, accelerated progress toward intra and extra familial equality of social and economic rights and equal access to occupational and educational statuses for women and men, and universal availability of comprehensive child care and child development services.

Summarizing these multi-faceted societal costs and benefits, it seems that the benefits of any one of the three policies would exceed real and perceived costs if humanistic, egalitarian, and collective interest criteria are used in the evaluation. The benefits-to-costs ratio, by these criteria, would be most favorable under the parents' wages policy, intermediate under the mothers' wages policy, and least favorable under the selective mothers' wages policy. One hidden opportunity cost item of all three policies, however, would be their failure to include among the recipients of direct income transfers poor and low income families and individuals in households without children under age 18. This shortcoming of the three policies could be corrected by adding to the parents' wages policy a special income transfer feature geared to the needs of this population segment, and assuring all its members an adequate annual income.

6. Finally, it should be noted that implementation of any one of the three policies would be feasible in American society in terms of physical and biological properties of the natural environment, biological and basic psychological properties of the population, the current stage of economic and technological development, and the size and institutional differentiation of society. However, in spite of objective feasibility, all three policies would be opposed intensely were they promoted in the political arena by a coalition of potential beneficiaries

and sympathizers committed to the objectives, value premises, and ideological orientations implicit in these policies. Opposition would derive from the perceived interests of powerful economic forces, and from dominant beliefs, values, ideologies, and traditions prevailing in the extant culture, and reflected throughout the existing system of social policies of American society. Because of this it does not seem too likely that any one of these three policies will be sponsored on the American political scene in the near future, nor that sufficient political support could be generated were some social action group willing to undertake such sponsorship.

The foregoing summary completes this illustration of the use of the conceptual model and the standard framework in the analysis and synthesis of social policies. It seems now indicated to return to the theoretical focus of this book and to consider implications of the conceptual model for social and political action aimed at structural social change.

PART
III
SOCIAL POLICIES AND SOCIAL PROVISION

CHAPTER FIVE

Resolving Issues of Social Provision in Our Society*

The notion "social provision" does not have a commonly accepted meaning. The *International Encyclopedia of the Social Sciences* and other important reference works do not mention the term. A discussion of issues related to social provision must, therefore, begin with an attempt to clarify the concept.

THE SOCIETAL NATURE OF PROVISIONS

The dictionary's derivations of the meanings of "provide" and "provision" make it clear that these terms refer to fundamental aspects of the life process, and more specifically of human life, i.e. conscious life in a societal context. "'Provide" and "provision" denote, according to Webster, anticipating and satisfying existential needs through foresight and forethought.

These meanings suggest certain biosocial observations. Life from the simple level of a single cell to the complex level of human societies always requires interaction and exchange between living organisms and their environment to obtain provisions for satisfying survival and

*Presented at the 1976 Annual Program Meeting of the Council on Social Work Education, Philadelphia, Pa., March 3, 1976.

other needs. Needs, experienced in the context of relative scarcities, and the pursuit of provisions to satisfy these needs, are, consequently, a major source of the evolution of human social orders. Indeed, any human social order, anytime and anywhere, be it simple or complex, can be understood as one particular response to the universal, existential imperative to provide life-sustaining and life-enhancing resources to members of the group.

The generation and distribution of provisions among humans living in groups always involve socially structured and sanctioned processes. All provisions are therefore intrinsically social, whatever their kind and manner of procurement, and whether they are used by individuals or collectively. Hence, qualifying the noun "provision" with the adjective "social," as is often done in professional and political discourse, reflects and perpetuates conceptual confusion; it implies that only certain provisions are social, while others are not. Limiting the designation "social" to selected types of provisions, e.g. provisions allocated to meet the needs of deprived segments of society, denies, by implication, that all provisions are socially sanctioned. It also denies that deprivation results from "legitimate" patterns of distribution of provisions, just as the reverse of deprivation, namely privilege, results from socially sanctioned patterns.

The current use of the notion "social provision" reflects a "blaming the victim" mentality,[1] for it implies that society needs to provide only for those who can not provide for themselves because of alleged inadequacies, imprudence, laziness, etc. Strong, industrious, thrifty, and wise individuals, on the other hand, are presumed to provide for themselves and not to require social provisions. Those who are perceived, falsely, as providing for themselves are also erroneously pictured as transferring social provisions to those identified as unable to provide for themselves, as an act of generosity, out of their "legitimate" property. In reality, however, their property is acquired, as is all property, in accordance with socially sanctioned patterns of distribution of provisions, patterns which are often grossly uneven and which thus cause the complementary conditions of deprivation and privilege.

The first issue to be settled, then, seems to be the semantic confusion implicit in the illusion-maintaining current use of the phrase "social provision." Language should convey unequivocally that all provisions of life-sustaining and life-enhancing resources in human societies are produced and distributed in accordance with socially established and sanctioned policies and processes, whether or not people are conscious of this fact, whether or not provisions are labeled "social," and whether they benefit all members of a society or merely selected individuals and groups.

KEY ISSUES OF PROVISION

Several key issues are implicit in the societal nature of provision. These are the issues which every human group must resolve, and which therefore require appropriate solutions in our society. These issues have always been central foci of social, economic, and political development, as well as of philosophical endeavors.

Choice of Kinds of Provision. Humans living in groups experience a wide range of biological and socially shaped needs. These include food, shelter, clothing; health, education, recreation; self-expression, creativity, recognition, communication, human relations; etc. These needs vary in urgency with reference to survival and other existential criteria, and they depend for satisfaction on different kinds of provisions. Human societies will, therefore, always confront fundamental choices and questions of priorities as a result of differences in type and urgency of needs, and corresponding differences in the kinds of provisions which satisfy acknowledged needs.

Modes of Production. The second set of issues concerns the modes of production which human societies evolve to secure provisions to match acknowledged needs. These modes affect circumstances of living, human relations, the overall quality of the existential milieu, and the flow and stock of natural resources and human products.

All production of provisions involves natural resources and human contributions. The former include solar energy, land, water, air, minerals, vegetation, wildlife, etc. The latter include the intellectual, emotional, and physical potential of past and present humans, their creativity, their accumulated stock of knowledge, and their labor. A mediating component of most productive processes is tools, which themselves are human-created products, involving natural resources, discoveries, inventions, and work.

Major choices which human societies face concerning modes of production include: ownership and control of natural resources and tools; development, transmission, ownership, and control of production technology and underlying basic science; division of labor and organization, management, and quality of work processes; quality of human relations in the workplace; location and size of production facilities; appropriate mix of human and other resources; scope of production and conservation of resources; etc.

Modes of Distribution. A third set of issues concerns the patterns evolved and legitimated by human societies for the distribution of provisions to their members as *rewards* for undertaking specific tasks in production processes, or as *entitlements* by virtue of belonging to society or to subgroups within it. Patterns of distribution of provisions also affect circumstances of living, human relations, and the quality of life.

Patterns of distribution may vary widely among societies. Provisions may be distributed equally or unequally; they may be designated for use by individuals, groups, or society as a whole; accumulation of "surplus" provisions beyond levels required for needs-satisfaction may, or may not, be sanctioned; control of certain types of provisions may, or may not, be granted to selected individuals or groups; transfer of provisions through gifts, inheritance, or trade with or without profit may or may not be sanctioned; market or other mechanisms may be utilized to administer the distribution of provisions; provisions may be distributed and transferred in kind or by means of symbolic equivalents, such as money.

Modes of Decision-Making. A final set of key issues concerns procedures societies devise for making the choices and decisions implicit in the selection, production, and distribution of provisions. Issues related to decision-making transcend, of course, the domain of provision and integrate it into the overall governance of a society and the conduct of its common affairs. The manner in which decisions are made on provisions and other public matters is obviously of central importance for circumstances of living, human relations, the quality of life, and the range of freedom in a society.

Major issues to be settled in this context include criteria for participation in various types of decision; degree of openness versus secrecy of decision-making processes; manner of accountability of decision-makers to the rest of society, etc.

The key issues concerning provisions noted here have been handled in a variety of ways by different human societies. By altering approaches to these issues, consciously or unintentionally, societies have attained significant modifications in existential circumstances and human relations. These issues continue to be the crux of policy development and of political action concerned with fundamental societal choices. Issues requiring resolution in any society should, therefore, be understood and defined in terms of types of needs and kinds of provisions corresponding to these needs, modes of production and distribution of provisions, modes of decision-making, interactions among these, and desired consequences for human existence and relations.

FORCES SHAPING AND MAINTAINING SYSTEMS OF PROVISION

Many factors have affected the manner in which human societies have resolved issues of provision in the course of evolution. Fear of death, the drive for survival and security in the context of scarcity and ignorance, trial and error, discoveries and inventions, basic characteristics of humans and the environment, conscious choices of policies as well as drifting along established paths—all these and many more have played a part in this process. Solutions at any point in time reflect a society's entire material and intellectual history up to that time, or rather the history of interactions among material realities, and perceptions, ideas, and actions concerning these realities. Furthermore, these solutions reflect the history of mutual aid and cooperation among humans who developed shared perceptions and definitions, and also the history of competition and conflict among individuals and groups who differed significantly in perceptions and definitions of interest.

Finally, solutions to the key issues of provision are always influenced and constrained by dominant conceptions concerning the worth, rights, and responsibilities of humans, and dominant positions on the following value-dimensions relevant to social policy:

equality	—	inequality
liberty	—	domination
cooperation	—	competition
collectivity-orientation	—	self-orientation

In turn, solutions developed by a society for the key issues of provision will tend to reinforce dominant philosophical concepts and dominant positions on policy-relevant value-dimensions.

Humans in any society tend to take for granted the principal features of established systems of provision. They usually view these features as "constants" beyond their influence and control. The reason for the ubiquitous tendency to accept, uncritically, the principal features of prevailing systems of provision is that these features, and the ideologies justifying and sustaining them, are internalized from the earliest stages of individual consciousness through processes of socialization and social control. People, therefore, tend to be unaware of the origin of these systems in past human choices and actions. They also tend to be unaware of their own ever-present potential to transcend and transform these systems, in spite of their apparent permanence, by means of new collective choices and actions.[2]

PATTERNS OF SYSTEMS OF PROVISION

Anthropological and historical studies reveal among human societies two principal tendencies in patterning systems of provision: the egalitarian, cooperative, collectivity-oriented and the inegalitarian, competitive, self-oriented.

The Egalitarian, Cooperative, Collectivity-Oriented Pattern. In societies organized according to this tendency, life-sustaining resources such as land, water, air, vegetation, wildlife, and minerals are considered to belong to God. ["The land is mine, says the Lord."] Humans are viewed as an integral part of nature. Nature's life-sustaining resources are for everyone's use, to sustain and enhance everyone's existence. While various resources may be used by humans, individually or in groups, appropriation of natural resources is not sanctioned.

Further, work tools are available to all, and knowledge of production technology circulates freely for everyone's use. Everyone participates in accordance with individual capacity in work aimed at procuring provisions for the satisfaction of acknowledged needs. Work tends to be carried out cooperatively, in a spirit of mutual aid, and all members of society are considered equally entitled to have their legitimate needs met. Natural resources are used thoughtfully, and conservation of the ecological base of life is an ever-present concern. Exploitation, destruction, and waste of natural resources are held to an irreducible minimum. A sense of harmony, belonging, and security tends to be promoted through institutionalized mutual responsibility of all for all, through collective management of production surplus and through widespread participation in open decision-making processes.

Societies whose systems of provision reflect, more or less, this tendency include many African, Asian, and American peoples prior to European conquests of their lands, as well as many ancient European peoples prior to the expansion of Greek and Roman civilizations; many medieval European villages; various religious and secular communal settlements in Europe, Asia, and America, past and present; contemporary communes in Israel and China; etc.[3]

Philosophical concepts sustaining this pattern are that humans are intrinsically equal in worth and ought to share equally in rights and responsibilities. Positions on policy-relevant value-dimensions reflected by this pattern are close to equality, liberty, cooperation, and collectivity-orientation.

The Inegalitarian, Competitive, Self-Oriented Pattern. In societies organized according to this second tendency, appropriation by individuals and groups of life-sustaining and life-enhancing material resources is the fundamental principle around which the system of provision and the entire social order are constructed.[4] Humans are viewed as masters over nature; they may use and exploit nature for their own benefit. Humans, therefore, do not view themselves, nor do they act, as an integral, harmonious component of nature's closed system, but as a unique species destined (by God) to rule this system.

The acquisitive, accumulative principle reflects the notion that all men are responsible to provide for themselves and their kin out of resources over which they manage to establish control. This notion usually gives rise to the desire to increase one's share of the aggregate available resources, as any increase in property is perceived as an increase in existential security. Collective responsibility for procurement of provisions to satisfy the needs of all members of society is usually not acknowledged under this pattern, as everyone is expected, and presumed to be able, to provide for one's own needs. As long as population size does not exceed the resource base and everyone controls sufficient resources to support himself by working with these resources, these expectations and presumptions correspond to reality.

However, an acquisitive mentality tends to result, over time, in increasing concentration of control over real wealth among decreasing numbers of owners and in an increase in the number of individuals whose share in the wealth of society decreases. This is the inevitable outcome of competitive dynamics in the context of limited resources: there are winners and losers. Eventually, large segments of the population end up without property, and thus without resources to provide for themselves. When this stage is reached they may either emigrate in search of new, uncontrolled territories and resources, choose to die for want of needed provisions, or work on property controlled by others on disadvantageous terms set by the owners. They become tenants, serfs, slaves, or wage-laborers and are forced to live on minimal provisions, as major portions of the products they create by their labor are appropriated by the owners, on whose property they work. The wealth of the latter continues to grow through constant appropriation of surplus produced by the former.

In a later stage of this pattern, tools and factories and even knowledge of production technology and skills are gradually appropriated and controlled by owners of wealth and their agents. By then the majority of the population owns little more than labor-power, often untrained and unskilled, which it is forced to supply to the owners in return for limited provisions. There usually are more property-less seekers of employment in the labor market than vacant work places. The share of the product allocated to workers can therefore be kept at a relatively low level.

During early stages of this process, society as a whole does not interfere to counteract evolving imbalances in control over life-sustaining resources, nor to assure provisions for the losers in the acquisitive race. On the contrary, the usual inclination is to blame the losers and to admire and reward the winners, especially since the latter tend to attain control over political institutions along with their growing control over society's basic wealth. Later on, various schemes are devised, e.g. charity and welfare, to allocate limited shares of essential provisions to disowned population segments, and to assure their survival and labor power, while checking rebellious tendencies and reinforcing the legitimacy of property rights and privileges.[5]

The mentality and dynamics of acquisitiveness tend to be reflected not only in exploitative attitudes towards other humans, who are perceived and treated as means towards further accumulation of wealth through profit, but also in equally exploitative attitudes towards the natural environment. As a result, irreplaceable resources are destroyed without concern for long-range consequences for future provisions and for human survival.

As a result of this pattern, human relations become increasingly competitive and antagonistic. Alienation, isolation, and various forms of deviance spread. The incidence of destructive and violent acts against property and people increases, and real security and personal fulfillment become unattainable. Eventually, increasing amounts of accumulated resources are channeled into futile efforts to defend the established order against internal and external challengers of privilege in order to regain an illusion of security.

Societies whose systems of provision reflect, approximately, the inegalitarian, competitive, self-centered, acquisitive, and exploitative pattern are ancient, medieval, and modern empires and would-be empires; slave-owning, feudal, and capitalist economic-political systems; and modern, industrial, urbanized, centralistic "welfare-states" of the pseudo-democratic, oligopoly-capitalist version, and the pseudo-socialist, state-monopoly-capitalist version.

Philosophical concepts which evolve along with this pattern and sustain it are that humans are intrinsically unequal in worth and hence entitled to unequal shares of rights and responsibilities. Essentially, they are entitled to what they manage to grab. Positions on policy-relevant value-dimensions reflected by this pattern are-close to inequality, domination, competition, and self-orientation.

The two tendencies of provision systems sketched here have rarely, if ever, existed in a pure form. Different human societies reflect varying combinations of these tendencies and can be imagined as located on a continuum. Comparative studies of actual societies suggest the hypothesis that in a society approximating the egalitarian, cooperative, collectivity-oriented pattern of provision, it is more likely that biological, social, and psychological needs of its members will be satisfied through sharing in the production and distribution of adequate provisions, and through participation in decisions affecting them. In such societies, it is also less likely that humans and natural resources will be exploited, wasted, and destroyed, and that people will feel insecure and alienated.[6]

Societies organized in accordance with inegalitarian, competitive, self-oriented, acquisitive, and exploitative tendencies have made important scientific and technological contributions and have achieved a large productive potential. But a study of societies approximating the egalitarian-cooperative pattern in the past, and also in the present, e.g. collective settlements in Israel and in contemporary Chinese society, reveals significant scientific and technological achievements as well as impressive levels of agricultural and industrial productivity. These have been attained at a lesser cost in human and natural resources, and at a higher level of evenly distributed human fulfillment, than in societies reflecting opposing tendencies in their structures and dominant values.

PROVISION IN MODERN, HIERARCHICAL, CENTRALIZED, INDUSTRIAL STATES

Before turning to issues of provision in our own society, some observations are indicated on certain attributes of provision systems in modern, hierarchical, centralized, industrial states, be they of the "democratic," oligopolist-capitalist or the "socialist," state-monopoly-capitalist version. In such states, most people are not self-directing, individually or collectively, in their lives and work, but are subject to controls of large, impersonal organizations with respect to many domains of existence, including production, consumption, health, education, leisure, etc. They work, usually for wages, in hierarchically managed enterprises. They have no meaningful share in the ownership and control of natural resources and production settings, nor do they play significant roles in determining the nature and quality of products and production processes, or of their share of the fruits of labor. Irrespective of legal definitions concerning ownership and control of resources and means of production, and irrespective of dominant political ideologies, the actual experience of people is not that of masters over their own lives and over production and consumption. What people do while creating provisions, and the scope of provisions to which they are eventually entitled, is determined largely by distant decision-makers, somewhere up the ladder of organizational command. As producers of provisions, workers usually lack a sense of mastery, creativity, pride, accomplishment, and fulfillment; they are not as fully human as they can become, being alienated in the deepest sense of this term. As consumers of services such as health, education, communications media, and recreation, and of mass-produced, standardized goods, people's relation to provisions is even less under their control, as it tends to be shaped by impersonal, political, and economic forces.

What is true for workers as producers and consumers is even truer for individuals and groups who, because of age, health, education, occupational, and personal qualifications, do not participate in the "work force," some of whom are at times considered and treated as surplus populations. Their relations to provisions are determined entirely through processes beyond their influence, and often beyond their grasp.

PROVISION SYSTEMS AND IDEOLOGIES IN CAPITALIST WELFARE STATES

Systems of provision in welfare states of the oligopoly-capitalist version involve varying combinations of elements of the principal tendencies sketched above, contradictions due to the pull of these tendencies, and conflicts which cannot be resolved unless the contradictions are overcome at their philosophical and institutional roots.

There are historical, philosophical, material, and institutional differences among democratic, capitalist welfare states in Western Europe, America, and other parts of the world, which are reflected in important differences in their respective systems of provision. However, in spite of these differences, all these societies sanction appropriation and control of important shares of natural resources, productive facilities, and human-created wealth by individuals, families, business enterprises, and other private formations. Humans are perceived as masters over nature, and an acquisitive, exploitative, competitive, selfish, and inegalitarian philosophy and mentality shape all social institutions and relations of humans to one another and to the environment. Wealth and political power tend to be correlated and concentrated. The majority of the population are practically propertyless; they possess few skills and limited knowledge. Their principal route to secure a meager share of provisions is through wage labor.

These societies expect all persons to provide for personal and family needs out of resources they own and work they do on these resources, or out of employment for wages on someone else's resources. However these societies also acknowledge with varying degrees of conviction that every human is entitled to a minimum of provisions to assure survival, and that such minimum provisions should be derived from taxes on wealth, income, production, trade, consumption, etc. This notion of societal responsibility for the survival and even well-being of all citizens has emerged gradually from many contradictory roots and has led to many controversies throughout the history of Europe and societies shaped by European civilization.

The roots of the welfare state notion include residues of communal tendencies toward mutual aid and collective responsibility; the Judeo-Christian beliefs in the sacrednesss of life, the brotherhood of all humans and their equality before God, and neighborly love as the ideal model for all human relations; monarchic and feudal, paternalistic traditions concerning responsibility for the life of one's subjects; the common-sense notion that basic human needs of a population ought to be satisfied, so that a stable and reliable work force and dependable military forces should be available on a regular basis; the realization that privilege tends to arouse challenge from deprived groups, and that rebellious tendencies might be pacified by assuring tolerable standards of existence to these groups; the relatively recent notion that a satisfied and well-trained population may, in fact, be an asset in the acquisitive drive of propertied groups, rather than an obstacle, and that, therefore, eliminating poverty in its worst forms may actually serve the interests of wealth; a vague sense of guilt for success in the competitive struggle of all against all; etc.

Controversies have centered on such issues as the following—what level of provision constituted an appropriate minimum that would assure survival but would not become a disincentive to unattractive, low-wage work? Should everyone in need be entitled to have his needs met by society or only the "deserving poor," to wit, individuals belonging to specified categories, e.g., children, aged, blind, handicapped, and sick persons, who lacked provisions through no fault of their own? Should strangers in need be assisted or only local residents? Should aid be provided by religious and other voluntary agencies or by government? From what sources should provisions for aiding poor people be derived, and who should shoulder that burden? Should provisions be made available in kind or in the form of purchasing power (i.e., money)? How thoroughly should applicants for aid be investigated before aid is granted; how much control should be exercised over the lives of those who receive aid; how should they be treated, and what should be expected of them? What kind of administrative and technical mechanisms would be most effective and efficient to achieve the ends of public welfare and what, actually were these ends?

Gradually these roots and controversies and the opposing tendencies crystallized into two philosophical-ideological positions concerning provisions for deprived groups in the population. These positions are labeled "liberal" and "conservative," respectively. These philosophies and ideologies continue to shape the politics, social policies, and programs of democratic, capitalist welfare states.

The "liberal" position. Present-day liberalism in the United States has little in common with 18th century liberal or "laissez-faire" philosophy which stressed individual freedom and free-enterprise in a truly competitive market, with minimal government intervention into the affairs of freely contracting parties. Liberalism now suggests an open, progressive mind-set on public issues, a fair, sympathetic, and humanistic attitude towards deprived population groups, and support for comprehensive government action to alleviate suffering and deprivation and to strengthen and stabilize economic activity. The modern liberal position in the United States seems, in many respects, akin to that of European social-democratic labor parties, who are committed to massive government intervention into capitalist economies to assure a wide range of health, education, and welfare services as well as transfers of purchasing power to population segments that fail to secure these services and a minimal income through conventional market mechanisms.

Liberals, during this century, have gradually come to acknowledge the roots of poverty and other social and economic problems in the unequal distribution of wealth and income. However, in spite of such understanding, liberals usually do not suggest strategies to overcome the social-structural roots of these problems. They tend to promote instead reforms aimed at ameliorating the symptoms through government-administered social services and financial assistance to those directly affected, and through "stimulating the economy"—a euphemism for channeling resources to owners of wealth whose investments are expected to cause benefits to "trickle down" to unemployed and poor persons.

Examples of liberal policies are the "New Deal" and "Great Society" programs, including Social Security, unemployment compensation, public housing, public assistance, Medicare and Medicaid, the War on Poverty, Headstart, Model Cities, etc. Clearly, these policies created mechanisms for the transfer of provisions to needy and deprived individuals and groups, to ameliorate their circumstances, but not to eliminate the structural inequalities which gave rise to, and continue to perpetuate, these circumstances. Besides, these programs generated huge, impersonal bureaucracies which became ever-present factors in the lives of people whose access to provisions they control.

Examples of another major type of liberal policies are fiscal and monetary interventions into the economy by government in accordance with theories developed in the twenties and thirties by the British economist John Maynard Keynes. These reforms, too, are essentially symptom-focused and ameliorative. They are meant to compensate for instabilities intrinsic to the existing economic order such as business cycles, unemployment, inflation, recessions, and depressions, but not to overcome the systemic roots of these instabilities and their unsettling consequences for the flow of provisions to the population.

The "conservative" position. This stance, in spite of its label, is actually closer than modern liberalism to eighteenth century liberalism. What conservatives seem eager to conserve are the sanctity and freedoms of property rights, and privileges resulting from the prevailing distribution of control over natural resources and productive facilities. Hence they tend to oppose, on principle, government intervention into the economy and into the no longer free play of market forces, especially when this intervention involves taxation for purposes of providing health and welfare services and purchasing power to deprived groups.

Conservatives believe, in spite of contrary evidence, that under the prevailing capitalist order everyone could provide for his own needs through work, savings, investments, and acquisition of property. They consider people who fail to do so unfit, lazy, and inferior, and hence deserving of blame rather than entitled to help from government and honest, hard-working taxpayers. In the view of conservatives, helping those who fail merely encourages others to avoid efforts to support themselves, and to depend instead on provisions from the government.

The conservative position usually disregards and denies structural sources of social and economic problems and interprets such problems as due primarily to individual shortcomings and faults. Policies derived from this position involve either "benign neglect" or measures to promote adjustment of individuals to prevailing realities, rather than adjustment of the social and economic order to the needs of people. Conservative policies will often also reflect authoritarian and punitive tendencies, and elements of crisis response, rather than prevention. Finally, conservatives prefer voluntary, charitable aid to government programs.

While conservatives tend to oppose government programs on behalf of deprived groups, they are no longer opposed to massive government intervention into the economy when such intervention is designed to improve the "business climate," to provide subsidies to industry and tax cuts for business investments, or otherwise to benefit the interests of owners of wealth.

The ideological positions sketched here which dominate political discourse on welfare state policies and provisions clearly do not confront the roots of social and economic problems in the prevailing inegalitarian distribution of ownership and control over natural resources, productive facilities, and human products, and of rights derived from such ownership and control. They also fail to deal with questions of human liberation, genuine human relations, and self-actualization.

The conservative position denies the existence of systemic roots. It perceives correctly, though for wrong reasons, the futility of symptom-oriented interventions, and objects to the creation of programs and bureaucracies, which are doomed to fail because of inadequate causal and intervention theories. However, though usually correct in their criticism of liberal welfare state policies and programs, conservatives do not offer a valid alternative.

A consistent, conservative position would have to acknowledge, as Karl Hess has done in a recent book,[7] that the prevailing system of provision excludes the majority of the population from sharing in natural resources and productive facilities, prevents them from providing for their own needs through self-directed work, and forces them, consequently, to depend for necessary provisions on government-controlled welfare state mechanisms until such time that natural resources and productive facilities will be freely available for everyone's use.

Liberals, too, do not challenge the all-pervasive inequalities which underlie our persistent social and economic problems, and tend to disregard the needs of people for self-actualization through meaningful work and genuine self-direction of their lives. Welfare state programs, however generous, remain subject to bureaucratic controls. Thus, while liberal reforms can and do reduce deprivation significantly, they can not bring about conditions essential to a free, fulfilling, and creative existence, for they avoid solving the key issues of control over life-sustaining and life-enhancing resources, self-direction at work, and participation by all in decisions affecting their lives.

It follows that in spite of important differences, the liberal and conservative positions serve a common function, to wit, to preserve the capitalist state, and the inequalities, privileges, and deprivations intrinsic to its social, economic, and political dynamics and system of provision. Whether, following the conservative position, dysfunctional aspects of capitalism are denied and attributed to the victims, or whether, in accordance with the liberal position, massive governmental programs for ameliorative intervention are devised, conservatives and liberals alike are committed to maintain the status quo, and their ideologies are conducive to the defense, legitimation, and perpetuation of capitalism.

SOCIAL SERVICES IN CAPITALIST WELFARE STATES

Social services and education for social service practice have evolved over recent centuries into widely accepted institutions in capitalist welfare states. Liberals and conservatives may favor different models of social services; yet every important group within the political spectrum of capitalism will approve some form of social services to distribute limited shares of provisions when market mechanisms fail to do so. This general acceptance of social services makes good sense within the internal logic of capitalist societies in view of the concrete benefits they now provide for many groups throughout society, and in view of the socialization, social control, and stabilization functions they perform on behalf of the prevailing social order by reinforcing the institutions, ideologies, and the entire symbolic universe.

Implicit in the social services in capitalist welfare states, and in the education for social service practice, is a tacit affirmation and legitimation of prevailing patterns of control over resources—i.e. over property rights, status allocation, and rights distribution—and of the consequences of these institutions for human relations and the existential milieu, for privilege and deprivation and for individual, social, and economic problems rooted in privilege and deprivation. Paradoxically, then, implicit in the social services is the affirmation of oppression and exploitation of humans by humans, and the negation of equality of rights, responsibilities, and dignity and of genuine liberty and self-actualization for all. The social services are thus revealed not as part of the solution of issues of provision in our society, but as a factor in the maintenance of the human problems they pretend to treat and prevent.

Intervention theories implicit in our social services frequently derive from the erroneous notion that social problems are functions of shortcomings of the very individuals and groups who suffer from these problems, rather than functions of prevailing social policies. In accordance with these faulty theories, services aim to change people rather than social institutions. The latter are taken for granted; they are considered "constants" to which people are being helped to adapt or conform. Furthermore, along with other professions and academic disciplines, the social services are organized as if social problems such as unemployment, poverty, crime, addiction, mental illness, etc., were discrete phenomena, each with a specific "professional" solution based in theory and involving skills which "experts" transmit through sophisticated educational processes. Obviously, such a fragmentary conception of social problems and corresponding practice disregard the common roots of those problems in prevailing social values, structures, and dynamics.

Professionals in the social services in modern, industrial capitalist welfare states tend to identify with the earlier sketched "liberal" ideology which, while never challenging the capitalist order, favors large-scale government programs to compensate for chronic and acute ills of that order, so as to ameliorate resulting suffering. In identifying with the ideologies and political efforts of liberals, social service professionals and their educators also accept, uncritically, the notion that more and larger social service programs within the capitalist system can overcome its multiple social problems. Having adopted this fallacious notion, social service professionals usually act in accordance with it, manifesting in doing so a high degree of faith and genuine commitment. They become planners, researchers, administrators, consultants, and staff and line workers of constantly growing service bureaucracies. Once involved in the agencies and programs, professionals are subject to the usual illusions and the social and psychological dynamics of large organizations. They come to believe in the validity of what they are doing in order to maintain their own sanity, and they develop blinders against the abundant evidence of constant failure. They will explain failures as due to inadequate budgets and staff shortages, and they will overlook the fact that the reported incidence of social problems tends to rise along with the growth of social service agencies, and that no social service agency has ever eliminated a social problem. The best one can reasonably expect of such agencies on the basis of past performance is some measure of amelioration.

The foregoing observations are by no means new to social service professionals who have experienced a sense of failure and futility for a long time. Furthermore, they are usually not unaware of being used to socialize and to control deprived human beings, and to administer often inhumane and oppressive services in the interest, not of their "clients," but of population groups whose privileged circumstances are the real source of the clients' deprivation and problems. And yet, social service professionals and educators continue the futile task of administering and reorganizing their services, designing forever new variations on the old theme of injustice, although, by and large, they are caring and thoughtful human beings. The reason for this contradiction is that social service professionals, like nearly all humans, are trapped in the institutional realities, the economic necessities, and the false consciousness of our society. They need their jobs to survive. Hence they develop illusions about, and vested interests in, the organizations which employ them; they are afraid to confront these organizations head on, and instead end up as apologists for them.

RESOLVING ISSUES OF PROVISION:
A PHILOSOPHICAL AND POLITICAL TASK

Analysis in this essay, so far, leads to one unambiguous conclusion. Resolving issues of provision in a fundamental sense is not, as is often assumed, a professional task involving technical innovations and adjustments within existing societal systems. Rather, it is a philosophical and political task, requiring strategies aimed at radical transformations of values, consciousness, and social institutions. The history of recent centuries all over the globe has demonstrated that there are no solutions to issues of provision in a manner that would satisfy the biological, psychological, and social needs of all humans within the framework of capitalist welfare states, since the values, structures, and dynamics of such states negate equality of rights and responsibility, genuine liberty, and self-actualization for all. Capitalism and other inegalitarian and oppressive systems, whatever their official designations may be, will have to be overcome and transformed thoroughly by philosophical and political means in order to assure the emergence of new value systems, consciousness, social structures, and dynamics conducive to an egalitarian, free, and non-exploitative existence for all. Fundamental solutions to issues of provision need therefore be discovered and realized through philosophy, political theory, and practice.

CURRENT TRENDS OF PROVISION SYSTEMS AND HUMAN PROSPECTS

The objectives of systems of provision in the future are the same as they were in the past: survival, enhancement of the quality of life, and self-actualization for humans everywhere. Yet present provision systems all over the world are shaped largely by zero-sum dynamics, by competitive, self-centered mentality, and by conflict models. These, plus the inegalitarian and selfish values from which they derive, and which they, in turn, reinforce, have brought humankind face to face with the possibility of extinction, at a time when scientific and technological development make a previously unattained quality of human life possible on a world-wide scale. Selfish, ethnocentric, narrow, and short-range perspectives and policies of major societies have caused, and continue to accelerate, critical conditions. Among these are those concerning population trends, production and distribution of food and other life-sustaining goods and services, waste and destruction of non-renewable, essential natural resources, chemical, thermal, and radioactive pollution of the biosphere, and the spread of thermonuclear and conventional armaments. Scholars with impeccable credentials have documented these interrelated, critical conditions, their sources and dynamics, and their likely consequences in countless reports.[8] They have also suggested courses which could lead humankind away from disaster toward survival and fulfillment for all. Yet prevailing political consciousness, dominant social values, short-sighted perceptions of interest, universal mistrust and fear, and existing institutional structures and dynamics constitute massive obstacles to bringing about fundamental transformations in attitudes and actions. Without these, humankind cannot overcome the multiple crises threatening its survival.

THE NEED FOR A NEW RENAISSANCE

When our planet was sparsely populated and societies existed in relative isolation from one another, solving issues of provision in accordance with selfish and ethnocentric principles may not have been just and satisfying to all, but it did not constitute a threat to survival. However, a densely populated planet in which human societies are in close contact with one another and in which levels of interdependence and of material and cultural exchanges are high can no longer solve these issues in this way. Satisfying one's needs and the needs of those close to one while remaining indifferent to the needs of others, or worse still, satisfying one's needs by exploiting and depriving others, accelerates the momentum of reciprocal processes which cause a constant decrease of need satisfaction for all societies and individuals. This is true whatever the level of development of these societies and however privileged they may be. To overcome this ultimately suicidal trend, sophisticated and comprehensive perceptions and definitions of self-interest are called for in the modern, crowded world.

In order to solve issues of provision effectively and satisfyingly, locally and globally, we need today a worldwide New Renaissance of egalitarian, libertarian, cooperative, and collective values and institutions shaped by these values. These are the conclusions reached in recent decades by progressive thinkers such as Martin Buber, Paulo Freire, Erich Fromm, Martin Luther King, Herbert Marcuse, Julius K. Nyerere, George Wald, and also by consistent, libertarian-conservative thinkers such as Karl Hess and George Cabot-Lodge.

To discover the essential elements of such a New Renaissance, we need to think through how issues of provision will have to be resolved locally and globally to assure not only survival, but also evenly shared enhancement of the quality of life, and free and full development and self-actualization for humans everywhere. Solutions to issues of provision today need to transcend prevailing political boundaries among communities, nation-states, and power blocks, since solutions which satisfy the needs of some parts of human-kind by exploiting and depriving others are merely pseudo-solutions; they constitute part of the very problems and obstacles which must be overcome.

Yet, while the global scope of issues of provision must serve as the frame of reference, solutions must be developed on different geographic and political levels, always with proper regard for issues of provision on more inclusive levels, so that local solutions should not constitute obstacles to trans-local and world-wide solutions. The search for solutions must be oriented, simultaneously, to one's own needs, the needs of one's group, and the needs of all groups, every-where. Satisfying the needs of everyone, everywhere—the needs of the "generalized other"—thus becomes the criterion, and the condi-tion, for satisfying the needs of the self and of the immediate group to which the self belongs. Self-interest, to fit the realities of the twen-tieth century and centuries to come, will have to be redefined to include the existential interests of all humans, everywhere, living now and in the future.

Solutions to issues of provision require a coherent set of interacting values and principles so as not to contradict the objectives of survival, evenly shared life enhancement, and self-actualization for humans everywhere. Such a set is suggested below:

- All humans and groups of humans ought to be considered intrinsically equal in worth.
- All resources, i.e. natural resources, human potential, and human mate-rial and non-material products, ought to be used, judiciously, to satisfy everyone's acknowledged needs, holding waste and destruction of re-sources to an irreducible minimum.
- All humans ought to be equally entitled to have their biological, social, and psychological needs acknowledged and satisfied, allowing, however, for differences in priorities related to types and urgency of needs, and for limitations in the aggregate of available need-satisfying resources.
- All humans ought to be equally entitled to participate in, and be responsible for, processes of production and decision making; these processes ought to be cooperative, collectivity-oriented, open, and non-secretive, and ought to preclude exploitation, domination, and control of humans by other humans.

FROM VALUES AND PRINCIPLES TO SOCIAL POLICIES AND INSTITUTIONS

The discussion of trends which threaten human survival, of the need for a New Renaissance to overcome that threat, and of the values and principles upon which such a renaissance is predicated, suggests that solutions to issues of provision for our society are unattainable through merely marginal adjustments of the existing system of provision. What is needed, therefore, is a radical transformation of this system. The centralized, nationalistic, militaristic United States, which rules hun-dreds of millions of alienated and competitive individuals at home, and which strives to maintain privileges abroad through pragmatic, un-principled power politics, must be transformed into a decentralized, humanistic, pacific commonwealth, a federation of truly democratic, self-governing, self-reliant, egalitarian communities in which all humans can attain autonomy and authenticity through cooperation and mutuality. How would such a commonwealth resolve issues of provision, and what would be its institutional structure?

Natural and Human-Created Wealth as Public Trust. The primary institution of a commonwealth of democratic, self-governing, self-reliant, egalitarian communities is a permanent Public Trust of all natural resources, productive facilities, scientific knowledge, and technological skill. These material, intellectual, natural, and human-created resources and products, the wealth or capital of all the people, would no longer be owned, controlled, transferred, exchanged, saved, invested, wasted, and destroyed by a small segment of the population to secure privileged circumstances of living for owners, their managers and professional aides—the propertied, bureaucratic, and intellectual elites. Nor could these currently powerful elites continue to exclude the remainder of the population from access to and use and enjoyment of natural and human-created wealth, and to exploit their productive potential by continuous appropriation of newly produced wealth. Instead, suitable shares of natural resources and productive facilities would be made available for use, not ownership, by all people, individually or in groups, to work with and to derive their livelihood from them. Scientific knowledge and technological skills would be freely available for use, enjoyment, and further development.

The Public Trust would have to be administered judiciously, in a manner assuring everyone's participation throughout life as equally acknowledged and entitled decision-maker, producer, and consumer. Everyone's potential and talents would be used fully, satisfying common and unique needs, subject to overall limitations on available resources and to the equal right of all others to satisfy their common and unique needs; there would be prevention, so far as possible, of waste and destruction of resources. Private ownership would be limited solely to items destined for personal use, such as clothing, homes, household equipment, etc.

The concept of the Public Trust, according to which everyone is equally entitled to use natural and human-created wealth, to derive livelihood from this use, and thus be truly free, is radically different from the welfare state concept. According to the welfare state concept, the sanctity of private ownership and control of capital—the permanent, dynamic source of inequalities and deprivation—is preserved essentially unchanged, while parts of income from capital and labor are allocated for transfers and government-administered human services to various groups in the population. Obviously, under this concept wealth-holding segments of the population continue their privileged circumstances, and the remainder of the people are not liberated from their dependence on government and on the elites that monopolize the control over all natural and manufactured wealth.

Production of Provisions to Be Geared to Need, Not Profit. Allocation of productive resources out of the Public Trust will have to be guided by flexible priority rules to assure that goods and services corresponding to the essential needs of the entire population are produced in appropriate quantities and quality before less essential items are produced. Furthermore, policies are required to balance population size and needs against ecological considerations and the reality of ultimate limits of natural resources by adjusting birth rates and by avoiding waste and destruction of human potential and other natural wealth. Such waste and destruction may be intrinsic to production processes shaped by the drive for profit and the accumulation of privately controlled wealth. When production is geared systematically to match population needs with high-quality, long-lasting goods and services, producers will not need to engage in irrational economic practices which are now induced by the competitive scramble for market shares and profits. Among these irrational economic practices are artificially inflated and manipulated patterns of consumption, model changes involving marginal variations rather than real improvements, built-in obsolescence, deceptive advertising, etc.

An effective system of provision also requires balanced integration of agricultural and industrial production and of rural and urban settlements. Reliable supply of high-quality food is obviously a *sine-qua-non.* Accordingly, policies ought to be avoided which impede food production and debase the quality of rural life by shifting human and material resources toward urban industrial centers primarily for the benefit of wealth-holding and other powerful groups. Such policies tend to result in mass migration from potentially healthy rural communities into urban slums, traditional breeding grounds for human misery, exploitation, and manifold individual and social pathology.

Industry must not be an end in itself, nor a means for the creation of privately controlled wealth. It must be a powerful instrument to promote the well-being of the entire population. Policies should therefore facilitate dispersion of industry to where people and natural resources are, and should steer industrial capacity toward high priority needs of the population and away from wasteful production of non-essentials.

Restructuring Processes of Production, Distribution, and Consumption. Once natural and human-created wealth are liberated for the use of all people, the modes of production, distribution, and consumption can be radically transformed. Everyone, regardless of sex, age, and other personal characteristics, will be entitled, as well as expected, to participate in the aggregate labor needed by communities to assure survival of the community and to enhance the quality of life for all. The manner of participation in work will be related to capacities, talents, and interests. Whether the amount of labor deemed needed by a community is large or small, it will be shared evenly by all. Human unemployment, including forced retirement, the exclusion of youth, and other forms of discriminatory exclusion from work, would thus be abolished. So also would be the waste, the deprivation, and the alienation which now result from such exclusion and unemployment.

All work deemed needed within a rationally designed system of provision should entitle workers to equal social recognition or prestige and to roughly equal claims against a community's aggregate product, adjusted flexibly to differences in individual needs. This policy reflects the fact that in a rational system of provision, "work" means activities required by communities for collective and individual well-being of all members. All such activities should be considered of equal worth and should, therefore, entitle workers to equal circumstances of living.

The experience of individuals engaging in different occupations would, nevertheless, vary widely in quality. Moreover, different individuals will also develop preferences for different types of work. Hence, different work roles will result in different levels of intrinsic satisfaction. Yet people should be entitled not only to equal social recognition for their work and to satisfaction of their material needs, but also to equal opportunities for subjective satisfaction, self-expression, and self-actualization in the process of production. Appropriate social policies are therefore required to compensate for differences inherent in occupations and in people, and also to overcome other potentially conflicting objectives intrinsic to processes of production, distribution, and consumption. A set of such policies is suggested below.

Firstly, all work should be directed by the workers engaged in it, whether it is carried out collectively or by an individual working alone. Next, production processes should not be split into minute, meaningless tasks; thus there would not be destruction of opportunities for expressing individual craftsmanship and creativity, and for deriving a sense of pride and accomplishment while producing goods and services of high quality and aesthetic value. Thirdly, unhealthy, dangerous, heavy, unpleasant, and routine work should be performed by machines before other, more desirable work is mechanized and automated. Work considered less desirable, or undesirable, that cannot be mechanized for various reasons but is nevertheless essential to a community's well-being ought to be shared evenly by all. This could be accomplished by assigning everyone during specified stages of the life cycle to the performance of such less desirable tasks, or by taking turns in undertaking these tasks throughout life. Fourthly, opportunities ought to be provided for all to change occupations at various stages of life, to engage in different occupations at the same time, or to rotate among different roles over time. Special efforts are imperative to overcome the prevailing, nearly absolute separation between physical and mental work, and the differential social valuation of these work domains. Fifthly, access to all occupations, and to preparatory channels for all occupation, ought to be completely open to all, and vestiges of role allocation by way of sex, age, caste, or class must be eliminated. Finally, societal structures which now bring forth competitive attitudes and practices at work must be transformed into structures conducive to cooperative attitudes and mutual aid in the course of production.

The distribution of provisions, or of shares of the aggregate product of the community, ought to be administered independently of the division of labor, once all work is considered of equal worth and hence the basis for equal entitlements. Provisions ought to be made available as needed and as universal entitlements, rather than through task-specific, differential wages and non-material rewards. Everyone will thus be entitled to an appropriate share of the aggregate product to satisfy all socially acknowledged needs throughout life by virtue of being a contributing member of a community, irrespective of the type and amount of one's work. Entitlement to provisions in accordance with individual needs is different from the welfare state concept, according to which welfare provisions represent transfers from privileged to deprived groups. Entitlements under the provision system discussed here are not one-way transfers but reciprocal exchanges over the life-cycle on the basis of equality and mutuality. For, with everyone entitled to use communal capital out of the Public Trust, and to derive a livelihood from such use, the goods and services created by self-directing, cooperating producers will be the peoples' to consume and exchange by right. Individuals will create only a limited range of products, but exchanges among producers whose labor is considered equal in worth will assure that everyone's needs are met. Everyone will be an equally entitled consumer.

Decision-Making, Coordination, Governance, Leadership. How would decisions be made, how would local, trans-local, and global needs be coordinated, and what governance structures are suited for humanistic, egalitarian, self-directing, and self-reliant communities? Choices and decisions affecting relations and circumstances of living ought to be arrived at in a thoroughly democratic fashion. Everyone who may be affected by a decision should be informed fully about all relevant aspects, and have an "equal voice," that is, equal rights, opportunities, and power in determining the outcome. Representative democracy, when practiced in an essentially inegalitarian context of interest group competition, inevitably falls short of these criteria. Hence it will have to be transcended, and replaced by political institutions conducive to genuine, participatory democracy.

The basic units of participatory democracy would not be isolated individuals, but self-governing communities. They would be small enough to permit personal relations, yet large enough to assure economic viability and social continuity. The communities would share social, economic, cultural, child-rearing, educational, and recreational functions and concerns. They would vary in size and in patterns and life-styles. They would be linked in local and trans-local networks or federations, which in turn would form more encompassing, democratic commonwealths. Coordination and integration would be achieved through local, regional, trans-regional, and global representative assemblies designed in a manner that would assure full and informed participation of all units and levels in decisions shaping their existence. Administrative units would be selected by and accountable to these assemblies. Issues for deliberation and decision could originate at any level, but would always have to be examined on all levels so that local and trans-local perspectives would be taken into consideration and reconciled before decisions are reached.

Such a multi-level, political-administrative system of decentralized, yet federated, coordinated, and integrated, self-governing communities could not function effectively unless every unit is guided by, and committed to, egalitarian and collectivity-oriented value premises. These premises would have to be primary decision criteria for internal and external issues, and there would have to be avoidance of competitive interactions derived from a scarcity mentality and the "zero-sum" model. Egalitarian values, non-competitive attitudes, and cooperative

practices in sharing and allocating productive resources and in producing and distributing goods and services will set in motion and
sustain a process of "plus-sum" dynamics.

Egalitarian-democratic institutions require widespread political
awareness and conscientious involvement in public affairs; these
would be facilitated by an unobstructed flow of relevant information.
Hence, such political institutions must not sanction secrecy and
confidential, privileged communications concerning public issues. If
people are to be their own masters, and if they are to share equally
responsibilities and entitlements, then individuals undertaking representative and administrative public service roles must under no
circumstances be permitted to withhold information from the sov-
ereign people. Behind all claims for secrecy and privileged communications lurks an evil purpose involving either the defense of existing
unfair and unjust conditions, or the intent to create, and benefit from,
such conditions. Just and fair objectives and purposes, on the other
hand, can always be discussed and confronted openly among equals.

Leadership in an egalitarian-democratic commonwealth means
service to people, not control and rule over people. It involves
performance of certain tasks deemed necessary to maintain and
enhance life. The social value of these tasks is equal to that of all other
tasks deemed necessary by communities. Hence individuals assigned
for a time to the performance of leadership functions should not be
entitled to privileged circumstances of living, but should share the
same life style and the same rights to goods and services as other
members of their community. Once leadership roles are defined as
service functions that do not entitle individuals performing them to
special rewards in the form of additional goods, services, and prestige,
people will be less eager to assume these roles and to hold on to them.
It may even become difficult to recruit volunteers for leadership roles,
as their performance would require commitment of extra time and
effort. Hence, these roles may eventually have to be filled by assigning
everyone to take a turn.

Qualifications for leadership roles are not as extraordinary and as
rare as people in inegalitarian, competitive societies assume. In such
societies, leaders invariably come from or are selected by, and
represent the perceived interests of, wealthy and powerful population
segments. Furthermore, leadership roles in such societies entitle those
who perform them to considerable privileges. They are a source of
patronage and corruption. Once secrecy and confidential, privileged
communications are abolished, and with them the monopoly on
information about public affairs, individuals who keep informed on

public affairs and who will participate in the study and disposition of public issues will soon develop the skills necessary for dealing with such issues, for representing their communities, and for assuming leadership positions. As with many other tasks that are monopolized in the prevailing social order by various power groups, the real issue concerning leadership roles seems to be access and opportunity rather than unique qualifications and abilities. It should be emphasized that in an egalitarian-democratic and pacific commonwealth the nature of leadership roles will be less complex than in a centralized, nationalistic and militaristic world power. The political institutions of egalitarian, participatory democracy will be designed in a manner which will preserve the right and responsibility of the people to make all decisions on policy in their communities and in their representative assemblies on local and trans-local levels. Accordingly, the responsibility of leaders will be the faithful execution of the people's decisions. They will be administrators, not rulers.

Global Relations. A commonwealth of federated, egalitarian-humanistic, and pacific communities is predicated upon avoidance of exploitation and domination of humans and natural resources in other parts of the globe. All forms of exploitation and domination abroad inevitably negate and destroy a just system of provision and of human relations at home; foreign exploitation and domination involve always exploitative and domineering human relations between powerful ruling elites and large segments of people. Internal and external exploitation and oppression complement and reinforce each other. They are manifestations of the same underlying principles and dynamics, to wit, commitment to inequality and hence readiness to use other humans as means or objects in the greedy pursuit of hegemony, privilege, and profit for oneself, one's family, one's tribe, or one's nation and state.

While foreign exploitation and domination in any form are incompatible with an egalitarian system of provision and of human relations, trade among communities living in different parts of the globe is not, as long as such trade involves coordinated, voluntary exchanges of different types of resources on the basis of equality among trading partners. Such exchanges as well as all forms of mutual aid among neighboring and distant peoples are apt to enhance the quality of life for all participants.

It is however not enough to avoid exploitation and domination of humans and natural resources beyond one's own community. This is an essential first step, but human survival on a global scale requires that the concept of Public Trust be applied to the entire human species and to the whole planet earth. Every human being should be equally entitled to make use of, and to derive a livelihood from, the total natural and human-created capital of the planet, to participate in processes of production, distribution, and consumption of provisions, and to participate in decision-making and governance. There are many technical problems of coordination and exchange to be worked out in transforming greedy and competitive nation-states into a world-wide, egalitarian, humanistic, democratic commonwealth. Reason suggests, though, that this is the logical course of sophisticated self-interest if there is to be a future for the human species. The right of every human being to a meaningful existence should no longer be left to chance and to determination by circumstances of birth. Human cooperation, and solutions to issues of provision derived from the principles and values sketched above, would enable us to overcome chance and parochialism by making full use of available natural and human-created resources, scientific knowledge and technology, and the power of reason and reflection. Narrow selfishness, tribalism, and ethnocentricity have run their disastrous course and have brought humankind to the brink of self-destruction. Sophisticated, humanistic self-interest can now guide us away from the abyss toward life and a meaningful existence for all.

A Unifying Philosophy. The suggestions presented here for solving the key issues of provisions in our society are not isolated fragments. In fact, they complement one another. Their combined impact should bring about the fundamental transformations of social values, structures, and dynamics implicit in the notion of a New Renaissance for survival of humankind and an enhanced quality of life for all. What unifies these policies is the underlying humanistic, egalitarian, democratic philosophy. According to this, all humans are intrinsically of equal worth, are entitled to equal rights in every sphere of life, and may not be exploited or dominated by other humans. The policies were developed by consistently applying these values and principles to the major domains of human existence and social organization, namely, the stewardship and allocation of all natural and human-created wealth, the design of productive processes and criteria for production priorities, the division of labor and the organization and valuation of work, the distribution of rights and claims to shares of the aggregate social product, and finally, the design of local and global political institutions.

THE ROLE OF SOCIAL WORK EDUCATION

Can education for social work practice play a role in solving issues of provision in our society, and if so, what is the nature of that role? Since genuine solutions to issues of provision were shown to involve radical transformations of the existing societal order, rather than merely marginal adjustments of that order, the questions to be explored now are whether, and how, social work practice and education can contribute to a radical transformation of the prevailing order into an egalitarian-humanistic one which would be conducive to the survival and self-actualization of all humans.

In answering these questions, one needs to recall that a radical transformation of the social order requires philosophical inquiry and political practice rather than merely technical innovations and professional processes. Social work practice and education would therefore have to be transformed into conscious philosophical search and political practice in order to make significant contributions to a radical transformation. Some educators and practitioners may think that perhaps we ought not to aim to make such contributions since social work practice and education are, and ought to be, politically neutral. Upon reflection, however, this claim to political neutrality of the profession appears to be fallacious, and to be in itself a myth, and a political act, by virtue of denying the political nature, sources, dynamics, and consequences of social work practice and education. The fact must be faced, that social work has never been politically neutral, although many practitioners and educators may not be conscious of the political nature of their work.

The political components of social work have many dimensions. Social work aids in the defense and maintenance of the existing social order in many ways. It does this by pacifying deprived and potentially rebellious segments of the population, by undertaking socialization and social control functions, by reinforcing the values, ideology, mythology, mental sets, and entire symbolic universe upon which the social order is founded, and by not challenging the prevailing societal order on a fundamental level; it thus actually supports that order passively while pretending to be politically neutral. To the extent that social workers are critical of prevailing social policies, their critique usually reflects a liberal-progressive position and thus does not transcend the broad consensus of capitalist ideology and institutions. Social workers tend to urge reforms which usually involve broadening the scope of welfare state programs such as income transfers and social service programs. When implemented, these reforms amount merely to new variations on the ancient themes of property rights and inequalities, and they usually bring about further growth of government bureaucracies and increased control over dependent populations. Needless to say, such reforms also serve the perceived interests of social service workers and educators, their institutions, and their professional organizations.

If, indeed, social work practice and education have always been political in nature, irrespective of the perceptions and interpretations of practitioners and educators, then the transformation of the profession suggested here involves merely shifting from an unintentional and often unconscious level of political action to an intentional and conscious one. Such a shift would require continuous reexamination of value premises, and clarification and development of political perspectives, objectives, and strategies, instead of taking for granted the prevailing social context and its value premises, and supporting its political objectives and strategies by passively drifting along with them.

Before we can consider how social work practice and education could incorporate a conscious political component aimed at fundamental societal transformations conducive to human survival and self-actualization, certain elements of an overall political strategy for such a radical transformation need to be explicated.

Transforming the prevailing system of provision and human relations into a humanistic, egalitarian, cooperative system on local, trans-local, and global levels seems to be in the true self-interest of all humans everywhere; the existing order oppresses not only deprived groups but prevents the vast majority of humans from leading meaningful, harmonious lives and from realizing their inherent human potential. If, then, a radical transformation is in everyone's true human interest, it does not seem valid to view it as a zero-sum game, in which currently deprived groups would be "winners" and currently privileged groups "losers." Rather, such a transformation is to be viewed and interpreted as a truly liberating process for all, with everyone coming out a "winner" in humanistic terms. Though acknowledged theoretically by past and present radical movements, this conception has, so far, not been integrated adequately into transformation strategies.

The major obstacles to a radical transformation at the present time

are existing social, economic, and political institutions and the dominant consciousness of large segments of the population in support of
these institutions. According to this dominant consciousness, the
prevailing capitalist system and its values either already serve their
interests or eventually will do so. Most individuals and groups are
ready to struggle for their perceived interests within the existing
system and assume that they will succeed eventually if they try hard
enough. They fail to see that such struggles can obviously not bring
success for everyone. Not only must there always be losers in a
competitive economic and political marketplace, but the winners too
cannot achieve self-actualization, meaningful human relations, and
meaningful existence because of the intrinsic social and psychological
dynamics of struggles within that system.

   Further obstacles to radical transformation are uncertainty about
the characteristics, reality, and feasibility of alternative social orders
and, related to this, fear of the unknown. There is also fear and
rejection of the little that is known from selective and often biased
information about various past and ongoing revolutions against capitalist systems. These fears, uncertainties, and misunderstandings are all
utilized in the defense of the existing order.

   In view of these considerations it seems that an essential component
of a transformation strategy is to overcome widespread, prevailing
misconceptions, or "false consciousness," concerning the realities and
the economic, psychic, and social "costs and benefits" of capitalism on
the one hand, and of humanistic, egalitarian, alternative social systems
on the other. Such reeducational, consciousness-enhancing efforts
should be directed at every segment of the population rather than
merely at oppressed groups, for, as suggested above, transformation is
to benefit everyone, as it is in everyone's truest human interest.

   Furthermore, no groups or individuals, whatever their current social
positions, should be cast in the image of enemies; such images tend to
turn into self-fulfilling prophesies. They prevent communication with
important and powerful segments of the population and undermine
the potential for consciousness change among those labeled enemies.
Such labeling also tends to intensify defense of the status quo through
repressive resistance to transformation efforts. The false consciousness
of powerful groups is thus merely reinforced. Although "personalizing
an enemy" and expressing hostility toward him may unify oppressed
groups, it seems counterproductive in terms of an effective overall
strategy. Political interpretation and reeducation as conceived here
should, therefore, identify as "enemy" not specific individuals and
abstract groups, such as a "ruling class," but the inegalitarian, com-

petitive, oppressive, and exploitative value premises and organizing principles of the prevailing social order, the institutions and social policies derived from these values and principles, and the destructive interpersonal and intergroup relations and conflicts generated by these institutions and policies. Such an interpretation should also reveal how all of us, oppressed and oppressors alike, are trapped in, and act in accordance with, the same dehumanizing, irrational institutions which humans have created and continue to maintain, and hence, how the liberation of every individual and group depends on the liberation of all individuals and groups from the shackles of the existing order.[9]

The transformation strategy advocated here is based primarily on reason and on human capacity to use intellect critically and creatively. Judicious use of civil disobedience, noncooperation with oppressive institutions, and dynamic, nonviolent resistance to such institutions and the development of alternative institutions would all be appropriate means in terms of this strategy. However, the use of physical force and violence would seem contraindicated on ethical, theoretical, and practical grounds, as force and violence are not only intrinsically incompatible with humanistic-egalitarian aims, but are also unlikely to change the perceptions and consciousness of people, especially those now holding power.

In summary, a true societal transformation requires fundamental changes of consciousness concerning social reality and perceptions of self-interest on the part of the population. Such a transformation is therefore a cultural change process and not merely an institutional and structural one. These two change processes are, of course, closely related to, and constantly interact with, one another. To advance such comprehensive cultural and institutional change processes in the United States, in spite of the prevailing mind-crippling and indoctrinating influences of our educational systems and our media of mass communication and entertainment, we need to organize a dynamic, nonviolent, radical liberation movement. A major function of such a movement would be to unravel and demystify, by means of systematic counter-communications and reeducation, the illusions and distortions disseminated perpetually by the dominant communications media. These tend to reinforce prevailing misconceptions concerning capitalism and possible alternative systems.

Social work, along with other human services, could become an important factor of such an evolving liberation movement if large numbers of practitioners in health, education, and welfare services would redefine their individual and professional roles in political terms. Professional practice in the various human services seems particularly well-suited to counter-communication functions aimed at overcoming false consciousness; its primary operational mode is communication and interaction around basic human needs and service programs, with individuals, groups, organizations, communities, or even larger and more complex human aggregates. The quality, content, and thrust of professional practice must, of course, be modified significantly if it is to unmask, rather than sustain, existing illusions; to unravel, rather than to cover up, the causes of social problems and human misery; and to promote identification with, and commitment to, a liberation movement, rather than adjustment to the status quo.

Politically informed practice in the human services, as conceived here, should be clearly distinguished from, and must never deteriorate into, indoctrination and manipulation. Such practice is meant to be truly liberating in the fullest sense of this concept; it aims to open up new vistas of choice for individuals and groups even while facilitating maximum utilization on their part of now-available resources and services. Practice from a radical perspective involves consistent attempts to bring into consciousness the multiple causal links between specific personal and social issues or problems addressed by a given service and the dynamics of the prevailing social, economic, and political order. Beyond thus fostering awareness of the causal context of issues and problems, such practice would also facilitate insights into options available to individuals and groups for organizing themselves and others into a liberation movement against the systemic causes of their specific problems, and the existing general oppression and exploitation.

The broad range of social issues, problems, and programs in which professionals in the human services are involved requires, of course, considerable flexibility, imagination, and creativity in adapting the general political-professional intervention model to specific situations. To work out these adaptations for different fields and levels of practice is the challenge now facing practitioners and educators in social work and other human services. By meeting this challenge, in spite of the strong resistance this radical thrust will arouse from defenders of the status quo, the human services professions could become truly relevant in terms of their original mission as conceived by Socrates and Plato—to serve the good of humankind rather than their own narrow self-interest.

The role of social work education in solving issues of provision in our society follows logically from the foregoing discussion. We have tried to analyze the potential contribution of politically conscious practice in the human services to the radical transformation upon which the solutions of issues of provision are predicated. Social work educators should aid students in developing the critical, intellectual attitudes and the penetrating analysis which are required for radical practice in the various domains and levels of the human services. Involved in this is a holistic analysis of the present workings of our society, of the institutional and philosophical roots of the breakdown of our system of provision, of the fundamental solutions that would lead us toward survival and liberation, of the contributions which radical practice can make to a liberation strategy, and of the nature and dynamics of radical practice in general terms and in terms of specific human services.

There are, of course, personal dilemmas and organizational conflicts implicit in the approach proposed here. Difficulties may be expected in translating it into the daily work of educators and practitioners. Universities, government, and community agencies will not be supportive; they will obstruct implementation of the approach, as these organizations are linked, directly or indirectly, to the existing social order and its policies and value premises. However, individual educators and practitioners can transcend the philosophy and the definition of reality of their organizations. This is the real meaning of individual responsibility for ethical professional practice. In contrast with "organization men" such as Lieutenant Calley at My Lai and Adolph Eichmann at Auschwitz, professionals are expected not to identify with organizational philosophies and not to follow blindly organizational directives when these philosophies and directives clash with basic human rights and social justice, to which they are committed. This means that individual educators and practitioners who accept the conceptualization of an integrated, conscious, political-professional role will have to act in accordance with their ethical commitments in spite of organizational resistance, and will gradually become focal points in a network of an emerging counterculture bent upon transforming from within the existing societal order, its values, and its institutional system.

REFORM AND RADICAL TRANSFORMATION: SHORT-RANGE AND LONG-RANGE TIME PERSPECTIVES

Solving issues of provision in a manner assuring the survival and the free and full development of humans everywhere has been shown to be predicated upon a New Renaissance involving a radical transformation of currently dominant selfish, competitive, oppressive, and inegalitarian values and institutions into community-oriented, cooperative, libertarian, and egalitarian ones. In the modern, crowded, and interdependent world, freedom, security, and self-actualization are simply not attainable for any individual or group unless they become available for all individuals and groups. Sophisticated self-interest must therefore pursue conditions conducive to survival, freedom, and fulfillment for all humans.

Such comprehensive transformations are obviously not realizable in one magic master stroke. A worldwide cultural revolution, without which the necessary institutional transformations can not become reality, requires consistent efforts by a liberation movement over an extended period of time. The movement must achieve massive reorientations of currently dominant ideas, perceptions of reality, and consciousness and corresponding fundamental redefinitions of self-interest among steadily growing segments of the population in our own and many other societies.

The time dimension implicit in this transformation process poses the difficult question of what to do in the meantime about acute human needs, suffering, and oppression, and more specifically, how to respond to now feasible reform measures. A valid solution to this dilemma seems to be not to reject the use of symptom-oriented, ameliorative reforms when they provide relief to suffering and oppression, but to expose openly and honestly their inadequacies and faulty assumptions, and their futility in terms of overcoming systemic causes of suffering and oppression. To reject reductions in suffering and oppression which can be obtained now through welfare state reforms would be cruel, inhuman, and unethical. Human suffering should never be used manipulatively in a humanistic strategy toward radical transformations.

Yet, misrepresenting reform measures which conform to the logic and institutions of capitalism as real solutions to the basic and complex existential needs of people, as promoters of reforms often do in political discourse, and refraining from exposing clearly their inadequacies in terms of the requirements of fundamental transformations, seems definitely counterproductive. Such misrepresentations and lack of openness and clarity will invariably strengthen the illusions and false consciousness which are essential to the perpetuation of the existing destructive societal order. On the other hand, unravelling the real nature and dynamics of now feasible reform measures, and openly criticizing their systems-maintenance function while using them to their limits, can even be turned into stepping stones in the struggle for fundamental transformations. Such activities can fit into a strategy of spreading consciousness of the dynamics of oppression and deprivation

and of alternative value premises and institutions. Such a consciousness would be conducive to real liberation and to the prevention of
further suffering and oppression. In this manner, reform measures
designed and initiated for the defense of the status quo can be turned
into tools for its subversion, while being used at the same time for
reducing the scope of deprivation inherent in that status quo.[10]

To move toward radical transformations by enhancing consciousness
around the use of ameliorative reforms may not be entirely satisfactory, especially with regard to the time dimension. This is only one
element of a comprehensive strategy, although it is an important one
for many severely deprived and oppressed human beings. Impatience
with the alienating, oppressive status quo is understandable, and so is
the yearning for an immediate fundamental solution, if need be, by
way of armed struggles. Yet studies of world history, of human
psychology, and of societal institutions and dynamics have a sobering
effect. Such studies reveal that quick social revolutions are unlikely to
be thorough enough in terms of real changes in values and institutions.
Human institutions and consciousness have evolved to their current
stage over very long periods of time, and fundamental changes, while
they can certainly be accelerated through systematic and consistent,
politically conscious efforts and practice, inevitably require much
time. All we can do is to carry on the movement and the struggle and
give it the intellectual and material resources at our disposal. To
become involved in that movement and struggle through our studies,
teaching, practice, and life-style, and to help our students understand
the context of this movement and struggle and the personal choices
which they must face in connection with their own involvement in the
movement for human liberation—these actions constitute, in my view,
the role of social work educators toward the solution of issues of
provision in our society.

EPILOGUE

POLITICAL ACTION
TOWARD SOCIAL EQUALITY

Implications for Social and Political Action

Now that one major objective of this study has been accomplished, namely, the development of a conceptual model of social policies and the design of a standard framework for systematic policy analysis and synthesis, it seems essential to explore implications of this conceptual model for a theory and practice of active social change, and, more specifically, for the evolution of an egalitarian and humanistic social and economic order. This exploration is of crucial importance since it is concerned with the application of the theoretical insights unraveled with the aid of the conceptual model to the world of real human problems. For, as suggested already in the introduction to this book, developing alternative social policies and understanding their dynamics and consequences are only first steps toward comprehensive, internally consistent, and humanly satisfying systems of social policies, steps which must be followed by consistent political action so that significant changes suggested by systematic policy analysis can become social realities. Conventional political approaches are, however, unlikely to suffice for this purpose, as shown in the analysis of the "Mothers' Wages" policy in the preceding chapter. That analysis clearly indicates that chances for promoting and implementing policies which involve significant departures from the established social order and its dominant value premises are slim, indeed, within the political system of that order. The central question to be addressed, therefore, in the present context is, what alternative guiding principles for social and political action toward an egalitarian and humanistic social order can be deduced from insights developed in this study concerning the common domain of social policies, societal key processes shaping this domain, and forces interacting with and constraining these key processes?[1]

Before answering, however, the foregoing challenging question it is important to clarify certain intrinsic dynamics of the established political system in American society, and of its conventional approach to the development and promotion of social policies, since they derive from, and perpetuate, the prevailing non-egalitarian, ruggedly individualistic, competitive, alienating and, in many respects, oppressive social and economic order. It is necessary to comprehend these dynamics in order to avoid being caught in them when designing alternative political approaches which should facilitate the evolution of a different societal order.

Development of social policies in American and in many other similarly organized societies tends to proceed in a fragmented and inconsistent manner in relation to different substantive elements of the common domain of social policies such as prices, wages, pensions, profits, and wealth; labor, commerce, industry, and agriculture; housing, education, health, and recreation; the needs and rights of children, women, families, and the aging; inter-group relations; social deviance; etc. The fragmentariness and inconsistencies of the "normal" processes of social policy formulation reflect their "political" nature, that is, their roots in conflicts of real or perceived interests of diverse groupings within society at large.

The various social groups which compete in the "pluralistic" political marketplace constitute, frequently, ad hoc, rather than stable organizations. They tend to organize, not around explicit values and ideologies such as liberty and equality which inspired political movements spearheading the American, the French, and several other social revolutions, but around pragmatic and concrete interests, related either to personal and group characteristics, such as age, sex, race, religion, social class and status, locality, etc., or to substantive issues, such as health, education, housing, income, taxes, etc.

Several observations concerning the foregoing organizing principles of political forces in American society seem indicated. Firstly, the personal and group characteristics, and the substantive issues around which political forces tend to crystallize, do not constitute mutually exclusive entities, but overlap in multiple ways. Consequently, individuals and groups tend to join different political organizations at the same, or at different, times, depending on the extent to which their perceived interests correspond to the objectives pursued by given "special characteristics" or "special issue" organizatons. Secondly, the apparent, relative stability of the "major political parties" in the United States does not negate the organzing principles of identity or similarity of perceived interests. For the durability of these parties seems to derive from their, by now, institutionalized function of building "grand electoral coalitions" among groups pursuing diverse interests, usually on the basis of vague and ambiguous promises, "trade-offs," and compromises. Thirdly, while then political forces tend to organize in the United States primarily around special, concrete interests, rather than around explicit sets of social policy relevant values and ideologies, the extant dynamics of political processes and organizations reflect, nevertheless, an intrinsic, very potent, though covert, commitment to an underlying ideological position. Not unexpectedly, the ideology and values implicit in these political processes correspond to the dominant value premises of American society, namely, pursuit of self-interest, competitiveness, and defense of established, and newly evolving, social and economic inequalities.

Social policies are thus shaped in the United States by an unceasing process of inter-group conflicts of interests, and competition, in the political arena, where, supposedly, every citizen and every group of citizens have equal opportunities and equal civil and political rights to promote their self-defined interests. Even if this image of the political arena were a true reflection of reality, this approach to the development of social policies would still be seriously deficient with respect to the promotion of policies concerning collective interests. For such policies, by definition, are no one's private interest, and they may, consequently, be left without adequate sponsorship in the competitive political marketplace.[2] The "ecology crisis," which has become such a prominent issue since the sixties, illustrates the serious neglect of overall societal and collective interests within the established political system. Such interests tend to be overlooked or short-changed until they reach critical dimensions.

Yet, as has been shown in many empirical studies of political processes in American society, the reality of the political marketplace bears little resemblance to the idealized image of "fair competition" under conditions of equal opportunities and equal civil rights and political power. For social and economic resources and opportunities have always been distributed unequally among individuals and groups in American society, and "real" civil rights and political power have tended to be highly correlated with the distribution of social and economic resources and opportunities. It is, therefore, not surprising that "free competition" in the political marketplace in pursuit of self-interest under existing conditions of inequality, tends to perpetuate or enhance advantages of individuals and groups who enter the competition from an advantageous position with respect to command over social and economic resources and opportunities, and tends to perpetuate disadvantages of individuals and groups who enter this free political competition handicapped by inferior social and economic opportunities.[3]

Several prominent characteristics of the American political system seem to derive from its principal source of energy, the continuous competition among different social groups in pursuit of their perceived self-interests. Perhaps most important among these characteristics is the fact that the social policy system is undergoing perpetual change as a result of ceaseless pressures and counter-pressures among various interest groups whose relative power shifts continuously as their political support increases or decreases, and as they enter into temporary coalitions or long-range alliances in pursuit of specific substantive objectives. Yet, paradoxically, in spite of perpetual changes of specific substantive policies, significant changes in the key processes of social policies — that is, in resource development, in status allocation, and, especially, in rights distribution — tend to be extremely rare. That does not mean that no changes occur in these processes for, by definition, any substantive change in a specific social policy reflects some underlying change in one or more of these key processes. However, the existing political dynamics of interest-group competition tend to facilitate merely minor, incremental changes of these key processes which are often also accompanied by compensatory changes such as special "loop-holes" in tax provisions for powerful, privileged interest groups. Thus, the eventual results of extended, and often frantic, political struggles tend to be merely new variations on long established patterns with respect to the allocation of statuses, the distribution of rights, and the development of overall societal resources. The entire process may well be summarized in the cynical adage: "the more things change, the more they remain the same."

Recent illustrations of this frustrating phenomenon are the "War on Poverty" and the "Model Cities Program" of the last Democratic administration, and the "Family Assistance Program" and the "New Economic Plan" of the current Republican administration. None of these programs has resulted, or is about to result, in thorough changes in the relative circumstances of living of major socio-economic subsegments of the population, in the overall quality of life in American society, or in intra-societal human relations.[4] Yet, all these policies have been promoted by their sponsors as measures designed to lead to major improvements in critical, social and economic conditions.

Explanations for the intrinsic futility of the perpetual changes of American social policies may be found in certain assumptions or, perhaps, illusions which seem to be shared by a majority of individuals and interest groups who compete in the political arena. These assumptions include the belief that the existing social, political, and economic systems of the United States are structurally sound, and that, therefore, policy reform should not concern itself with structural elements of the society, but should deal merely, one by one, with specific deficiencies which may exist in certain areas such as housing, health, education, etc., and which may be corrected through specific technological and professional interventions in each of these separate areas. This approach leads to a preoccupation with isolated symptoms, but leaves underlying structural causes and sources of social and economic problems untouched.

Related to the foregoing assumptions, concerning the essential soundness of the institutional structure of American society, is the corollary that social problems tend to result from personal failings of the individuals affected by these problems, rather than from the societal context in which these individuals find themselves. The widespread notions that "poor people are lazy," and that "their poverty results from their laziness," illustrate this way of thinking about social problems. Such an approach leads unavoidably into dead-end streets in terms of social policy development and intervention, for it generates policies and programs aimed at changing individuals rather than the social reality with which they are confronted.[5]

Further explanations for the futile nature of most changes in American social policies can be detected in the strategies and tactics used by the various competing interest groups, or in what is often referred to as the "rules of the political game." Central to these strategies and tactics are such notions as "feasibility," "flexibility," "compromise," "a little is better than nothing," etc.[6] Implicit in these notions is a tacit acceptance of the power relations existing in the established order, and a questionable readiness to forego the responsibilities of political leadership and political education, based on unambiguous commitment to a set of humanistic values and principles. These notions may, at times, also reflect a certain ambivalence concerning the "costs" of real changes in social policies, which may be higher than even the sponsors of the changes are willing to pay. Thus, while many reform-minded, "liberal" individuals and groups would like to eliminate poverty, exploitation, and discrimination, they seem reluctant to forego the material advantages made possible for them by the continued existence of these conditions. Because of this they may be inclined to accept "feasible compromises" which involve merely minor improvements in the circumstances of poor, exploited, and discriminated against segments of the population, but do not affect adversely the advantageous position of privileged groups. It should be noted here that while political compromises under the current system may, at times, yield limited benefits for disadvantaged groups, and may have to be accepted temporarily on this basis, it seems important not to get caught in illusions, and to mistake such incremental improvements as real and meaningful changes.

One further characteristic of the existing approach to social policy development needs to be mentioned here since it, too, derives from the dynamics of interest group competition, and since it, too, is an important factor in keeping the social policy system essentially unchanged as far as the key processes and common domain of social policies are concerned. This element is the manipulative approach employed by political leaders and organizations in order to generate support for themselves and their objectives from individuals and groups in society. Essentially this approach involves telling people what they like to hear, whether one believes in it or not; creating the impression that one agrees with, and would promote, the perceived interests and biases of potential supporters, even if one has no intention of doing so; and, in general, using any handy means to obtain support and votes for one's political endeavors, whether these means are honest and ethical or not. This manipulative approach is often rationalized by futile expectations, according to which, once one achieves political power, one would use it to promote the "common good." However, in reality, political leaders and organizations who make ambiguous and vague commitments to groups pursuing different and even conflicting interests, in order to gain political support from these groups, will find their options greatly constrained after gaining power and office, as these diverse supporters will rightfully demand fulfillment of campaign promises. And, as many political leaders and organizations may often be more concerned with the effects of their actions on their future political fortunes, than on the quality and circumstances of life in society, they are likely to be reluctant to disappoint their various political supporters. Hence, they will be caught in their own, past, manipulative schemes and promises, and will hesitate to promote real changes in the social policy system. Instead, they will "play it safe" by promoting policies involving merely incremental, non-significant changes, yet they will tend to present these policy proposals as major advances.[7] Campaign promises are rarely specific under this manipulative approach, and it is thus not too difficult to present such incremental steps as fulfillment of vague promises made in the past to groups of varying political persuasions.

There would be little reason to explore alternative approaches to the development and promotion of social policies if the existing system would result in a social and economic order in which all members of society would lead meaningful, satisfying, and self-fulfilling lives. Since, however, the circumstances of living of large segments of American society, as well as the overall quality of life and of human relations, continue to be unsatisfactory in many respects and to varying degrees, it seems imperative to search for alternative political strategies, and for approaches to the development and promotion of social policies which would assure equal rights and opportunities for self-realization to all members of society. The tentative ideas sketched below for such an alternative political approach presuppose an interdependence between the dynamics of political systems and the nature of social policies they generate, an assumption which is supported by observations of the workings of the American political system and its social policy output. To the extent, then, that this assumption is valid, it seems necessary to modify the established approach to political action if one desires to replace the now prevailing societal order with one actully based on social, economic, civil, and political equality, and on humanistic value premises.

Perhaps the most important change in this context concerns the organizing principle of political movements. The existing principle of organization which reflects a model of competition in a pluralistic marketplace among groups in pursuit of their perceived self-interests needs to be replaced by an alternative principle, namely, commitment to an explicit set of social policy relevant value premises. For equal rights and opportunities for all individuals and groups, and the collective interests of society as a whole, can simply not be realized as long as social policies are left to emerge from a process of intrinsically unfair competition among social groups commanding unequal resources and power, and striving to perpetuate and enhance advantageous positions. Thus, the existing competitive model of political action sustains, implicitly, an ideology of inequality, as each competing individual and group merely seek to improve their own circumstances of living relative to other individuals and groups, but no one promotes equality of rights for all members and groups of society.

One destructive consequence of the competitive approach tends to be that deprived groups perceive each other as threats to their respective, narrowly defined, interests, rather than realizing that the real threat to their joint interests is the principle of inequality which pervades the entire structure and fabric of society. These perceptions or, rather, mis-perceptions of deprived groups in society result often in fierce conflicts among them, with respect to the limited resources which powerful and privileged groups permit to "trickle down" through conventional, incremental social policies. The animosity between "poor Whites" and "poor Blacks," and local conflicts surrounding "Model Cities" and "O.E.O." funds and programs, reflect these sad consequences of the competitive approach, as well as the underlying, ancient, and cynical device of powerful ruling groups: "divide et impera."

Explicit value premises such as equality of social, economic, civil, and political rights and liberties, would provide a political movement organized around them with definitive criteria for evaluating existing or newly proposed social policies, and for developing its own alternative policies, irrespective of the substantive content of given policy issues. It would thus no longer be necessary to mobilize separate political action groups and lobbies whenever different issues or interests demand attention. The inefficient use of political energy, and the self-defeating fragmentation and inconsistencies which now characterize political action, could thus be avoided. A political movement committed to such value premises would also eschew existing tendencies of social policies to deal merely with the symptoms rather than the causes of social problems, and the futility of incremental, illusory changes in policies. Such a movement would focus policy development on the key issues of rechanneling resource development, reallocating statuses, and redistributing rights, and it would work for an adjustment of these key variables to levels implicit in the notion of equality. While such a movement might have to accept "feasible compromises" on a temporary basis so as to ease the circumstances of living of deprived population segments, it would neither mistake nor misrepresent such compromises as real solutions, and would continue to work for policies which conformed in every respect to its egalitarian ideology.

A political movement of the kind envisaged here would be guided in policy development by assumptions concerning the causation of social problems, which differed from the assumptions implicit in the political actions and social policy proposals of the majority of existing political forces. Its assumptions would derive from the application of egalitarian yardsticks to the analysis of social issues and problems in America and throughout the world. Such analyses would systematically bare the causes of existing individual, social, and economic problems in the structure and fabric of society, rather than disguise these causes, as is done now, by blaming individuals and groups for their problems, and deprived circumstances. Social policy proposals derived from this kind of analysis would, therefore, avoid futile programs for rehabilitating the victims of destructive social and economic conditions without simultaneously eliminating these conditions. They would focus instead primarily on restructuring society as a whole, so that all members and groups would live in circumstances conducive to the fullest possible development of their innate human potential.

Intrinsic to the egalitarian and humanistic philosophy of such an alternative political movement would be the unequivocal rejection of intergroup political competition in pursuit of special interests. For true equality of rights is only possible when no single individual or group maintains a privileged position in relation to all other individuals and groups. Consequently, a political movement committed to equality would have to work for the rights of all groups rather than merely for the special interests of some groups such as the currently deprived segments of society. Such a movement could not be directed against any segment of society. What it should be directed against is the principles of privilege, inequality, exploitation, injustice, oppression, and inhumanity, but not individuals and groups who at present derive advantages from the workings of these principles. Perhaps a major source of failure of many past and present political movements committed to egalitarian principles has been their tacit or explicit acceptance of competitive and manipulative political models. They thus tended to become involved in destructive, and often violent, conflicts with powerful and privileged interest groups and the latters' political allies from deprived population strata, rather than engage in comprehensive, constructive efforts to eliminate the principles of inequality and privilege, so as to benefit all members and groups in society, and to establish a social order truly conducive to self-realization for all. It should be emphasized in this context that the use of inter-personal and inter-group physical coercion and violence in any form would be contrary to egalitarian values implicit in the political approach suggested here as coercion and violence always involve inequalities between their agents and victims.

The ideas discussed here raise questions concerning appropriate strategies and means to be utilized by such an alternative political movement. Important departures from the existing political system are indicated in this respect. The overriding guiding principle seems to be that the strategies and means must never be in conflict with the egalitarian and humanistic philosophy of the movement. Manipulation in any form, exploitation, deception, dishonesty, and physical force, be they directed against opponents or potential supporters, are therefore ruled out as acceptable means. Clearly, then, an alternative political movement would have to evolve a radically different political style from the one fitting the existing political system and its competitive philosophy. If all human beings are valued for their intrinsically equal worth and dignity, and if they are respected by political leaders and by a movement, it is inconceivable that such a movement and its leaders should deceive and manipulate them, nor that they should withhold from them significant information.

What options, if any, for constructive, non-violent political action are then available to a movement committed to egalitarian and humanistic value premises? One most appropriate focus of intervention for political action, based on man's innate capacity for reason and for rational judgment of verifiable facts, seems to be the system of dominant beliefs and values of society. When discussing in Chapter Two the conceptual model of social policies it was suggested that a society's dominant values and ideology exert a constraining influence on the malleability of its social policy system. Therefore, if policy changes are sought beyond the range set by existing dominant value premises, these premises need first to be changed, so as to widen the scope of options for the development of alternative policies. A movement committed to the establishment of an egalitarian social order needs, therefore, to attempt to gain acceptance of its ideology among large segments of society.

Changing a society's dominant value premises is, of course, a complicated undertaking since these values pervade all aspects of its culture, its institutional structure, and its system of socialization and education. Social and behavioral sciences offer only uncertain guiding principles for large scale value change. It seems, however, valid to proceed on the assumption that self-interest as perceived by the majority of a population constitutes a major source of energy for maintaining, as well as for changing, a society's system of values. Changes in dominant values may therefore depend on changes in the perceptions of self-interest of large segments of a society. Accordingly, a crucial issue to be raised, and examined, by a political movement interested in radical change of the American social policy system, by way of thorough modifications of its dominant value premises, is whether the existing value premises of competitiveness, pursuit of narrowly perceived self-interest, and inequality of rights and opportunities are indeed conducive to the realization of the self-interest of the American people. Characteristic features of the existing social policy system which reflect these dominant value commitments are attitudes and practices of exploitation toward the natural environment and toward human beings, inequalities in circumstances of living of members and groups of society, and a high incidence of alienation in human experience and relations. The question to be examined then is whether these values and these aspects of the social policy system serve indeed the true interests of Americans.

There is, of course, no "correct" way for selecting criteria to establish the "true" interests of an individual and of an entire society or its subsegments. Any criteria one selects would involve certain value positions. The criteria suggested here are derived from an intrinsic aspect of the human condition, namely, man's innate bio-psychological drive to survive, and the value premise that all men are entitled equally to realize this basic, common, human drive. Based on this primary, common drive of perhaps all human beings, it is submitted that only those social policies which sustain life, and which enhance the quality of life and the circumstances of living of all members of a society, meet the test of true or real interests; and that social policies which undermine life, and which adversely affect the quality of life and the circumstances of living, even of some members of a society, do not meet that test.

Were one to apply this test of true interests to conditions prevailing at present in the United States, it would become obvious that the existing dominant values, and the social policies based on them, certainly fail to promote the true interests of deprived segments of the population. Their very state of deprivation, exploitation, and alienation provides ample evidence for this judgment, whatever their own perceptions concerning the realization of their interests may be.

It may help to get at this point a sense of the scope of material deprivation in America's affluent society. Using as a rough measure the "low" standard of living of the Bureau of Labor Statistics which was $7214 in the fall of 1971 for an urban family of four, one realizes that approximately one-third of the population is deprived in a material sense, for their purchasing power is below that low standard of living. Furthermore, over half the population live in households with incomes below the BLS "intermediate" standard, which in the fall of 1971 was $10,971 for an urban family of four. No doubt, then, the true interests of the majority of the population, the deprived and near-deprived segments, would benefit from policy changes aimed at eliminating their deprived circumstances by equalizing rights and opportunities for all.

Turning next to the less than 50 percent of the American population who constitute the non-deprived and privileged segments, one soon realizes that material affluence in itself does not assure a satisfactory quality of life, and realization of true interests. The American middle and upper classes seem to be in a state of social and cultural crisis. This statement could be supported with recitations of ample evidence. It should suffice, however, to mention here the serious drug problems and the alienation and disaffection among middle and upper class youth, and the "rat-race syndrome" of white-collar, professional, and managerial strata. These are, no doubt, symptoms of a social crisis. The conclusion suggested by these brief observations is that America's privileged classes fail under current conditions to realize their true human interests just as the deprived classes fail to realize theirs. The existing system of social policies and the value premises underlying it seem thus to have destructive consequences for all segments of this society. Accordingly, major changes in values, and in the social policies derived from these values, would seem to be in the true interest of all segments of society. The commitment to rugged individualism, competitiveness, and inequality seems detrimental to the well-being of all, the deprived and the privileged, and those in between. This analysis suggests that a political movement interested in promoting radical changes of values and policies through non-violent means would have to engage in active interpretation and education among all population groups in order to facilitate a more realistic understanding of the social context and its destructive and alienating dynamics, and of the extent to which the true human interests of all Americans are now not being realized. Such political re-education or re-interpretation would have to be thorough, factual, and honest, rather than superficial, misleading, and manipulative, and it would have to be mainly on an intellectual, rather than on a charismatic, emotional, non-rational basis.

The major difficulty to be coped with in this re-educational and interpretational effort are the misconceptions and the "false-consciousness"[8] which most Americans tend to develop through exposure to often stultifying and mind-crippling educational systems, mass media of communications geared to a below-average mentality, and exhortations by public officials and political leaders from the President downward, all involving oversimplified presentations of complex issues, and avoiding responsible, intellectual inquiry into such issues. These combined, lifelong influences tend to indoctrinate large segments of the population into the dominant value system of the society by constantly reinforcing the notion of the structural soundness and the superiority of "the American way of life," its "free enterprise, capitalistic system," its "competitive spirit," and a broad range of social and economic inequalities intrinsic to this way of life and system. Eventually these influences add up to an utterly distorted view of America, the world, and reality.

An alternative political movement would endeavor to overcome the false consciousness of the population, and to counter the foregoing destructive influences through overt political activities involving recruitment and organization of support on local, regional, national, and international levels, and through personal influence by its members on everyone they come in contact with, be it in an informal, social, or a formal occupational context. Teachers on all levels of educational systems, and other professionals working with individuals and groups, are likely to have many opportunities for re-educational and interpretative work, since students and intellectuals appear to be most ready to respond to such efforts. However, the message of such a movement must reach eventually every member of society. Elitism must, therefore, be avoided at all costs, and efforts would have to be made to involve all strata of society, and to organize political support on the broadest possible level.

All members of such a movement would have to view themselves as "educational agents," since the movement's principal strategy would consist of political education and re-education. Lest this notion be viewed as unethical by teachers and other professionals who might consider education a politically neutral process, it needs to be emphasized that education involves always overt and covert political components. Education involves preparation for life in society, through expansion of understanding and awareness of societal processes. In this sense it is a political process both by what it communicates, and by what it fails to communicate. It seems entirely ethical to recognize and affirm this political reality of education, and to assume consciously responsibility for this important function, rather than to deny its existence and to let it happen subconsciously. Furthermore, it should be re-emphasized that political education, as suggested here, is not to be confused with propaganda or indoctrination. Rather, it is to be a serious, intellectual process leading to thorough understanding of the dynamics of American and world society.

Adherents of such a political movement who would have to be its educational agents would assume this role in addition to their other social, occupational and professional roles. This would be similar to undertaking missionary work for religious movements, except that it would concern a mission on behalf of a secular, political, humanistic movement. Adding to one's occupational role the role of educational agent for a political movement may lead to conflicts in occupational settings, since nearly all such settings are linked in various ways to the existing social order and its policies and value premises, and since they also obtain their resources from within that order. There is no simple solution to this dilemma, yet individual responsibility for ethical action in accordance with one's conscience may have to take precedence over blind loyalty to the organization in which one is employed. By engaging in political education in their social and occupational settings movement members could gradually become focal points for an emerging counter culture.

The approach to political action sketched here seems to follow logically from the preceding line of argument, according to which social problems are products of extant social policies which must be changed radically if the problems are to be eradicated; that such radical changes of social policies require prior changes in the dominant value premises of society, and that such changes in value premises depend in turn on revisions in the perceptions and consciousness of large segments of the population with respect to their true interests and the reality in which they live.

Critics of the political philosophy and approach presented here may argue that man cannot overcome his narrow self-centeredness, that he is greedy and competitive by nature, and that the proposed political movement would be working against human nature. Science offers no definitive answers to the hypotheses implied in such claims and counter-claims. Man certainly seems to have an innate potential for self-centeredness, greed, and competitiveness. Yet he also seems to have an innate potential for acting cooperatively and for sensing fairness and justice. Besides, he has intellect and a capacity for learning from past experiences and future possibilities, and he can distinguish between different levels of interest, immediate and long-range. Which of man's many innate potentialities become dominant, manifest traits, seems to depend on socializing influences in his environment. There certainly have always been human societies which practiced high levels of cooperation, and in which man does not act as greedily, and does not compete as savagely, as he tends to do in today's American culture.[9] It consequently seems that the movement may not be going against human nature after all. Certainly, until more definitive scientific evidence becomes available, it would seem as valid to assume that environmental conditions can be designed to bring out man's potential for living cooperatively in a just and egalitarian social and economic order, as would be to assume that man is incapable by his very nature to live in such a way.

What chances to achieve its goals does then such an alternative political movement have within the existing context of American society?
Is it not naive to assume that a small, politically conscious, intellectually
oriented, and ideologically committed minority movement could
stem and reverse an overwhelming tide, and bring about a radical restructuring and reorientation of American society, especially when this
movement is also committed to avail itself only of non-violent and
ethical means? Perhaps so; therefore, no assumptions are made here
concerning the probabilities of success of such a political movement.
The dynamics and motivations of this gradually evolving and growing
movement, in America and abroad, are not based on calculations of
probabilities of success. Such a movement is coming into being because its time is here and now, because it stands for social justice which
requires no justification and no assurances of success, because an ever-
growing number of Americans and others realize that certainty of
destruction looms ahead if we continue to live by the dominant value
premises of this culture, its inhumane system of social policies, and the
competitive and manipulative political processes through which the
system perpetuates itself.

Once a thinking person fully comprehends the true situation in
America today, he no longer seems to have a choice but to turn
around and join a movement for radical change, and to ask others to
do the same, even though he is aware of the odds against such a movement, and even though he knows nothing of probabilities of success.
The road ahead for such a movement is uncertain, of course, and would
have to be determined mainly by avoiding the route which leads
with certainty toward destruction, and by being guided by principles
of social justice, equality, and humanism. Groping its way in that direction this movement would know that it has turned away from the direction of death toward the probability of life.

To broaden the scope of this discussion beyond the United States
it should be noted that social problems and social policies within any
society tend to interact in many ways with that society's worldwide,
international relations. Because of this general linkage between social
and foreign policies, solutions of extant social problems within the
United States, in accordance with the philosophy suggested here, seem
to depend also on the pursuit of foreign policies shaped by the same
egalitarian, cooperative, humanistic, and nonviolent principles implicit in that philosophy. To clarify further the linkage between social
and foreign policies, several observations are indicated concerning
"boundaries" of national societies and the general domain and functions of foreign policies.

International boundaries constitute man-made lines which reflect the workings, over time, of ecologic, biologic, psychologic, social, cultural, economic, and political forces within, and between, separate human societies. Such boundaries seem to fulfill on a worldwide scale the same functions as variously defined dividing lines between segments of national societies. In either context boundaries identify, and set apart, one aggregate of human beings from other aggregates, in order to establish, promote, and defend, exclusive claims with respect to certain rights and statuses for members of specified groups. Hence, from the perspective of mankind, the relations of national societies to worldwide society are analogous to the relations of segments of national societies to their respective national societies. The dynamics of international relations and of "foreign policies" on a worldwide scale are consequently similar, in principle, to the dynamics of inter-group relations and of social policies within national societies.

The foregoing argument suggests that the conceptual model of social policies, the framework for policy analysis and synthesis, as well as the implications of the conceptual model for social and political action, can be extrapolated to a worldwide scale by expanding the notion of "society" to encompass all of mankind. The key-variables of the conceptual model and the foci of the framework can, therefore, be used in the analysis and development of foreign policies, the common domain of which includes (a) the overall quality of life on earth, (b) the circumstances of living of various segments of world society, and (c) the relations among nations. Such analyses would reveal that many worldwide social problems and international conflicts are rooted in the ethnocentric and competitive dominant value premises of nations, and in a world order involving multi-faceted inequalities with respect to the development, distribution and allocation of life-sustaining and life-enhancing resources, rights, and statuses, just as social problems within the United States are rooted in the fabric of its non-egalitarian social and economic order, and in its dominant value premises of rugged individualism, competitiveness and inequality. The United States, it may be noted, occupies a highly privileged position in the existing world order as it controls roughly 40 percent of the world's resources and annual output, while constituting less than six percent of the world's population. It thus shares major responsibility for maintaining worldwide social and economic inequalities.

Problems in international relations seem, at times, even less amenable to reasoned solutions than social problems within national societies, since forces involved in international affairs tend to be more complex, uninhibited, and violent, and less susceptible to rational influences than intra-societal forces. However, since intra-societal and international problems seem to involve identical dynamics, though on different scales, and since both types of problems can be understood in terms of the same conceptual model, the guiding principles derived from that model for dealing with social problems within American society seem equally valid for developing constructive, just, humane, and peaceful foreign policies. For, in spite of uncertainties concerning probabilities of eventual success, the political action philosophy based on principles of equality, cooperation, humanism, and active non-violence seems to constitute, over time, the most promising approach to resolving social problems and conflicts not only on the level of local communities and national societies, but also on the international, worldwide level.

In concluding these observations one important source of resistance to social and foreign policies, based on the political philosophy advocated here, should be noted: a widespread fear, on the part of more affluent societies, and privileged segments within many societies, of significant reductions in their accustomed standards of living. Such reductions in living standards are feared to ensue, should an egalitarian social and world order replace the prevailing non-egalitarian order. This fear seems rooted in certain, long established, cultural patterns and attitudes which reflect one dominant trait of man's response to conditions of real scarcity, to wit, fierce competition for limited, essential resources, to satisfy immediate needs, and to provide security from future want for oneself, one's family, and one's social group by accumulating wealth ("securities"). Over time such competitive and acquisitive patterns became thoroughly institutionalized in many societies. By now these traits pervade many aspects of intra-societal and international human relations, and they are widely perceived as intrinsic to human nature and as essential to survival. Yet there is ample evidence that modern science and technology, and the existing worldwide economic potential could enable mankind, through cooperation rather than through competition, to organize the development and distribution of life-sustaining and life-enhancing resources in a manner which would assure to all adequate living standards and meaningful, satisfying life experiences. The fears noted above would thus seem to be largely unfounded.

It thus appears that competition and acquisitiveness in human relations within and among national societies may no longer be necessary or appropriate, but may, by now, be definitely dysfunctional, and may pose serious threats to human well-being and survival. Yet irrational fears, based on "false consciousness" with respect to existing human realities on the part of large segments of the world population, sustain the continued dominance of these dysfunctional and potentially destructive patterns. Constructive changes in consciousness, attitudes, policies, and actions become thus very difficult to achieve. Social and political action and education, aimed at establishing a just world order, need, therefore, to counteract the widespread ignorance, misconceptions, and fears which now underlie resistance to necessary changes in social and foreign policies, by demonstrating the feasibility and long-range advantages for all individuals and all nations, of an alternative order involving worldwide cooperation toward social and economic equality and justice. For it seems, a political movement promoting the implementation of egalitarian, non-competitive, non-acquisitive, and humanistic social and foreign policies will gather momentum only if, and when, ever increasing numbers of people all over the world will come to realize that a social and world order based on such policies would serve their best interests, since it could indeed assure to all mankind peace, adequate and enriching circumstances of living, improvements in the overall quality of life on earth, and enhanced opportunities for meaningful human relations and self-fulfillment.

NOTES TO FOREWORD

1. For examples from United States see:
   Howard E. Freeman and Clarence C. Sherwood, *Social Research and Social Policy*, Englewood Cliffs, N.J.: Prentice-Hall, Inc., 1970.
   S. M. Miller and Frank Riessman, *Social Class and Social Policy*, New York: Basic Books, Inc., 1968.
   Martin Rein, *Social Policy: Issues of Choice and Change*, New York: Random House, Inc., 1970.
   Alvin L. Schorr, *Explorations in Social Policy*, New York: Basic Books, Inc., 1968.

For examples from Great Britain, see:
   A. Macbeath, *Can Social Policies be Rationally Tested?*, L. T. Hobhouse Memorial Trust Lecture No. 27, King's College London, 2 May 1957, London: Oxford University Press, 1957.
   T. H. Marshall, *Social Policy*, London: Hutchinson University Press, 1965.
   Richard M. Titmuss, *Problems of Social Policy*, London: His Majesty's Stationery Office, 1950.

For example from the Netherlands, see:
   J. A. Ponsioen, ed., *Social Welfare Policy — Contributions to Theory*. The Hague, Netherlands: Mounton & Company, Publishers, 1962.

For example from Hungary, see:
   Susan Ferge, *Social Policy in Connection with Maternity and Children in Hungary after 1945*. Paper presented at an International Conference on Family Poverty and Social Policy, Manchester, England, 1969.

International studies of social policy are being undertaken by the United Nations Research Institute for Social Development, Geneva, and the sixteenth conference of the International Council on Social Welfare, held at The Hague, August 1972, had as its theme "Developing Social Policy in Conditions of Rapid Change."

NOTES TO INTRODUCTION

1. R. H. Tawney, *Equality*, London: George Allen and Unwin Ltd., 1964 (with a new introduction by Richard M. Titmuss). — First published in 1931.
2. Bernard Shaw, *The Road to Equality, Ten Unpublished Lectures and Essays, 1884-1918*, Boston: Beacon Press, 1971.

NOTES TO CHAPTER ONE

1. Alvin L. Schorr, *Explorations in Social Policy*, New York: Basic Books, Inc., 1968.
2. S. M. Miller and Frank Riessman, *Social Class and Social Policy*, New York: Basic Books, Inc., 1968.
3. S. M. Miller and Pamela Roby, *The Future of Inequality*, New York: Basic Books, Inc., 1970.
4. Frank Riessman, Editor, *Social Policy*, published six times a year by Social Policy Corporation, New York, N. Y. First issue May/June 1970.
5. T. H. Marshall, *Social Policy*, London: Hutchinson University Press, 1965, p. 7.
6. Howard E. Freeman and Clarence C. Sherwood, *Social Research and Social Policy*, Englewood Cliffs, N.J.: Prentice-Hall, Inc., 1970, p. 2.
7. Martin Rein, *Social Policy: Issues of Choice and Change*, New York: Random House, Inc., 1970, p. 3.
8. Freeman and Sherwood, *Social Research and Social Policy*, © 1970, p. 2. By permission of Prentice-Hall, Inc., Englewood Cliffs, New Jersey.
9. Rein, *Social Policy: Issues of Choice and Change*, p. 4.
10. Richard M. Titmuss, *Problems of Social Policy*, London: His Majesty's Stationery Office, 1950.
   Richard M. Titmuss, *Essays on the Welfare State*, Boston: Beacon Press, 1969. (First published 1958.)
   Richard M. Titmuss, *Income Distribution and Social Change*, London: George Allen and Unwin, Ltd., 1962.
   Richard M. Titmuss, *Commitment to Welfare*, New York: Pantheon Books, 1969.
   Richard M. Titmuss, *The Gift Relationship*, New York: Pantheon Books, 1971.
11. Rein, *Social Policy: Issues of Choice and Change*, p. 4.
12. Rein, *Social Policy: Issues of Choice and Change*, p. 5.
13. Eveline M. Burns, "Social Policy: The Stepchild of the Curriculum" in *Proceedings, Ninth Annual Program Meeting, Council on Social Work Education*, New York: Council on Social Work Education, 1961.
14. Charles I. Schottland, personal communication.
15. National Association of Social Workers, *Goals of Public Social Policy*, New York: National Association of Social Workers, 1963.
16. Kenneth E. Boulding, "Boundaries of Social Policy," *Social Work*, Vol. 12, No. 1, January 1967, p. 3-11.
17. Marshall, *Social Policy*, p. 7.
18. Titmuss, *Commitment to Welfare*, p. 192.
19. Titmuss, *Commitment to Welfare*, pp. 192-93.
20. Peter Townsend, "Strategies in Meeting Poverty," paper presented at the International Conference on Family Poverty and Social Policy, Manchester, England, September 20, 1969.
21. A. Macbeath, *Can Social Policies be Rationally Tested?*, L. T. Hobhouse Memorial Trust Lecture No. 27, King's College London, 2 May 1957. London: Oxford University Press, 1957.
22. J. A. Ponsioen, "General Theory of Social Welfare Policy," in J. A. Ponsioen, ed., *Social Welfare Policy — Contributions to Theory*, The Hague, The Netherlands: Mounton & Company, Publishers, 1962 (Volume III, Series Maior, Publications of the Institute of Social Studies), p. 18.
23. Harold L. Wilensky and Charles N. Lebeaux, *Industrial Society and Social Welfare*, New York: Russell Sage Foundation, 1958, pp. 138-40.

NOTES TO CHAPTER TWO

1. George A. Theodorson and Achilles G. Theodorson, *A Modern Dictionary of Sociology*, New York: Thomas Y. Crowell Co., 1969, p. 261.

2.   See Theodorson and Theodorson, *A Modern Dictionary of Sociology*, p.398, for a similar definition of society. (The phrase between quotation marks is borrowed from that work.)

3.   Eleanor B. Sheldon and Wilbert E. Moore, eds., *Indicators of Social Change — Concepts and Measurement*, New York: Russell Sage Foundation, 1968; Jan Drewnowski, *Studies in the Measurement of Levels of Living and Welfare*, United Nations Research Institute for Social Development, Report No. 70.3, Geneva 1970; Jan Drewnowski, Claude Richard-Proust & Muthu Subramanian, *Studies in the Methodology of Social Planning*, United Nations Research Institute for Social Development, Report No. 70.5, Geneva 1970; Donald V. McGranahan, "Analysis of Socio-Economic Development Through a System of Indicators," *The Annals*, Vol. 393, January 1971; Jan Drewnowski, "The Practical Significance of Social Information," *The Annals*, Vol. 393, January 1971.

4.   The following discussion of "status" and "role" is based in part on Ralph Linton, *The Study of Man*, New York: Appleton-Century-Crofts, Inc., 1936, pp. 113-115.

5.   David Macarov, *Incentives to Work*, San Francisco: Jossey-Bass, 1970.

NOTES TO CHAPTER THREE

1.   Frances Fox Piven, Richard Cloward, *Regulating the Poor: The Functions of Public Welfare*, New York: Pantheon Books, Random House, 1971.

For an interpretation of the important concept of "secondary labor market" see Michael J. Piore, "Jobs and Training," in Samuel H. Beer and Richard E. Barringer, eds., *The State and the Poor*, Cambridge, Mass.: Winthrop Publishers, Inc., 1970.

2.   Mollie Orshansky, "Counting the Poor: Another Look at the Poverty Profile," *Social Security Bulletin*, January 1965, pp. 3-29.

Mollie Orshansky, "Who's Who Among the Poor: A Demographic View of Poverty," *Social Security Bulletin*, July 1965, pp. 3-32.

U. S. Department of Commerce, Bureau of the Census, *Current Population Reports*, Series P-23, No. 28, August 12, 1969 — Revisions in Poverty Statistics, 1959 to 1968.

3.   Eleanor B. Sheldon and Wilbert E. Moore, eds., *Indicators of Social Change — Concepts and Measurement*, New York: Russell Sage Foundation, 1968; Otis Dudley Duncan, *Toward Social Reporting: Next Steps*, New York: Russell Sage Foundation, 1969; U. S. Department of Health, Education, and Welfare, *Toward a Social Report*, Washington, D.C.: U. S. Government Printing Office, 1969; Raymond A. Bauer, Editor, *Social Indicators*, Cambridge, Massachusetts, and London, England: The M.I.T. Press, 1966; Jan Drewnowski, *Studies in the Measurement of Levels of Living and Welfare*, United Nations Research Institute for Social Development, Report No. 70.3, Geneva 1970; Jan Drewnowski, Claude Richard-Proust & Muthu Subramanian, *Studies in the Methodology of Social Planning*, United Nations Research Institute for Social Development, Report No. 70.5, Geneva 1970; Donald V. McGranahan, "Analysis of Socio-Economic Development Through a System of Indicators," *The Annals*, Vol. 393, January 1971; Jan Drewnowski, "The Practical Significance of Social Information," *The Annals*, Vol. 393, January 1971.

4.   Mike Reddin,"Universality Versus Selectivity" in William A. Robson and Bernard Crick, eds., *The Future of the Social Services*, Harmondworth, Middlesex, England: Penguin Books Ltd., 1970.

NOTES TO CHAPTER FOUR

1.   David G. Gil, "Mothers' Wages — One Way to Attack Poverty," *Children*, Vol. 15, No. 6, November-December 1968. Reprinted in *Social Service Outlook*, Vol. 4, No. 4, April 1969.

"Mothers' Wages — An Alternative Attack on Poverty," in *Social Work Practice*, 1969, New York: Columbia University Press, 1969 (published for the National Conference on Social Welfare).
2.   See Chapter 2, p. 25.
3.   See Chapter 2, p. 25
4.   See this chapter, pp. 65-67.
5.   Mike Reddin, "Universality versus Selectivity" in William A. Robson and Bernard Crick, editors, *The Future of the Social Services*, Harmondsworth, England: Penguin Books, 1970.
    Eveline M. Burns, editor, *Children's Allowances and the Economic Welfare of Children*, New York: Citizens' Committee for Children of New York, Inc., 1968.
    Christopher Green, *Negative Taxes and the Poverty Program*, Washington, D.C.: The Brookings Institution, 1967.

Note: To avoid misunderstandings it needs to be pointed out, parenthetically, that the assumptions concerning the advantages and disadvantages of universal and selective income transfer mechanisms oversimplify a complex technical issue. First of all, the differentiation between the two approaches is not absolute since each approach contains elements of the other. Thus, universal entitlement programs such as the Children's Allowance involve a "delayed" means test and also "indirect" work incentive features through the income tax mechanism. Negative income taxes, on the other hand, involve "universal entitlement" since all individuals within a category defined by income are entitled to benefits. Secondly, as far as the economic efficiency argument is concerned, negative income taxes lose efficiency because of the direct work incentive feature. Because of the indirect work incentive feature of Children's Allowances this approach may, in fact, result in higher economic efficiency than is generally realized. This would depend on the provisions of the income tax. Thirdly, the arguments concerning societal cohesiveness and solidarity are also inconclusive since these social phenomena depend less on technical aspects of an income transfer system than on the general value orientations of a society. Given an overall egalitarian and humanistic value system, either transfer mechanism would be conducive to social cohesiveness and solidarity. On the other hand, an individualistic, non-egalitarian value system is likely to result in tension and conflict between recipients of transfer payments and taxpayers, irrespective of the transfer techniques employed. In summary then, important as the technical aspects of income transfers are, the more significant issues seem to be the size of the transfers, the extent to which they are intended to eliminate inequalities, and the value premises underlying the transfer policy.

6.   U. S. Department of Commerce, Bureau of the Census, *Consumer Income, Current Population Reports*, Series P-60, No. 78, May 20, 1971, p. 1.
7.   U. S. Department of Labor, News Release USDL-11-606, December 21, 1970, p. 1.
8.   U. S. Department of Commerce, Bureau of the Census, *Consumer Income, Current Population Reports*, Series P-60, No. 77, May 7, 1971, Tables No. l, p. 2; No. 4, p. 5; No. 6, p. 6.
9.   U. S. Department of Health, Education and Welfare, Social Security Administration, *Social Security Bulletin*, Vol. 34, No. 6, June 1971, Table M-24, p. 46.

The apparent discrepancy between the number of poor families headed by women in 1970, namely 1.7 million, and the number of families participating in the AFCD program at the end of 1970, namely 2.6 million, seems due to the following circumstances: AFDC payments are available in many states not only to female-headed families but also to male-headed families when fathers are unemployed and have exhausted unemployment benefits. Furthermore, poverty figures are estimates based on annual sample surveys and are subject to sampling errors, whereas figures of AFDC recipients are based on actual counts. There has been a steep increase in the number of AFDC recipients during 1970 from 1,875,000 families at the beginning of the year to 2,553,000 families at the end of that year. Finally, eligibility for AFDC is determined on the basis of circumstances prevailing at the point of application while poverty is measured on the basis of income in the course of an entire year. Hence, families whose

total income during 1970 exceeded the poverty level may, nevertheless, be entitled to AFDC payments at any time during the year when they may be without sufficient income.

10.   U. S. Department of Commerce, Bureau of the Census, *Consumer Income, Current Population Reports*, Series P-60, No. 77, May 7, 1971, Table No. 9, p. 8.

11.   U. S. Department of Commerce, Bureau of the Census, *Consumer Income, Current Population Reports*, Series P-60, No. 77, May 7, 1971, Table No. 1, p. 2 and Table No. 4, p. 5.

12.   U. S. Department of Commerce, Bureau of the Census, *Consumer Income, Current Population Reports*, Series P-60, No. 77, May 7, 1971, Table No. 1, p. 3 and Table No. 4, p. 5.

13.   U. S. Department of Commerce, Bureau of the Census, *Consumer Income, Current Population Reports*, Series P-60, No. 78, May 20, 1971, Table No. 2, p. 3.

14.   U. S. Department of Commerce, Bureau of the Census, *Statistical Abstract of the United States*, 1970, Table No. 44, p. 38.

15.   U. S. Department of Commerce, Bureau of the Census, *Consumer Income, Current Population Reports*, Series P-60, No. 76, December 16, 1970, Table No. 8, p. 51.

16.   U. S. Department of Commerce, Bureau of the Census, *Consumer Income, Current Population Reports*, Series P-60, No. 76, December 16, 1970, Table No. 8, p. 51.

17.   U. S. Department of Commerce, Bureau of the Census, *Consumer Income, Current Population Reports*, Series P-60, No. 75, December 14, 1970, Table 11, p. 26.

This table reveals that since 1947, the lowest fifth of families received consistently about 5 percent of aggregate income, the second lowest fifth about 12 percent, the third fifth about 18 percent, the fourth fifth about 23 percent and the highest fifth about 41 percent. The top 5 percent of families received consistently about 15 percent of aggregate income. The income distribution for black families is even more skewed, and so is the distribution for unrelated individuals.

18.   To shorten this illustrative analysis actual projections of the numerical size of target segments have been omitted. The technique for obtaining these estimates is quite simple. It involves applying general population projections of the U. S. Bureau of the Census to portions of the population included in the target segments, e.g., children under age 18, mothers, families with children, percentiles of the income distribution, racial minorities, etc.

19.   See this chapter, p. 68.

20.   U. S. Department of Commerce, Bureau of the Census, *Consumer Income, Current Population Reports*, Series P-60, No. 77, May 7, 1971, Table 6, p. 6.

21.   Florence A. Ruderman, *Child Care and Working Mothers*, New York: Child Welfare League of America, Inc., 1968, p. 153.

22.   The New York Times, January 18, 1969: "Treasury Secretary Warns of Taxpayers Revolt."

23.   Eveline M. Burns, Editor, *Children's Allowances and the Economic Welfare of Children*, New York: Citizens' Committee for Children of New York, Inc., 1968.

24.   New York Times, Editorial, "Reversing a Welfare Trend . . .," July 10, 1971.

25.   Florence A. Ruderman, *Child Care and Working Mothers*, New York: Child Welfare League of America, Inc., 1968.

Child Welfare League of America, *The Changing Dimensions of Day Care: Highlights from Child Welfare*, New York: 1970.

Seth Low and Pearl G. Spindler, *Child Care Arrangements of Working Mothers in the United States*, Washington, D.C.: Superintendent of Documents, 1968, (Children's Bureau Publication No. 461-1968).

Marvin Bloom and Frank J. Hodges, "Day Care Centers?," *The Humanist*, Vol. 31, No. 4, July/August, 1971, p. 33.

26.   See this chapter, p. 92.

27.   David G. Gil, "Mothers' Wages—One Way to Attack Poverty," *Children*, Vol. 15, No. 6, November-December, 1968, pp. 229-230; reprinted in *Social Service Outlook*, Vol. 4, No. 4, April 1969, pp. 1-2.

David G. Gil, "Mother's Wages—An Alternative Attack on Poverty," in *Social Work Practice, 1969,* New York: Columbia University Press, 1969, pp. 187-197.

For a sampling of press reactions to the Mothers' Wages policy proposal see: *The Christian Science Monitor,* July 29, 1968; *The Evening Star,* Washington, D.C., May 27, 1969; *Daily News,* New York City, June 2, 1969; *The Times,* London, England, June 3, 1969; *Daily News,* Philadelphia, Pa., August 1, 1969; *Family Weekly,* February 1, 1970; *Sunday Express and News,* San Antonio, Texas, October 3, 1971. For a similar proposal see: William V. Shannon, "A Radical, Direct, Simple, Utopian Alternative to Day Care Centers," *The New York Times Magazine,* April 30, 1972.

28. Pierre Larogue, editor, *Les Institutions Sociales de la France,* Paris: La Documentation Francaise, 1963. English translation: M. M. Philip Gaunt and Noel Lindsay, *Social Welfare in France.* See especially: *Part II:* French Family Policy and its Achievements, *Section B:* The Equalization of Family Liabilities, *II Family Benefits:* The Single Wage Allowance, pp. 455-456, Mother in the Home Allowance, p. 457.

29. Susan Ferge, *Social Policy in Connection with Maternity and Children in Hungary after 1945.* Paper presented at an International Conference on Family Poverty and Social Policy, University of Manchester, Manchester, England, September 1969.

30. James C. Vadakin, *Children, Poverty, and Family Allowances* with a Foreword by Daniel P. Moynihan, New York and London: Basic Books, Inc., 1968.

31. The following publications during the late 1960s reflect these efforts: Alvin L. Schorr, *Poor Kids,* New York and London: Basic Books, Inc., 1966.

James C. Vadakin, *Children, Poverty, and Family Allowances* with a Foreword by Daniel P. Moynihan, New York and London: Basic Books, Inc., 1968.

Eveline M. Burns, Editor, *Children's Allowances and the Economic Welfare of Children,* New York: Citizens' Committee for Children of New York, Inc., 1968.

Children's Allowance Project, *Why We Need Children's Allowances in the United States—A Proposal,* New York: Citizen's Committee for Children of New York, Inc., 1969.

Vera Shlakman, *Children's Allowances,* New York: Citizen's Committee for Children of New York, Inc. (A publication of the Children's Allowance Project) 1969.

32. Evidence for the government's interest in the children's allowance concept is reflected in the following excerpt from the *Fiscal Year 1969 Plan, Research and Demonstrations, Community Action Program, Office of Economic Opportunity.* This document is dated October 14, 1968, and was approved by Mr. Bertrand M. Harding, Acting Director of OEO on November 25, 1968. The excerpt is from pages 47 and 48:

FY 1968 $1,279,886
FY 1969 $1,950,000

V. Income Maintenance—Nearly half of those in poverty are children. In the consideration of strategies for income maintenance, children's allowances similar to those in effect in Canada and European countries have been much discussed. There is as yet, however, no operational children's allowance model in the United States on which to base a comparison with alternate income maintenance systems. R&D will fund a children's allowance demonstration in an urban model cities neighborhood together with related research to provide a model for comparison with other systems, and to answer the numerous speculative questions which have so far been unanswered by individual prejudices and conjecture. The question of particular relevance is the effect, if any, on birth rates associated with a system of children's allowances, and particular attention will be placed upon this question in the research design of the project. Other research questions would be the effects of such an allowance on consumer behavior; effects on patterns of child rearing; whether it might vary patterns of labor force participation differently than under income maintenance programs (such as the Graduated Work Inventive Experiment); and the effects of a direct transfer of money to families in the poverty environment. This project will be developed with other Federal agencies, with each sharing resources and talent in order to develop a well-designed

children's allowance model, and to participate in financing transfer payments and related research and evaluation. The groundwork for such an effort is already being laid. (1. Model Children's Allowance $500,000)

Additional funding of our graduated work incentives experiment will be required in Fiscal Year 1969. (2. Graduated Work Incentives Experiment $1,400,000)

Income Maintenance Priority List

1. Model Children's Allowance	500,000
2. Graduated Work Incentive Experiment	1,400,000
TOTAL:	1,950,000
REFUNDING TOTAL:	1,400,000

As further evidence of the government's interest in experimenting with the children's allowance policy see the following news story:

Martin F. Nolan, "U.S., Brandeis Eye Family Allowance Trial," in *The Boston Globe*, May 1, 1969.

33. Richard L. Strout, "Nixon Aides Argue Merits of Family Aid Plans," *The Christian Science Monitor*, New England Edition, Weekend Edition, June 21-23, 1969.

34. See this chapter, pp. 75-76.

35. See Chapter 2, pp 27-28.

36. See this chapter, p. 68.

37. See Chapter 3, pp. 55-56. Readers with special substantive interest in the issues dealt with by the mothers' wages policy may, however, wish to conduct a comprehensive analysis of the two alternative policies, and in doing so would obtain a more valid and reliable basis for comparing and evaluating the several policies, and would also gain experience with, and further insight into, the analytic approach.

NOTES TO CHAPTER 5

1.   William Ryan, *Blaming the Victim*, New York: Pantheon Books, 1971.
2.   Peter L. Berger & Thomas Luckmann, *The Social Construction of Reality*, Garden City, New York: Doubleday & Co., 1970.
3.   Peter Kropotkin, *Mutual Aid — A Factor in Evolution*, Boston, Mass.: Porter Sargent, 1956. Originally published in 1902. Martin Buber, *Paths in Utopia*, Boston, Mass.: Beacon Press, 1958; Rosabeth M. Kanter, *Commitment and Community*, Cambridge, Mass.: Harvard University Press, 1972.
4.   R.H. Tawney, *The Acquisitive Society*, New York: Harcourt, Brace, & Co., 1920.
5.   Frances Fox Piven, Richard A. Cloward, *Regulating the Poor: The Functions of Public Welfare*, New York: Pantheon Books, 1971.
6.   Ruth Benedict, "Synergy," *American Anthropologist*, 1970, pp. 320-333; Reprinted in *Psychology Today*, June 1970, pp. 51-77.
7.   Karl Hess, *Dear America*, New York: William Morrow, 1975.
8.   e.g., for more recent works, see Robert L. Heilbroner, *An Inquiry Into the Human Prospect*, New York: W.W. Norton, 1975; Barry Commoner, *The Closing Circle*, New York: Alfred Knopf, 1971, Nicholas Georgescu-Roegen, "Energy and Economic Myths," *Southern Economic Journal*, January 1975; Mihajlo Mesarovic and Eduard Pestel, *Mankind at the Turning Point*, New York: Dutton & Co., 1974, George Wald, "Arise Ye Prisoners of Extinction," 20th World Conference Against A & H Bombs, 1974, also in *New York Times*, 8/17/74; E.F. Schumacher, *Small Is Beautiful*, New York: Harper & Row, 1973.
9.   Paulo Freire, *Pedagogy of the Oppressed*, New York: Herder and Herder, 1970.
10.   André Gorz, *Strategy for Labor*, Boston: Beacon Press, 1967; idem, *Socialism and Revolution*, Garden City, N.Y.: Anchor Press/Doubleday, 1973.

NOTES TO THE EPILOGUE

1. See Chapter 2, especially Chart 2.2, p. 29.

2. Roger Strait, "We CAN Become Responsible," *Journal* (United Church of Christ), Vol. 9, No. 4, Jan.-Feb. 1971, pp. 4-11.

3. Gabriel Kolko, *Wealth and Power in America—An Analysis of Social Class and Income Distribution,* New York, Washington, London: Praeger Publishers, 1962.

    C. Wright Mills, *The Power Elite,* New York: Oxford University Press, 1956.

    S. M. Miller, Pamela Roby, *The Future of Inequality,* New York and London: Basic Books, Inc., 1970.

4. Peter Marris and Martin Rein, *Dilemmas of Social Reform,* New York: Atherton Press, 1967.

    Stephen M. Rose, *The Betrayal of the Poor,* Cambridge. Schenkman Publishing Co., 1972.

    Roland L. Warren, "The Sociology of Knowledge and the Problem of the Inner Cities," *Social Science Quarterly,* December, 1971.

    Eveline M. Burns, "Welfare Reform and Income Security Policies" in *The Social Welfare Forum, 1970,* New York and London: National Conference on Social Welfare, Columbia University Press, 1970, pp. 46-60.

    Alvin L. Schorr in "Two Views on the Welfare Plan," *New York Times,* December 1, 1970.

5. William Ryan, *Blaming the Victim,* New York: Pantheon Books, 1971.

6. Robert Morris and Robert H. Binstock, with the collaboration of Martin Rein, *Feasible Planning for Social Change,* New York and London: Columbia University Press, 1966.

7. An apt illustration of this tendency is Dr. Daniel P. Moynihan's article "One Step We Must Take" (Saturday Review, May 23, 1970, pp. 20-23), in which he describes President Nixon's Family Assistance Program in the following manner:

    ". . . Then came the Family Assistance Plan, the single most important piece of social legislation to be sent to the Congress in a generation (or really two generations as we count them today) and the social initiative that will almost surely define the beginning of a new era in American social policy. The legislation establishes a floor under the income of every American family with children. It provides incentives for work and opportunities for work training, job placement, and child care.

    The Family Assistance Plan is not an incremental change—a marginal improvement in an old program. It is a new departure in social policy, emerging from a new mode of analysis of social processes. Indeed, it is something more than just that. The Social Security Act, the only comparable legislation in American history, was after all mostly a compendium of ideas we had got from Lloyd George, who had got them from Bismarck. With Family Assistance, the United States takes its place as the leading innovator in the world in the field of social policy. Soon, I expect, we shall be seen as an exporter of social programs to Europe, reversing a century in which the flow has been from Europe to us.

    . . . Yet at this very moment it is within the power of that great majority of the American people who love their nation—who wish to see it healed and whole—to enact a social program that will cause future generations to regard us as an anguished and often agonizing people who were somehow touched with glory. Others would say, and I would not deny, that recognizing it or not, what posterity will in fact be contemplating is a generation of Americans who for all their failings were capable of great things and did great things."

When writing this article Dr. Moynihan was Counselor to President Nixon and was actively promoting the administration's welfare reform plan which he had helped to design. The income floor referred to in this excerpt was to be $1600 in cash and $894 in foodstamps per year for a family of four. This amount was merely two-thirds of the government's own, unrealistically low, poverty threshold ($3720 in 1970). It was also lower than public assistance rates prevailing at the time in 42 states. Thus, in spite of the

rhetoric in this article, implementation of the Family Assistance Plan as proposed by President Nixon and passed by the House of Representatives in 1970, and again in 1972 in a somewhat different version would have hardly changed the relative distribution of rights, statuses, and resources among socio-economic strata of the U.S. population.

8. For a discussion of the concept "false consciousness" see: Karl Mannheim, *Ideology and Utopia*, New York: A Harvest Book—Harcourt, Brace and Company, 1936. (First published in Germany in 1929.) See especially Chapter II, section 9: The Problem of False Consciousness, pp. 94-97.

9. Petr Kropotkin, *Mutual Aid—A Factor of Evolution*, Harmondsworth, Middlesex, England: Penguin Books Limited, 1939, also Boston, Mass. Extending Horizons Books, Porter Sargent (no date), originally published in 1902.

   Ruth Benedict, "Synergy—Patterns of the Good Culture," *Psychology Today*, June 1970.

INDEX

Abortions, 80
Aid to Families with Dependent Children (AFDC), 72, 74, 77, 80, 82, 85, 105
Alcoholism, 92
Alienation, 149, 150, 187, 188
Alternative social orders, fear of, 169
American way of life, The, 188
Auschwitz, 172
Automation, 79, 82, 111, 133
Automobiles, 51

Bill of Rights, 45, 111
Birthrate, 79, 90, 97, 112, 160, 200
Boundaries, international, 192
Boulding, Kenneth E., 6
Buber, Martin, 157
Budgets
    defense, 109-110; federal, 108
Bureau of Labor Statistics (BLS), 54, 70, 187
Burns, Eveline M., 5

Capitalism, 67, 154
Capitalist system, 154
Capitalist Welfare States, 148-149, 153-155;
    society in, 144; social services in, 153-155
Census, U.S. Bureau of, 42, 71
Childbearing, 59, 60, 62, 93
Child care, 66, 68, 69, 70, 71, 85, 114, 120, 124, 131, 202;
    alternative societal, 116; services, 84, 121, 122, 123, 124, 126, 127, 128, 130, 131, 132, 133, 134; sharing of, 115-116; wages for, 120
Child development, 122, 123, 124, 134
Childrearing, 59-60, 93, 108, 111, 114, 123, 129, 200
Children, 63, 85, 126;

with exceptional needs, 121; exploitation of, 65; and families, 95; number of, 90-91; and parents, 65, 94, 95, 102, 103, 128, 132; rights and status of, 63, 64, 65-66, 69, 71, 85, 108, 111, 124, 129
Children's allowances, xvi, 48, 54, 68, 69, 74, 86, 87, 100, 101, 113, 121, 124, 126, 132-133, 198;
    aggregate amounts of, 76; analysis of, 59-177; financing of, 61; history of, 96-98; research on, 200; standard rate for, 70; table of, 75; tax policies and, 103-104
Circumstances of living, xiv, xvi, 13, 16-17, 18, 20, 24, 25, 35, 36, 43, 46-48, 51, 71, 114, 116, 125, 133;
    of children and families, 113; indicators of, 14, 47; and key processes, 15; and Mothers' Wages policy, 88-96; worldwide, 192-194
Collectivism, 27, 67, 68, 109, 110, 113, 130, 144
Common domain, 12, 13-15, 25, 32, 34-35, 37, 43, 47, 52;
    definition of, 13; and Mothers' Wages policy, 83-96
Common Law, 45
Competition, 27, 67, 113, 114, 130, 178-179, 183, 185, 186, 188, 189, 192
Compromises, political, 182, 184
"Conservative" position, 151-152
Constraints, 21, 34, 46
Consumption, 84
Cooperation, 27, 67, 113, 114, 193
Cost of living, 97
Counter culture, 188
Crime, 92
Cybernation, 79, 82, 111, 133

Day care, 84, 107
Decision making, 142-143;
  criteria for participation in, 142, 143
Declaration of Independence, xvi, 111
Democracy, xiii
Demogrants, universal, 45, 48, 53
Deprivation, 64, 78, 107, 140, 187
Deprived segments of society, 140
Discrimination, 181-182
Distribution, patterns of, 140;
  and deprivation, 140; of provisions, 144
Division of labor, *See also* Status allocation, 19-20, 24, 25;
  in families, 120, 122, 123; and inequality of rights, 22; as key process, 15-16; sex as basis for, 65
Dominant philosophical concepts, 193;
  reinforced by societal solutions to issues of provisions, 144

Ecology crisis, 179
Economists, 101
Economy, 133
Education, 63, 85-86, 90, 91, 112;
  in America, 188; as political process, 151; special programs, 107
Egalitarian society, 144-145, 164;
  vs. inegalitarian society, 147
Egalitarianism, 109, 110, 114, 130, 144-145, 185, 193
  and Mothers' Wages policy, 114-116; and Parents' Wages policy, 127, 128
Eichmann, Adolph, 172
Elitism, 151
Entitlements, 21, 23, 34, 44, 45, 46; 142
  universal, 69-70, 87, 195

Equality, xvi, 27, 67, 68. 122, 156, 191, 193, 194
  vs. inequality, 113-114
Equality of rights, 156
Ethnocentric principles, 156, 157
European social-democratic labor parties, 150
Exploitation, 66, 115, 181, 182, 187

Fair Labor Standards Act, 60
Familial relations, 48, 91-92, 93
Families, 59;
  headed by women, 73, 74; life in, 125-126, 131, 134; Mothers' Wages policies and, 99-100, 113; of racial minorities, 73; single parent, 94-95
Family Assistance Program (FAP), 74, 77, 98, 105, 180, 202
Fathers, 68, 82, 94, 120, 122, 134; status of, 85, 124
Fertility, 79, 112
Food stamps, 105, 202
Food supply, 160
Framework for policy analysis and synthesis, 31-56, 135, 136;
  analytic objectives of, 32; chart of, 33-35; illustration of, 59-139; interpretation of, 36; worldwide scale of, 192
Free enterprise system, 101, 106, 109, 113, 188-189
Freeman, Howard E., 4
Freire, Paulo, 157
Fromm, Erich, 157
Future provision trends, 156

Goods and services, 18-19, 21, 26, 46, 83-84, 111, 124, 132
"Great Society," 151
Gross National Product (G.N.P.), 9, 60, 77, 87;
  as index of resource development, 18-19
Group, definition of, 11

Headstart, 40, 107

Health, 82, 90, 91, 103;
  maintenance policies, 108; mental, 91, 134

Hess, Karl, 157

Hierarchial states, 147-148

Highway construction, 38

Homemaking, 114, 115

Housing, 82, 91, 105, 111, 134; public, 38, 105-106

Human condition, 16, 25

Human nature, 152

Human potential, xiii, xvi

Human societies, 143;
  mutual aid and cooperation among, 143; shared perceptions and definitions among, 143; patterns evolved for distribution of provisions, 142; needs of as affecting choices and priorities, 141; dominant conceptions concerning worth of, 143

Humans, role of in resolving issues of provision, 143

Hunger, elimination of, 39

Income, distribution of, 54, 71, 73, 78, 92;
  of families with children under 18, 71; low, 72; mean, 70; median, 70, 74; transfers, 70, 96, 101, 109, 116, 117, 119-120, 160

Income maintenance, 37, 41, 48, 98;
  work incentives in, 49, 54, 70, 198, 201, 202

Income tax, 44, 61, 69, 70, 78;
  children's allowances and, 97-98; negative, 48, 53, 54, 69, 98, 100

Individual, early internalizing of established systems of provision, 144;
  potential for new choices and actions, 144

Individualism, 27, 67, 68, 113, 130, 188; 192

Inegalitarian society, 144, 145-147;
  human relations in, 145; vs. Egalitarian societies, 147

Inequality, 45-46, 67, 68, 114, 130, 188, 192
  and child care, 122; economic 83, 85, 179; vs. equality, 113-114; ideology of, 183; Mothers' Wages policy and, 116; principle of, 184, 185; of rights, 120, 125, 131, 186; social, xvii, 3, 27, 66-67

Information, withholding of, 164

Interest groups, 180-183

Internal Revenue Services 119-120

International Encyclopedia of Social Sciences, 139

International Institute of Social Studies, 8

International relations, 192-193

Intra-societal relationships, 13, 14-15, 17, 18, 24, 25, 35, 36, 43, 46, 48, 126, 180;
  and key processes, 15; and Mothers' Wages policy, 88-96; types of, 14

Juvenile delinquency, 92

Key processes, 15-23, 27, 32, 34-35, 47, 48, 55;
  interaction between, 22-23; modifications of, 18, 43, 52; Mothers' Wages policy and, 83-96

Keynes, John Maynard, 151

King, Martin Luther, 157

Labor unions, 48

"Laissez-faire" philosophy, 150

Leadership, qualifications for, 164-165

Lebeaux, Charles N., 9

"Liberal" position, 150-153

Life styles, 90, 92

Loan guarantees, 101
Lobbies, 184

Macbeath, A., 7-8
Magna Charta, 45
Manpower training, 107
Marcuse, Herbert, 157
Marriage, 93
Marshall, T. H., 4, 6
Mass media, 150
Means tests, 100, 106, 119, 127,
    128,   198
Medicaid, 105, 151
Medical services, 90, 108
Medicare, 90, 118, 151
Mental retardation, 82, 134
Miller, S. M., 3
Minimum wage, 41, 44, 53, 60, 70,
    74, 87
Models, definition of, 11
Model cities, 151
Motherhood, 61, 85;
    and child care, 114-115, 120,
    129, 132
Mothers, 104, 115, 120, 122, 127;
    and employers, 95; employ-
    ment of, 75, 76, 78-79; ex-
    ploitation of, 113, 115, 131;
    self-image of, 80, 82, 94, 133;
    status of, 85, 124
Mothers' Wages, 124;
    aggregate amount of, 76-77;
    standard rate for, 70; table of,
    75; uniform rate of, 71
Mothers' Wages policy, xvi, xvii,
    48, 54;
    and alternative policies, 118-
    135; analysis of, 59-135, 177;
    benefits of, 81-82, 83; and
    child development, 80, 82, 95;
    and common domain, 83-96;
    costs of, 82-83, 134; and cul-
    tural development, 111-112;
    and economy, 88-89, 111;
    effects of, 74-83, 102, 103;
    and employment, 60-61; and
    extra-societal forces, 108-111;

financing of, 61, 77-78; and
    foreign policies, 108-111; his-
    tory of, 96-98; and institu-
    tions, 111; issues dealt with
    by, 62-67; and key processes,
    83-96; and marriage and
    family life, 80, 82; and natural
    environment, 102-103; non-
    target segments of, 72, 88, 89,
    116; objectives of, 68; politi-
    cal reaction to, 68-69, 98-102,
    105, 116-118; and population,
    112; sex bias of, 115-116,
    118, 120-121; target segments
    of, 71-74, 88; and taxes, 80-
    81, 103-104; theories under-
    lying, 69-71; value premises
    of, 68-69, 112-116, 120
Mothers' Wages policy, selective,
    xvi;
    analysis of, 121-130; conclu-
    sions and predictions for, 129-
    130; cost of, 123, 129, 134;
    effects of, 123-125; and
    foreign and defense policies,
    128; history of, 126; issues
    dealt with by, 121; and key
    processes, 124-125; and natu-
    ral environment, 127; objec-
    tives of, 121-122; and other
    policies, 127; political reac-
    tions to, 126-127, 129-130; and
    societal development, 128-129;
    target segments of, 123;
    theories underlying, 122; value
    premises of, 122, 129
Motivation, human, 23
Moynihan, Daniel P., 202
Myrdal, Gunnar, 4

National Association of Social
    Workers, 5-6
National Conference on Social
    Welfare, 96
National health service, 44, 48,
    108

Needs, 146;
  and evolution of human socie-
    tal order, 140; of humans in
    groups, 141; satisfaction of,
    140, 157
Neighborhoods, 82, 91, 105-106,
  134
"New Deal," 151
New Economic Plan, 180
New Renaissance, 157;
  aggregate labor in, 161; alloca-
    tion of productive resources,
    160; coordination under, 163;
    entitlement to provisions
    under, 163; decision making,
    163; essential elements of, 157-
    158; equal opportunities, 161;
    governance under, 163; leader-
    ship under, 163-165; mech-
    anization of work, 162; occu-
    pation changes, 162; produc-
    tion processes under, 161;
    restructuring processes under,
    161; satisfaction of material
    needs, 157; separation of
    mental and physical work,
    162; social policies in, 161;
    social recognition in, 161;
    work roles, 161; work sharing,
    162
Need satisfaction, 157;
  amount of humans living in
    groups, 141
Non-target segments, 46
Nutrition, 90, 91
Nyerere, Julius K., 157

Office of Economic Opportunity
  (OEO), 77, 98, 106, 184
Oil depletion allowances, 101
Opportunities for Families Pro-
  gram (OFF), 105

Parents, 121;
  roles of, 102, 103; status and
    rights of, 63, 64
Parents' wages, 116, 120, 124

Parents' Wages policy, xvi;
  analysis of, 121-130; conclusions
    and predictions for, 130; cost
    of, 124, 127, 130, 134; effects
    of, 123-126; and foreign and
    defense policies, 128; history
    of 126; issues dealt with by,
    121; and key processes, 124-
    126; and natural environment,
    127; objectives of, 121-122;
    and other policies, 127-128;
    political reactions to, 127, 130;
    and societal development, 128-
    129; target segments of, 123;
    theories underlying, 122-123;
    value premises of, 122, 129,
    130
"Plus-sure" dynamics, 164
Policies
  anti-poverty, 100; definition of,
    of, 12; defense, of U.S., 109-
    110; foreign, of U.S., 109-110;
    reform of, 143
Political action, 177, 178, 183,
  188-194; alternative, xiv,
  185, 186; competitive model
  of, 183, 184; and human rela-
  tions, 193, 194
Political forces, in American
  society, 178, 179
Political leaders, 182-183, 185-186
Political parties, in U.S., 141
Ponsioen, Father J. A., 8
Population, 90-91
Population trends, 156
Poverty, 40-41, 53, 59, 72, 78, 79,
  81, 88, 93-94, 98, 107, 129,
  131, 132, 133, 181-182, 202;
  gap, 53-54
Prerogatives, 20, 34
Present provision systems, 156;
  failure of, 156
Prestige, 19, 20, 21, 46
Prevailing systems of provision,
  143;
  tendency toward uncritical
    acceptance of, 143

Price increases, 79, 83
Private enterprise, 106
Privilege, 140
Privileged population groups, 155;
    as source of social deprivation,
    155
Production, 111, 133, 141-142;
    agricultural and industrial, 160;
    modes of, 141
Productive resources, allocation
    of, 160
Profit motive, The, 23
Propaganda, 151
Provide, meaning of, 139
Provision, analysis of term, 139-
    174;
    systems of 143-144; forces shap-
    ing and maintaining key issues
    implicit in societal nature, 141;
    qualifying with adjective "so-
    cial," 140; solution to key
    issues of, 143
Provision systems, 144-148;
    current trends of, 156
Provisions, as intrinsically social,
    140;
    production of, 141-142, 160;
    societal choices in selection,
    production and distribution
    of, 142; rejection of society's
    material and intellectual his-
    tory, 143
Public assistance, 63, 85, 86, 95,
    104-105, 113, 151, 164
Public housing, 151
Public services, 82, 84, 87, 91,
    133
Public trust, 159-160
Purchasing power, 34, 71, 74, 81,
    85, 103, 127, 132, 187;
    redistribution of, 73, 114; transfer
    of, 62, 67, 68, 69, 75-79, 83-84,
    87-88, 101, 107, 111, 131

Quality of life, xiv, xvi, 13, 16-17
    18, 24, 25, 35, 36, 43, 46-48,
    51, 125, 133, 180, 183, 187

of American middle and upper
    classes, 188; indicators of, 14,
    47; and key processes, 15; and
    Mothers' Wages policy, 88-96;
    worldwide, 192-194

Radical transformation, obstacles
    to, 168
Rat-race syndrome, 188
Reeducation, political, 188-190;
    educational agents for, 188-190
Reform and radical transforma-
    tion, 172;
    time perspectives, 173-174
Rein, Martin, 4, 5, 6
Resolving issues of provision, 155;
    as philosophical and political
    task, 155
Resource development, 16, 18-19,
    24, 25, 26, 34-35, 40, 42, 52,
    124, 132, 133, 180;
    as key process, 15; Mothers'
    Wages policy and, 83-84, 103
Resources, distribution of 179-180,
    193, 202
    necessity of, 140; national, 44,
    109; world, 109
Rewards, 21, 26, 34, 45, 46, 62,
    67, 68, 87, 142
Riessman, Frank, 3
Right-equivalents, 18, 21, 34, 45
Rights, xvi-xvii, 18, 34, 92, 125, 202;
    civil, 45, 46, 179-180; and con-
    straints, entitlements, and re-
    wards, 21; economic, 87;
    equal, 183, 185; minimum, 45;
    and prerogatives, 20; property,
    26; redistribution of, 62, 64,
    68, 131; unequal, 26, 27
Rights distribution, 20-22, 23, 24,
    25, 26-27, 34-35, 40, 42, 44-46,
    52, 66-67, 69, 125, 132-133,
    180;
    as key process, 16; and Mothers'
    Wages policy, 86-88, 103, 120;
    sex as basis for, 64-65

Roby, Pamela, 3
Roles, 20, 34, 67, 68, 80, 82;
    age, 44; sex, 44, 65

Schorr, Alvin, 3
Schottland, Charles I., 5-6
Scientists, social and political, xiii,
    xvi, 101
Security, economic, 93
Selectivity, principle of, 101, 119,
    122, 125, 126, 127
Self-interest, 27, 113, 114, 158,
    179, 186.
Settlement and land use, 91, 105-
    106, 134, 160
Sexes, equality between, 62-69,
    93, 115, 116
Shaw, George Bernard, xvi
Sherwood, Clarence C., 4
Slum clearance, 38
Social change, xiv, 177;
    political action for, xv
Social equality, xvii;
    principal of, xvi; and political
    action, 177-194
Social groups, xvi;
    conflicts between, 179, 180, 185
    organization of, 178
Social justice, 191, 194
Social order, egalitarian and
    humanistic, xiv, xvii, 96, 177,
    178, 183;
    as means of providing re-
    sources for group members,
    140; as source of evolution,
    140
Social policies
    alternative, 30, 32, 35, 36, 52-
    54; analysis of, xiv-xv, 18, 19,
    28, 30-56, 59-135; analysts of,
    xiv-xv, 3-10, 17, 32, 55; bene-
    fits of, 32, 34, 42, 55; com-
    mon domain or focus of, 3-4,
    8, 12, 13-15, 32-33, 36, 178,
    182; comparison and evalua-
    tion of, 35, 54-55; conceptual
    model of, xiv, xv, xvii, 8, 10,
    11-30, 31, 42, 135, 136, costs
    of, 32, 34, 42, 55; definition
    of, xiii, 3, 24-25; development
    in America, 178-188; and eco-
    nomic policies, 9, 13-14;
    effects of, 31-32, 34, 36, 42-
    48; framework for analysis
    of, xiv, xv, xvi, xvii, 31-56;
    functions of, 3-4, 8; force
    field of, 25-27, 29 (chart), 32,
    35, 36, 48-54; and foreign
    policies, 50, 191-193; history
    of, 48-49; incremental changes
    in, xiii, 180-183, 202; inter-
    national studies of, 195, and
    issues, 31, 33, 36-38; key proc-
    esses of, xiv, xv, 3, 8, 15-23,
    140, 142, 144; literature on, 3-
    9; means of 38, 54; non-target
    segments of, 41, 42, 46; objec-
    tives of, 31-32, 33, 40, 42, 52,
    53-54; and other policies, 50,
    91; and political systems, 183;
    and social problems, 9-10, 17-
    18, 36, 153; and social ser-
    vices, 8-10; and societal devel-
    opment, 50-51; strategy of, 40-
    41, 42; system of, xiii-xiv, 12,
    28; target segments or popula-
    tions of, 32, 33-34, 38, 41-42,
    46; value premises of, 27-28,
    33, 39-41, 51, 142, 183, 184
Social problems, 143, 154, 184-
    185, 190, 192
Social provision, 139-174;
    choice of kinds of, 141; clarifi-
    cation of concepts of, 139;
    semantic confusion involving,
    140-141
Social security, 53, 69, 90, 103,
    104, 118, 151
    Act, 164; benefits, 61, 82, 85,
    86, 93; deductions, 61
Social Security Administration, 6,
    45, 61
Social service, education for, 154

Social service agencies and programs, failure of, 155

Social service professionals, 154; fallacious notions of, 154; relation to privileged groups, 155; sense of failure and futility, 155

Social services, in capitalist welfare states, 153-155; intervention theories implicit in, 154

Social stratification, 64

Social welfare, 3; iceberg phenomenon of, 6-7; International Council on, 195

Social work, political components of, 167

Social work education, 167; contributing to transformation of prevailing order, 167; societies comparative studies of, 147; patterns of distribution among, 142

Solutions to issues of provision, 158

Society, beliefs, values, and ideologies of, 27, 28, 39-40, 92; definition of, 12-13; restructuring of, 185; types of, 49; worldwide, 192

Standard of living, 54, 86, 89, 187, 193

Status, 34, 125, 202; definition of, 19, 85; and prerogatives, 20; and prestige, 19; and rights, 22, 62; and roles, 20

Status allocation, *See also* Division of labor, 19-20, 23, 24, 25, 26-27, 34-35, 40, 42, 52, 124, 125, 132, 133, 180; changes in, 44-45; criteria for, 20; as key process, 15-16; and Mothers' Wages policy, 84-86, 108, 115, 120; sex as basis for, 64-65; types of, 43

Status symbol, 19

Subsidies, 101; agricultural, 39

Surpluses, agricultural, 39

Surveys, 47

Target segments or populations, 32, 33-34, 46

Tawney, R. H., xvi

Taxes, 79, 82, 83, 109, 123, 124; cuts in, 101; federal, 61; increases in, 89; loopholes in, 180; policies of, 127-128; reduction of, 49; reform of, 86-87; revenue from, 81-82; structure of, 133; system of, 77-78, 82

Titmuss, Richard M., 5, 6-7

Townsend, Peter, 7

Transfer payments, 123, 124, 126, 127, 133, 201

Transformation strategy, 170

Unemployment, 79, 81, 133

United Nations Research Institute for Social Development, 195

Universality, principle of, 101, 119, 125

Upward-bound, 40

Urban renewal, 105-106

U.S. Constitution, 45

U.S. Department of Agriculture, 77

U.S. Department of Health, Education, and Welfare, 6, 77, 98, 106

U.S. Department of Housing and Urban Development (HUD), 77; Model Cities Administration of, 106, 180, 183

U.S. Department of Labor, 77

Value premises, xvii, 28, 32, 33, 83, 129-130; of American society, 122, 179; 186-191; of nations, 154; of policy analysts, xiv, 54; of a society, 43, 110, 177, 198

Wages, 82, 95
Wald, George, 157
War on Poverty, 151, 180
Wars, 109
Wealth, 159
Welfare services, 98, 100, 103, 106-108
Welfare state, 149-153;
  programs, 153; the "liberal" position, 150-151; the "conservative" position, 151-153
Wilensky, Harold L., 9
Women
  discrimination against, 62-64, 69; economic dependency, 93; and employment, 68, 95; exploitation of, 62-64, 65, 68, 69, 93, 95, 115; and husbands, 63, 68; men and, 134; and Parents' Wages policy, 126; status and rights of, 62-67, 68, 71, 88, 93, 108, 111, 116, 122-123, 126, 127, 128, 129, 131, 132
Women's rights groups, 127, 130; Mothers' Wages policy and, 100-101
Work, 62-64, 66-67, 87, 104, 111, 202;
  conditions of, 133; and distribution of rights, 114-115; mothers' 131
Work force, composition of, 124
Work guarantee programs, 41

Zoning, 105-106